Eurasia Rising

Eurasia Rising

Democracy and Independence in the Post-Soviet Space

Georgeta Pourchot

PSI Reports

PRAEGER SECURITY INTERNATIONAL
Westport, Connecticut · London

Library of Congress Cataloging-in-Publication Data

Pourchot, Georgeta.
    Eurasia rising : democracy and independence in the post-Soviet space / Georgeta Pourchot.
        p. cm.
    Includes bibliographical references and index.
    ISBN 978–0–275–99916–2 (alk. paper)
1. Russia (Federation)—Foreign relations—Former Soviet republics. 2. Former Soviet republics—
Foreign relations—Russia (Federation) 3. World politics—1989– I. Title.
DK510.764.P67   2008
327.47—dc22   2008009950

British Library Cataloguing in Publication Data is available.

Library of Congress Catalog Card Number: 2008009950
ISBN-13: 978–0–275–99916–2

First published in 2008

Praeger Security International, 88 Post Road West, Westport, CT 06881
An imprint of Greenwood Publishing Group, Inc.
www.praeger.com

Printed in the United States of America

The paper used in this book complies with the
Permanent Paper Standard issued by the National
Information Standards Organization (Z39.48–1984).

10 9 8 7 6 5 4 3 2 1

To the memory of those who fought oppression and tyranny,
and to my son in hopes he never knows either

Contents

Acknowledgments   ix

Abbreviations   xi

  Chapter 1: Sovereignty from Within   1

  Chapter 2: The Vanguard Central European States   11

  Chapter 3: The Vanguard Former Soviet Republics   40

  Chapter 4: The Late-Bloomer Republics   64

  Chapter 5: Russia and Eurasia—Where To?   118

Appendix I: Postcommunist Parliamentary Election Turnout Results in   143
Central Europe and the Baltic Countries

Appendix II: Economic Freedom of the World Index (EFW), Fraser   145
Institute Ratings

Appendix III: Reporters without Borders Index of Press Freedom   147

Appendix IV: Gazprom Fees for Gas to Europe and Central Asia   149

Notes   151

Index   173

Acknowledgments

Special thanks go to my family, who has supported me through the arduous process of research and writing. My husband Eric, who provided valuable content and editorial suggestions, and my son Michael, who asked me daily "how many more pages I had" to write, were my pillars in completing this project.

Thank you to Anders Aslund, Jim Dunton, the embassies of Estonia, Latvia, Poland, and Romania in Washington DC, and the Center for Strategic and International Studies, who helped with supporting materials regarding this project.

Thank you to George Handy, Ilja Luciak, Tim Luke, Daniel Nelson, and Simon Serfaty, who over the years believed in me and were supportive of my ideas.

Thank you to Robert Hutchinson and Hilary Claggett for editorial and production support.

Abbreviations

AIOC	Azerbaijan International Operating Company
BALTBAT	Baltic countries multinational peacekeeping battalion
BALTDEFCOL	Baltic regional qualified defense officers
BALTNET	Baltic combined air-surveillance networks
BALTRON	Baltic navy squadron
BSEC	Black Sea Economic Cooperation Organization (1992): Albania, Armenia, Azerbaijan, Bulgaria, Georgia, Greece, Moldova, Romania, Russia, Serbia, Turkey, and Ukraine
BTC	Baku-Tbilisi-Ceyhan pipeline
BYuT	Yulia Tymoshenko Bloc
CACO	Central Asian Cooperation Organization (1991 or 1994 CHECK): Kazakhstan, Kyrgyzstan, Russia, Tajikistan and Uzbekistan
CDC	Community of Democratic Choice: Estonia, Georgia, Lithuania, Latvia, Republic of Macedonia, Moldova, Romania, Slovenia, and Ukraine
CEE	Central and Eastern Europe: Bulgaria, Czech Republic, Hungary, Poland, Romania, and Slovak Republic
CEFTA	Central European Free Trade Area
CIS	Commonwealth of Independent States (1991): Armenia, Azerbaijan, Belarus, Georgia (1993), Kazakhstan, Kyrgyzstan, Moldova, Russia, Tajikistan, Turkmenistan (through 2005), Ukraine, and Uzbekistan
CPC	Caspian Pipeline Consortium
CSTO	Collective Security Treaty Organization (1992): Armenia, Azerbaijan (through 1999), Belarus, Georgia (through 1999), Kazakhstan, Kyrgyzstan, Russia, Tajikistan, and Uzbekistan (1994–99, rejoined 2006)

Duma	Russia's lower house of parliament
EC	European Community
EEC	Eurasian Economic Community (2000): Belarus, Kazakhstan, Kyrgyzstan, Russia, Tajikistan, and Uzbekistan
EFW	Economic Freedom of the World index
EU	European Union
GDP	Gross Domestic Product
GUAM	Organization for Democracy and Economic Development (1997): Georgia, Ukraine, Azerbaijan and Moldova, Uzbekistan (1999 through 2005)
IGC	Intergovernmental Conference (EU)
IPAP	Individual Partnership Action Plan (NATO, 2002): Armenia, Azerbaijan, Georgia, Kazakhstan, and Moldova
K-2	Karshi-Khanabad military base in southern Uzbekistan
LITPOLBAT	Combined Polish-Lithuanian battalion
NATO	North Atlantic Treaty Organization
NGO	Nongovernmental Organization
PCA	Partnership and Cooperation Agreement (EU)
PfP	Partnership for Peace (NATO)
PHARE	Pre-EU accession program to assist applicant countries join the EU
Rada	Ukrainian Parliament
RwB	Reporters without Borders
SCO	Shanghai Cooperation Organization (2001): China, Kazakhstan, Kyrgyzstan, Russia, Tajikistan, and Uzbekistan
SES	Single Economic Space
SSR	Soviet Socialist Republic
TACIS	Technical Aid to the Commonwealth of Independent States, democracy assistance program of the European Commission
TB/LNNK	Latvian Fatherland and Freedom/Latvian National Independence Movement
TSFSR	Transcaucasian Soviet Federative Socialist Republic
UN	United Nations
UPA	Ukrainian Insurgent Army
USSR	Union of the Socialist Soviet Republics (the Soviet Union)
UTO	United Tajik Opposition
WTO	World Trade Organization
WWII	World War II

1 ———————————————

Sovereignty from Within

In the post–Cold War world, Russian politicians and analysts blame the United States and "the West" for trying to isolate Russia by co-opting countries of Central Europe and Central Asia into "the Western sphere of influence." They point to NATO (North Atlantic Treaty Organization) "expansion," Central Asian color revolutions, and the placement of U.S. bases and weapons in the area of "Russian traditional strategic interests," and argue that Russia is being deliberately surrounded by a new *cordon sanitaire*.[1]

On the other hand, some Western circles argue that Russia, after a period of disarray following the collapse of communism, is pursuing a neo-expansionist agenda across these same countries, to reestablish its past sphere of influence. From warnings of a "neo-imperialist Russia," to fears of an imminent second Cold War, politicians and analysts in American and European circles fear the resurgence of a powerful, heavily militarized, and undemocratic Russia.[2]

In between these typical balance of power arguments, there is little room for a third position: That Central European, Baltic, and Central Asian countries are no longer pushover pawns, acting or reacting to the tug of war between two super-powers. From Poland to Kazakhstan, countries of Eurasia show that they have minds of their own,[3] and national interests they define and pursue in their own capitals, whether the traditional centers of power in the Kremlin, Washington, or Brussels approve or not.[4]

This book takes the position that the concept of "assertive sovereignty" captures an emerging, interstate dynamic in this vast region since the end of communism in 1989. Without neglecting any of the nuances of democratic transitions developed by scholars throughout the nineties, assertive sovereign states define domestic and foreign policy priorities in home capitals. They do not conform to the traditional subordination to the Kremlin illustrated by the core-periphery approach and main-tain a strategic relationship with Russia while pursuing integration in regional or global structures of their own choosing. The national interest is formulated at home, not in Moscow, nor in other centers of power, and is defined by popularly elected governments. The rise of assertive sovereign states is not monolithic, nor unidirectional, it varies based on perceived interests defined by leaders of respective countries. This dynamic has, however been perceived in the Kremlin as an attempt to "encircle" or "isolate" Russia, with subsequent diplomatic fallouts that did not help Russia's relations with these countries, or with the Euro-Atlantic community. A continued interpretation of sovereign-mindedness as pro-Western and anti-Russian is likely to become a self-fulfilling prophecy and lead to Russia's isolation, at least from the Eurasian countries under discussion.

The information gathered in this book is not new, but it is presented from the vantage point of Eurasian countries' interests. In so doing, this book hopes to provide fresh perspective to the polarizing rhetoric that dramatizes the actual state of relations between Russia and Eurasia, on one hand, and between Russia and the Euro-Atlantic community on the other hand.

HISTORICAL BACKGROUND

In 1989, the fast and peaceful collapse of the communist bloc in Eastern Europe was considered the single most dramatic, unexpected, and groundbreaking event of the post-WWII (World War II) period. With the exception of Romania, peaceful mass demonstrations or negotiated agreements led to the overthrow of communist governments from Poland to Bulgaria. With no exceptions, populations across a geographic area representing over one hundred million people rejected the communist system imposed on them by the Soviet Union at the end of WWII and demanded transition to a political system that would allow freedom and economic rights. In most cases, elections were organized within one year. Constitutions were rewritten to reject the premise of the Soviet-style single party systems, and to incorporate principles of Western democratic governance and free markets.

The Kremlin witnessed these fast-paced developments without intervening, and on March 11, 1990, Lithuania gave the Soviet Union the first fatal blow by declaring independence.[5] Initial Soviet political and military intervention generated large crowds of Lithuanians gathered in the capital Vilnius, vowing to reclaim their sovereignty. International pressure also mounted on the Soviet administration of Mikhail Gorbachev to recognize the sovereignty of this Baltic country. Other Soviet republics started demanding further autonomy or downright independence from Moscow. A year later, negotiations with constituent republics led to a nationwide referendum on the preservation of the Soviet Union. Boycotted by the Baltic countries (Estonia, Latvia, and Lithuania), two of the Caucasus countries (Armenia and Georgia), and Moldova, the referendum approved a "renewed Soviet Union" and a New Union Treaty. If approved by all constituent republics, the Soviet Union would become a federation of independent republics, with the same president, common foreign policy, and military.

Hard-line communists in the Kremlin feared that the New Union Treaty while designed to salvage the Soviet Union would in fact lead to its demise. They orchestrated a coup during President Gorbachev's absence from Moscow in August 1991 and briefly took over power. The coup backfired. Large popular demonstrations inside and outside Moscow, and the leadership of then president of the Russian Republic, Boris Yeltsin, led to the quick defeat of the coup leaders. Yeltsin strongly opposed the coup and appeared on national television to call for the restoration of order. The military troops sent to defend the coup openly sided with the demonstrators and the coup collapsed in two days.

While trying to stop the unraveling of the Soviet Union, the hard-liners in fact speeded it up. A month later, the independence of all three Baltic republics was recognized by the Kremlin. In December 1991, Ukraine held a referendum and over 90 percent of the population voted in favor of independence. On December 8, the leaders of Russia, (independent) Ukraine, and Belarus met in Minsk to sign the creation of the CIS (Commonwealth of Independent States) and annul the 1922 union treaty that established the Soviet Union. Two weeks later, they met again in Alma-Ata to expand the CIS to include Armenia, Azerbaijan, Kazakhstan, Kyrgyzstan, Tajikistan, Turkmenistan, and Uzbekistan. On December 25, 1991, Mikhail Gorbachev resigned as the president of the Soviet Union and the union *de facto* disappeared off the map.

With the disappearance of the core that held communism and its institutions together, countries on the periphery started to act more independently, asserting their national priorities with or without Russian permission. Central Europeans convened quickly and voted the self-dissolution of the Warsaw Pact, the military bloc that the Kremlin created as a counter to NATO. On July 1, 1991, the Pact ceased to exist.

Furthermore, Central Europeans and later Central Asian republics called for the withdrawal of Soviet troops from their territories. The Kremlin ordered the withdrawal of its Soviet troops in Central Europe. The withdrawal of approximately half a million military stationed in East Germany started in 1990 and was fully completed by 1994. Approximately 130,000 Soviet soldiers were withdrawn from the Baltic countries by 1994. Withdrawal of 7,000 Russian troops from Georgia was negotiated for ten years, started in 2006, and remains under way. Russian troops were stationed in southern Tajikistan until 2005, to guard the border with Afghanistan.

In the middle of this turmoil, the reunification of Germany in October 1990 was as astonishing and unexpected as the collapse of the Soviet Union a year later. Yet events moved so fast that many analysts now call them inevitable—in hindsight. Soon, these dramatic changes would be overshadowed by years of civil war in the disintegrating Yugoslavia. Never a part of the Soviet Union sphere of influence, Yugoslavia disintegrated in its constituent, ethnic-based republics by mid-1991 and succumbed to secessionist civil wars that lasted until 1995. Despite a peace agreement brokered by the United States known as "The Dayton Accords," Serbia's continued claim to and military activities inside the province of Kosovo eventually led to the involvement of NATO in its first ever combat operation in 1999.[6]

By 1999, the process of dismantling the institutions of communist power was over in Central Europe and the Baltic countries. Repeated orderly, free elections were organized across the region. One country broke up peacefully—Czechoslovakia—and two countries replaced it on the map: the Czech Republic and the Slovak Republic (also known as Slovakia). All Central European and Baltic countries applied for NATO and EU (European Union) membership, adapted their legal and administrative regulations to qualify, and were eventually admitted in both organizations. In 1999, at the fiftieth anniversary of NATO, the Czech Republic, Hungary, and Poland were the first former communist countries to be admitted into the alliance, less than a month before the NATO operation in Kosovo. In March 2004, Bulgaria, Estonia, Latvia, Lithuania, Romania, and Slovakia also joined, in a second wave of postcommunist NATO enlargement. In May 2004, Estonia, the Czech Republic, Hungary, Latvia, Lithuania, Poland, and the Slovak Republic were admitted into the EU. In January 2007, EU enlargement was further extended to Bulgaria and Romania. While Russia opposed NATO enlargement, by and large it refrained from its traditional mode of operation which was to intervene militarily and pressure countries out of arrangements not approved by the Kremlin.

In Central Asia, Russia and the newly independent republics struggled after 1990.[7] Russia traditionally played the role of political and economic "core" to the surrounding republics, sometimes called "the periphery" or "the near abroad." In mid-eighties, then Soviet leader Mikhail Gorbachev introduced two policies to salvage the communist system, *glasnost* and *perestroika* respectively. The former referred to an "openness and transparency" in the communist system, which would lead to more freedom of speech and dissent, and would preclude the widespread corruption endemic in the system. The latter referred to the restructuring of the communist economy along more competitive and accountable practices.[8] The ultimate result of Gorbachev's actions to reform the communist system and make it work better was its self-destruction.

The reunification of Germany, the withdrawal of Soviet troops from Eastern Germany, and a united Germany member of NATO were conditions agreed between Gorbachev and Western powers in exchange for significant loans from Germany, the EC (European Community), and then Group of Seven industrialized countries.[9]

Yeltsin's leadership in the nineties was characterized by incomplete political and economic reforms that hurt the country more than it helped. It was during his time in office that NATO enlarged to accept the first three former communist countries, the process of EU enlargement started, and Russia strengthened relations with the Euro-Atlantic community through NATO-Russia consultative arrangements and U.S.-Russia high-level systematic consultations. It was also during Yeltsin's terms in office that Russia witnessed recession, a degree of privatization, more freedom for the media, and more freedom for the former periphery states to make their own decisions.

Vladimir Putin's leadership since 2000 focused on reclaiming a great power status for Russia and reasserting a measure of political and economic influence over the periphery. To a certain extent, Putin's legacy will be a stronger Russia, domestically and internationally.

The process of decoupling from the core had mixed and uneven results in the newly sovereign countries of Central Asia, the Caucasus, Belarus, Ukraine, and

Moldova. During the nineties, governments focused on rewriting constitutions and the rules governing the economy. In many cases, political leadership was a rollover from Soviet times.

Most former Soviet republics carry historical baggage in the form of territorial and political disputes that led the region to recurrent unrest. Central Asian countries witnessed either civil war or further disintegration. Tajikistan went through civil war between 1992 and 1997, with an estimated loss of one hundred thousand people and many more refugees. Georgia continues to suffer from separatist movements in North and South Ossetia and Abkhazia. Azerbaijan went through the war of independence of its constituent region, Nagorno-Karabakh. Russia still bleeds from two wars in the separatist region of Chechnya. In Moldova, the separatist region of trans-Nister demands independence.

The beginning of the twenty-first century brought about further changes in the region, with a series of popular revolutions that overthrew incumbent administrations. Georgia was the first country to witness a popular revolution, known as "the Rose Revolution" against the regime of incumbent president Eduard Shevardnadze. Ukraine followed with an "Orange Revolution" against perceived fraud during presidential elections. The "Tulip Revolution" in Kyrgyzstan was yet another popular uprising against perceived power abuses by the incumbent president Askar Akayev. Peaceful transfer of power occurred in Turkmenistan, after the passing of president for life Saparmurat Niyazov in 2006.

Unlike Central European transitions, Russian interference was noticeable in the way some of the Central Asian countries handled their transfer of power or resolved their territorial disputes, particularly during Putin's two terms in office. The Kremlin used economic leverage in some cases to "discipline" the Euro-Atlantic preferences of some leaders of the periphery. However, even Putin chose not to send military troops to settle disputes outside of Russia's territory, as was the tradition in Soviet times. Putin also discontinued the tradition of forcefully installing puppet regimes in neighboring countries whenever the choice of domestic populations was not favored by the Kremlin. As of the writing of this book in 2007, the Russian government remains opposed to Euro-Atlantic tendencies in its former sphere of influence, translates further membership in NATO for former Soviet republics as a foreign plot directly affecting its security, and is ambivalent about treating any of the former communist countries in this region with the respect they request.

POLITICAL AND SOCIOECONOMIC TRENDS

The overthrow of communist regimes and their replacement with a different brand of political and economic system was a watershed event that proved a lot more challenging than populations or politicians seemed to realize in the early days of 1990. Across the region, elected or negotiated noncommunist governments rejected the Marxist-Leninist doctrine that the Kremlin forced upon them in 1945, declared themselves "democracies," elected to become "market economies," rewrote constitutions, adopted human rights legislation in line with those of Western countries, and overall led a conscious effort to redefine themselves according to their perceived national interests.

Politicians and the people who elected them thought they knew what they wanted but behaved as if they were not always sure. Publicly and privately, everyone seemed to want the degree of personal freedoms and wealth of Western developed countries, yet few had concrete plans to bring about massive prosperity, and even fewer had an understanding of the consensus-building mechanisms that were necessary to introduce effective change. Slowly, the political and economic transition from a closed, state-centered system to an open, democratic, and free market system proved not only difficult but also uneven, with periods better described as one-step-forward-two-steps-backward. Poland sacked six cabinets in the first two years of postcommunist transition. Czechoslovakia split into two sovereign states due to the inability of politicians to negotiate a formula for shared government. By mid-nineties, the trend of elections across the region was to return Socialist parties to government. Popular participation in elections started to go down, in a sign of disillusionment with the democratic process. Economic growth, while briefly rejuvenated by an opening to foreign direct investment, and a few uneven liberalization policies started to slow down. Unemployment was high throughout the area and corruption flourished.

As open societies already know, debates about reforms, new Constitutions, the limits of government authority, transparency, and accountability yield a variety of views, some of them mutually exclusive. In this vast region emerging from a Soviet-imposed period of one-party rule, where only the view of the Communist Party counted, political debates were not part of the political culture. Parliamentary debates tended to focus on what to do with the economy and how to do it, how to create wealth without instituting social inequality, how to insure that communist practices would not be reinstated, and how to insure that freedom of speech and of movement would be upheld. The debates were contentious, often acrimonious and often times inconclusive.[10]

To Western observers and analysts, the situation in the region was a conundrum. Much of postcommunist scholarship focused on appraising the state of democratization in these countries relative to Western standards of democratic institutional behavior. Scholars and analysts focused on assessments of stages in the transition of these countries to open, democratic systems; on the degree of openness and competition of their markets; and on the degree of corruption and respect for human rights relative to Western democracies and market economies. In fact, the focus on comparisons with hundred-year old democracies pushed the analyses so far that in the early nineties, the puzzle over exactly what was happening in the region led to analyses with self-explanatory titles. "Pluralism in Eastern Europe: Not Will It Last but What Is It?"[11] or "Economic Chaos and Fragility of Transition"[12] were followed by titles such as "The Rise of Illiberal Democracy"[13] and "Why Did Some Nations Succeed in Their Transformations While Others Failed?"[14] Western analysts agreed that these dilemmas were a function of the low to inexistent level of political culture in the region and warned that it could take generations to change the communist mind-set of populations and their elected leaders.

Yet none of these and many other progressive or regressive events were orchestrated in Moscow. To Russia's credit, Kremlin leaders discontinued the past practice of dictating how elections should be held, who should win, how the victors should govern, or how dissidents should be dealt with. Russia was collapsing itself but even before the disintegration of the Soviet empire, a decision of noninterference in the former communist countries was made in the Kremlin and carried out by successive administrations.

From Gorbachev to Putin, Russia discontinued the practice of dictating Central and East European countries how to run their affairs. In 1987, Gorbachev first introduced the revolutionary notion that countries had a right to decide for themselves what kind of society they wanted to live in. "Every nation has the right to decide whether these [communist] principles are good for it and whether it wants to adopt them in restructuring its life... 'The victorious proletariat cannot impose on any other nation its own ideal of a happy life without doing damage to its own victory.' This statement by Marx is an accurate definition of our attitude to all kinds of 'exports of revolution.'"[15] His top officials restated and amplified this apparent change in foreign policy. Vadim Loginov, an official in the Central Committee's International Department, stated in a 1988 interview that "every people and every country has the right to choose its own economic and political social system and its own aspirations, and no one has the right, in this regard, to impose, whether it be through a revolution or a counterrevolution."[16] Appearing on a U.S. morning show in 1989, foreign ministry spokesperson Gennady Gerasimov told his interviewers that the Brezhnev Doctrine was dead, "we now have the Frank Sinatra doctrine. He has a song, *I Did It My Way.* So every country decides on its own which road to take." Asked whether this would include Moscow accepting the rejection of communist parties in the Soviet bloc, he replied, "That's for sure... political structures must be decided by the people who live there."[17]

Gorbachev, Yeltsin, and Putin kept true to the so-called Sinatra Doctrine in Central Europe, allowing the region to handle their affairs "their way," without interference from "the core," even if at times unhappiness with the region's choices was voiced loud and clear.

Much of the Russian unhappiness with developments in these countries stems from an incomplete reconciliation with historic facts. When communist regimes came abruptly to an end in Eastern Europe in 1988–89, the Soviet leadership was taken by surprise by the extent of popular rejection of a system that it cultivated—and forced—on Eurasia. The Soviet leaders trying to revamp and energize the ailing state-run economy and the one-party system with *glasnost* and *perestroika* hoped that most of the countries of Eastern Europe would welcome and follow their lead. In a recent interview, Gerasimov articulated Gorbachev's belief that given the choice,

the Poles, the Czechs, you name them, would vote for socialism and friendship with Moscow. [Gorbachev] underestimated nationalistic tendencies. When he traveled to Lithuania shortly thereafter [January 1990], he used an unusual-even dangerous-tactic, which was to stop the car in the street. And of course people surrounded him. And he was trying to convince them that it was better to be with Moscow for many reasons-economic, social, you name it you will be better off and so on, we are going to change. It will be worse for you to go at it alone. But they said, "We want freedom, we want to go our own way." It was a very big surprise for him, especially when this kind of talk happened at a gathering of the party in Vilnius, when [Algirdas] Brazauskas was in charge of the party there. And he also said, "We want to go our own way." That was a big surprise for Gorbachev.[18]

None of the Eastern European countries were interested to fix the communist system, they were interested to abandon it and switch to a market economy and a democratic system.

More startling to the Kremlin, once Eastern European countries rejected communism the Soviet Union itself started to do the same. The fast and peaceful dissolution of the Soviet Union led to the overnight loss of a geographic identity that Russians regarded with pride. Ever since those events, Russia has been coming to terms with new historic realities such as having to treat its former republics as equals in the political and economic process. That has proven to be a daunting task.

The policy of noninterference in former communist countries' affairs also applied to European centers of power such as the EU or NATO. In fact, when CEE (Central and Eastern Europe) not only rejected communism and the state-run economic system but started talking about joining the EU and NATO, the Brussels bureaucracy was caught by surprise. Neither the EU nor NATO had enlarged in several decades, they had no process or institutional framework to start cooperating with former "enemies." As a former U.S. policy maker put it, "...in the long row of [National Security Council] file cabinets...there was no drawer labeled 'in case of German unification, open file and follow instructions,' nor were there any policy papers on 'what to do if the Soviet Union disintegrates.' We were entering uncharted territory."[19] As former communist countries one by one reached out to new centers of power of their own choosing in Brussels and Washington, Euro-Atlantic leaders moved fast to accommodate the new wave of interest in democracy and open markets.

In that spirit, this book argues that while much scholarship focused on processes of democratization and transition in the former communist space, or on the typical "spheres of influence" division, much less attention was paid to how the traditional subordination of these countries to a focal point of power, the Kremlin, influenced countries' sovereign decisions. Assertiveness in foreign and domestic policy has been a means of shaking off political dependencies and establishing full sovereignty, a long held a dream for these countries. Assertiveness in selecting domestic and foreign policies considered the best choices for these countries was more than a matter of national identity, it was a matter of growing up and walking on their feet rather than being held by the hand by "big brother" Russia. The dynamic of sovereign assertiveness is incomplete and its direction is not to be taken for granted. This dynamic explains aspects of economic and political transitions that have not yet been fully accounted for in the region. It is the task of this book to contribute to that endeavor.

BOOK STRUCTURE

The remainder of this book presents information about economic and political choices made by Eurasian countries from the vantage point of the countries themselves. Chapter 2 gathers information about the transition of vanguard Central European countries. The chapter argues that the fast pace of domestic and foreign policy reforms of the early nineties set the tone for a thorough transformation of the former communist space and emboldened countries further east to take similar steps toward their own affairs.

Central Europeans were assertive both in domestic and in foreign policy. Domestically, the region chose to develop democratic institutions, introduce market economy mechanisms, and civil society reforms of their choosing. In foreign policy, they pursued membership in Euro-Atlantic institutions such as NATO and the EU. They also chose to self-dissolve the Warsaw Pact, NATO's Cold War military counterpart in the communist world. Interestingly, Central Europe was also assertive toward its new allies in the West, which further strengthens the thesis that sovereign assertiveness in the region was not necessarily anti-Russian.

Chapter 3 analyzes the spread of sovereign assertiveness further east, among former Soviet republics. The Baltic countries were the first former Soviet republics to assert their national interest in terms of a Euro-Atlantic choice. Russia lobbied against further NATO expansion, and argued that membership was a choice "against Russia." Baltic countries' integration into NATO and the EU speeded up domestic reforms and demonstrated that Russia's fears of encirclement were unwarranted.

Domestically, Baltic countries developed democratic institutions, transitioned to market economy, and introduced civil society reforms. By comparison to Central Europe, the Baltic countries vigorously defended their version of the historical record of Soviet occupation, a process that left Russia further alienated. In foreign policy, the Baltic countries refused the traditional core-periphery format of relations with Russia, and led successful bids to join Euro-Atlantic institutions.

Chapter 4 highlights signs of assertive sovereignty in Central Asia, in countries that remain incomplete democracies or downright authoritarian regimes by Western standards. From Ukraine to the Caucasus, select former Soviet republics slowly set a course for Euro-Atlantic integration and started implementing domestic reforms that would enable them to qualify for membership. Even in cases where Euro-Atlantic membership was not pursued, such as in Kyrgyzstan, Kazakhstan, or Turkmenistan, assertiveness took the form of standing up to Russia and defining the terms of the political and economic discourse rather than succumbing to Moscow's pressure. Russia continued to regard these developments as attempts at encirclement and started to counter countries' assertiveness with political pressure in the field of energy. By 2006, leveraging energy resources to dampen the assertiveness of its former republics became a Kremlin tool to reassert Russian power in the region.

Late-bloomer republics tried to assert their interests in domestic and foreign policy but Russia yielded sufficient influence in their affairs to block or delay further decoupling of the periphery. Domestically, they attempted to reduce national dependence on Russian energy resources, reestablish the historical record of Soviet occupation, resist pressure from the Kremlin on a host of issues, and develop political and economic systems of their own choosing. In foreign policy, some refused the core-periphery format, established regional cooperative agreements with and without Russia, established bilateral regional agreements, or led (successful) rapprochement with NATO and the EU.

Final chapter 5 revisits Russia's Western conspiracy theories, and calls for a double toning down of the rhetoric of encirclement, and that of Russia's neo-imperialism. Russia tends to translate the assertiveness of Eurasia either as anti-Russian or as a Western conspiracy. If persistent, this state of affairs will further damage Russia's relations with its former periphery, and with its Euro-Atlantic allies.

NATO and EU enlargement to former communist countries, the color revolutions in Central Asia, the planned positioning of military bases in Romania and Bulgaria, and a missile defense site in Poland and the Czech Republic, Western criticism of Russia's state of democracy, and Russia's reluctance to make amends for Soviet abuses in Eurasia add up to the reasons why Russian politicians believe in a Western plot. None of these developments are seen as genuine, sovereign choices of the countries under discussion, but as skillfully orchestrated stages of an anti-Russian plot.

Polarized rhetoric about the imminence of a second Cold War among Russian politicians, and of the expanding neo-imperialism of Russia among Western analysts, can lead to an inimical state of affairs that is avoidable. Russia and the Euro-Atlantic community could find ways to eat humble pie together to get past historical and current differences, and make a conscious effort to modify the way they think about one another. Only then, can this vast area speak of renewed trust, based on mutual respect and cooperation toward common goals. Until then, dangerous rhetoric can grow into alternative realities that do not serve anybody.

The Vanguard Central European States

The countries of Central Europe led the movement to greater assertiveness relative to the former core of political power in the region, Russia. Unlike countries that had been incorporated in the Soviet Union before or at the end of WWII, such as the Baltic and Central Asian countries, Central Europe had territorial integrity after WWII. The core, however, did not permit the region to have a political or economic system of its choosing. The Kremlin orchestrated communist electoral victories in Central European countries as the war came to an end, then maintained political leverage behind the Iron Curtain. When the Berlin Wall fell and the Curtain was lifted, the region took immediate advantage of the window of opportunity to liberate itself from foreign influence in its affairs. One by one, countries redesigned their political and economic systems to correspond to their populations' demands for freedom and economic opportunity. Ten years after communism fell, three of them were admitted into the military alliance that they opposed during communist times. Fifteen years after the collapse of communism, the six Central European countries that make the subject of this chapter were members of both NATO and the EU. Relations with Russia tensed up as the Kremlin opposed NATO membership for the region but they never amounted to the traditional political and military intrusion in countries' affairs. Central Europe retained trade and diplomatic relations with Russia, as it developed relations of its choice with the Euro-Atlantic community.

HISTORICAL BACKGROUND

Bulgaria, Czechoslovakia (later the Czech and the Slovak Republics), Hungary, Poland, and Romania have historically been bitter about what they considered "the injustice of Yalta." At the end of WWII, the leaders of the Allied forces, Joseph Stalin for the Soviet Union, Winston Churchill for the United Kingdom, and Franklin D. Roosevelt for the United States, met at Yalta,[1] to discuss and agree on a postwar world order. Even as Stalin impressed on FDR and Churchill the necessity of having Soviet-friendly governments in these countries considered a security buffer zone against potential future attacks on the Soviet Union, all three agreed that governments in these countries should be elected by the people. Part II of the Protocol of Proceedings of the Yalta Conference states that

> The establishment of order in Europe and the rebuilding of national economic life must be achieved by processes which will enable the liberated peoples to destroy the last vestiges of nazism and fascism and to create democratic institutions of their own choice. This is a principle of the Atlantic Charter—the right of all people to choose the form of government under which they will live—the restoration of sovereign rights and self-government to those peoples who have been forcibly deprived of them by the aggressor nations.[2]

The Yalta agreement never recognized the Soviet Union's right to interfere in the affairs and elections of neighboring Central Europe. Yet when Kremlin appointees did interfere in rigging results to create the appearance that communism was overwhelmingly popular in the region, the Western Allies did nothing. There were diplomatic protests, hardening of positions, and much talking past one another on both sides of the Atlantic. The Soviet interference in the affairs of Eastern Europe led Churchill to declare that "an Iron Curtain" descended between the countries in the "Soviet sphere of influence" and the Western part of the continent. The famous Fulton Address is considered the official beginning of the Cold War.[3]

Much of the Western protest was relatively unknown to the region's populations during the Cold War; information about the world outside the Soviet sphere of influence was carefully filtered by domestic governments with Moscow's guidance. The perceived lack of Western reaction against the rigged elections of 1945 and 1946 was assumed to be the result of the Yalta agreements, hence there was a popular sense that "the West" betrayed the region. It was telling that in 1990, if an American wandered around in a Romanian village and talked to older locals, he would get the following reaction, "What, an American?? We have been waiting for the Americans since 1945, welcome!"[4]

Between 1946 and the collapse of communism in 1989, there were strong indications that communism was not popular across the region. In 1956, as a result of the de-Stalinization process initiated by then Soviet leader Nikita Khrushchev, the communist system seemed to be challenged to the core. In the "secret speech" of 1956, the Soviet leader criticized the abuses of the Stalin era in an attempt to gain further legitimacy for the communist ideology inside and outside the Soviet Union. The processes of de-Stalinization that followed brought about popular demonstrations against the system particularly in Poland and Hungary.

In Poland, worker riots in June 1956 marked the first significant anticommunist unrest. For a while, communist leaders seemed to lose control of domestic developments. The government then instituted a (temporary) liberalization of political life in an effort to keep the lid on the workers' movements. Later in the year, popular demonstrations in Hungary turned into a full-scale revolution, with the new communist party leader Imre Nagy declaring an end to Hungary's alliance with the Soviet Union. That declaration prompted the Kremlin to send Soviet troops into Hungary and squash the revolution. Soviet troops were thereafter stationed on Hungarian territory through the end of the Cold War.

In Poland, anticommunism led to the rise of the Solidarity movement in 1980.[5] In Czechoslovakia, the 1968 liberalization of the political regime under the leadership of Alexander Dubcek known as the Prague Spring resulted in the invasion of the country by Warsaw Pact troops. Dubcek introduced freedoms that worried the authorities in the Kremlin, who feared that any challenge to the supremacy of the one-party rule would threaten the communist system.[6] In the eighties, playwright Vaclav Havel initiated the "Charter 77" movement, a civic nonpolitical organization that criticized the Czechoslovak communist government's human rights abuses.[7] In Romania, the state security apparatus, the Securitate detained, tortured, and executed anticommunist dissidents, and stifled their ability to organize a strong national movement.[8] Bulgaria appeared the most in tune with the Soviet values; few cases of opposition to the communist regime were recorded.[9]

When the events of 1988 and 1989 started unfolding, the region saw a window of opportunity to reset the course of history. Populations across the region showed determination to change the communist system by showing up in massive numbers at street demonstrations to support the anticommunist events.

Hungary led the way to fundamental anticommunist change. Starting in late 1988, change from within the communist party amounted to the creation of new, noncommunist political groups pressing for democratic change, free elections, and civic freedoms. In October 1989, the communist party held its last Congress and transformed itself into the Hungarian Socialist Party. The parliament then adopted legislation for multiparty free elections which were held the following year.

In Poland, after almost a decade of challenge to the communist regime, the Solidarity trade union secured negotiations with the communist government. The Round-table Talks led to agreement on semi-free elections according to a formula where the communist party and its satellite groups retained 65 percent of seats in the lower chamber (Sejm), and all the seats in the Senate were up for electoral competition. The results of the subsequent June 1989 elections in Poland were a preamble of things to come across the region. Of one hundred Senate seats up for election, none were won by the communist party. Communists further lost all the seats up for election in the lower chamber. This produced a new hybrid government made up of a majority of communists in the lower chamber, and a noncommunist majority in the Senate.

November 1989 was the month in which the anticommunist movement picked up momentum across the region. In Prague, thousands of students and citizens staged what was later known as "the Velvet Revolution," a peaceful protracted vigil in front of the governmental central offices, to demand an end to communist rule. In Romania, anticommunist demonstrations in the western city of Timisoara acted as catalyst for the December street demonstrations in Bucharest and throughout the country. In Bulgaria, environmental degradation with serious safety concerns led to public demonstrations in the northern part of the country. The communist regime of Todor Zhivkov acted quickly in Sophia, to replace the old communist leader with a fresh face. In February 1990, the Bulgarian communist party voluntarily gave up its preeminent role in politics and opened the door for political reforms.

May 1990 witnessed free, multiparty elections in Hungary and Romania. Free elections in Bulgaria and Czechoslovakia followed in June 1990. Poland held its first full free elections in 1991. Across the region, domestic and international media reported that populations showed strong support for a political and economic system "resembling the West," and free of Kremlin influence.

The remainder of this chapter presents evidence of countries' choices in domestic and foreign policy, to support the argument that the transformation of the region from a buffer zone under the Kremlin's influence to one of sovereign-minded states is not anti-Russian, nor pro-West, but pro-national interest as defined by each country's elected leaders. While the choices in domestic and foreign policy were certainly influenced by pro-Western values, these choices did not translate into blindly following Western models of transition and consolidation of democracy and market economy. In fact, Central Europeans stood up to the powers that be in Brussels,[10] Washington, and Moscow, when their national interests dictated it. This indicates that sovereign assertiveness is a phenomenon in its own right and whether countries choose a pro-Russian or pro-Western approach to their politics, their choices should not be taken for granted.

DOMESTIC POLICY ASSERTIVENESS

Domestically, Central Europe chose to reject the one-party system, develop democratic institutions, reject the state-run economy, and introduce market economy mechanisms. Civil society reforms and freedoms were also introduced. All these reforms were in blatant contrast to the system that the soon-to-collapse Soviet Union would have preferred. Reforms also went much further than postcommunist Russia chose in its own transformation, as chapter 5 will show.

Development of Democratic Institutions

The first significant indicator that Central Europe was going to set its own priorities and reject the Moscow model of politics was the immediate initiation of democratic reforms in all the countries under discussion. Democratic constitutions, free elections, and a multiparty system are three minimum conditions to start the democratization of a country, according to Western standards.[11] All three conditions were implemented in Central Europe since 1990.

In the span of four years after the collapse of communism, Central and East European countries rewrote their constitutions to eliminate provisions regarding the single-party system and the primacy of the socialist or communist system.[12] All countries stipulated that the foundation of their political system was going to be democratic and law-abiding, with respect for individual freedom and human rights. Some countries such as the Czech Republic went even further to insure that the foundation of the democratic state remained enshrined by stipulating that "no change shall be permissible in the essential foundation of the democratic state."[13]

All countries stipulated that "the people" were going to express their political choice through free elections,[14] from a multitude of political parties.[15] In communist times, countries' constitutions also referred to freedom of elections but for all practical purposes, that provision was meaningless. There was only one political party, the communist party, which submitted lists of candidates to the electoral commission. There were as many names on the lists as positions to fill so the vote was not an expression of choice, but one of endorsement of preselected people for specific jobs. Presidential elections consisted of one ballot, with one name on it; there was no choice of voting for or against someone, just a box to place the "vote" stamp. This experience made Central Europeans particularly sensitive to the issue of political competition and prompted them to enshrine it in their countries' most fundamental document.

All countries recognized individual rights such as the right to practice any religion, equal rights for minorities, and equal legal rights with no discrimination for gender, age, or social status. Some countries referred to "international human rights to which the country adhered," while others wrote entire chapters dedicated to individual rights.[16]

Another right that was specified precisely because it did not exist in the communist system was freedom of movement.[17] Past communist leaders were weary of defections to the West and stalled tourism abroad to avoid embarrassing testimonies about the realities of the system that occasional defectors gave the Western media. Freedom of speech and freedom of the media were also landmark Constitutional rights in all countries.[18] While in theory the people and the media were free to speak their mind in communist times, in reality saying anything against the communist system landed people in jail. Freedom of association, or peaceful protest and petitioning the government was also enshrined in postcommunist constitutions.[19] This freedom had been severely stifled in communist times to the point where state security agencies raised informants to spy on regular people and report any civil unrest associated with anticommunist feelings. In Poland, Solidarity had to go underground to be able to continue its antigovernment activities.

Finally, all Constitutions stipulated that the basis for the Central European economic system was going to be that of a free market.[20] In fifty years of communism, the state-run economy led to labor and leadership practices that *de facto* segregated managers from workers in socioeconomic status, and left large masses of people with no choice for alternative revenues. Private property was seen as the fundamental evil of the capitalist economy and forbidden. Some countries allowed limited numbers of small enterprises in the hospitality industry and some Polish farmers retained their right to land. But the state-run economy was by and large centralized in the hands of the government, produced according to "the needs of the people" determined by the government, and spread the wealth among the people according to a government plan. This planned approach to individual needs left Central European populations impoverished, with no alternative sources of income and little upward mobility. Only communist party members could advance professionally in a manner that permitted them to make more money than the average citizen. The philosophy of the state-run economy promised to make "everybody equal in rights and responsibilities," but in fact made everyone equally poor.

Free elections, a second hallmark of democratic governance, were held across the region, based on postcommunist constitutional rules and associated legislation. Popular participation was generally high by Western standards, as evidenced by election turnouts. By late nineties, disappointment with the pace and depth of reforms and increasing corruption led to voter apathy mirrored in lower turnouts. At no point during this process were election results hijacked by force, as had happened in 1945. Nor did losers contest the elections, as was the case in Central Asian republics (to be discussed in chapter 4). If Sam Huntington's two-turnover test was applied to these new democracies, critics would have to agree that the region was walking the road to democracy, and doing so without interference from Moscow.[21]

Appendix I lists voter turnout in consecutive postcommunist parliamentary elections relative to the total population of the country. The results show that popular participation through election turnout remained high by Western standards, even if it declined since the revolutions of 1989.

The third basic element of a democratic system, political competition through a multiparty system, was evident in the large numbers of political parties and groups that were formed in a short period of time.

In Bulgaria, Freedom House found 205 political parties registered by 1997 elections.[22] In the 2001 Bulgarian elections for the National Assembly, 36 parties competed and 4 passed the minimum legal threshold of 4 percent of the popular vote to enter the assembly. In the 2005 elections for the same body, 22 parties competed and 7 won representation in the assembly.[23]

In the Czech Republic, Freedom House counted the formation of over 50 parties after 1989. Four out of 29 parties competing for seats entered the Chamber in 1996. Twenty-six parties competed in 2006 and 5 gained representation into the Chamber.[24]

In Hungary, Freedom House found that by 1998, over 200 political parties had registered with the Budapest City Court.[25] In the 1990 and 1994 elections, 7 parties won representation in the parliament. In 1998, 5 out of 26 political parties won seats in the National Assembly.[26]

In Poland, Freedom House counted over 300 political parties by 1997.[27] Nineteen political groups competed the 2005 parliamentary elections for Sejm, only seven won seats.[28]

In Romania, 200 political parties were formed by May 1990.[29] That number went drastically down to 50 in 1996, when a law was passed requiring a party to have at least 10,000 members before it could register.[30] In 1996, of 38 parties who participated in elections, 6 passed the required 3 percent threshold to gain representation in the Parliament.[31]

In Slovakia, Freedom House found approximately 90 political parties by 1998.[32] In 1992, 5 out of 23 parties passed the 5 percent threshold to gain seats in the parliament. In the 1994 elections, 7 out of 18 parties won representation. In 1998, 6 out of 17 parties won representation in the parliament. In 2002, 25 parties competed, 7 won seats. In 2006, 21 parties competed and 6 won parliamentary seats.[33]

Overnight, hundreds of small political parties were formed with various mission statements and aspirations. Some were focused on reenergizing the historical parties that were banned by the Soviets and the local communists in 1945. Others were intent on offering alternative, issue-driven platforms such as the green agenda. Candidates competed for the people's votes door-to-door and through media exposure. The amount of campaigning, public speaking, and diversification of media sources and information provided the public with a plethora of new thinking, and made the political stage lively.

In most countries, the first round of postcommunist elections produced two or three front-runner party majorities and dozens of smaller, one- or two-person representation from the multitude of competing parties. Except for the parties made up of large numbers of former communists with new political names, few of the new parties had a good sense of self-management or organization. Under the "socialist democratic" or "democratic socialist" labels, former communists and their sympathizers consolidated a body of managerial know-how that permitted them to run successful campaigns. Most of the newer parties disappeared from national parliaments by mid-nineties. The assets of former communist parties were seized by governments and some were redistributed to new political formations to help them get started in politics. Party headquarters endowed with minimal technology were initially offered to new parties by national governments, to support a plurality of political voices. With time, some parties became financially self-sustaining, while others dissolved from lack of public support or convincing political platforms.

None of these processes were smooth, nor did they follow a particular "model" of transformation. Some institutional changes were quite contentious, hotly disputed by the parties that would have to relinquish power. Many legislative freedoms were implemented in a manner different from that intended by elected bodies. Yet all along, each of these developments was a moment on a continuum of democratic transition. At no point during these processes did Russia reiterate its past mode of operation of sending special ideologues to rig the results, to favor pro-Russia candidates. There were no Vyshinskys or Ana Paukers to tell countries how to run the elections.[34] Overall, Russia stayed out of these developments.

Introduction of Market Economy Mechanisms

A second indicator of domestic assertiveness in Central European countries was the unanimous rejection of the state-run economy. Simultaneously with the eradication of communism as political foundation, countries stated their intention to adopt principles and practices of free market economies. They wanted competition to replace state planning, liberalization of markets instead of economic power in the hands of the government, and the ability to earn and accumulate private property. The communist economy, in line with Marxist precepts, viewed private property as particularly damaging to the ideals of communism; with few exceptions, irrespective of how much people worked or produced, they had equally low pay and benefits. After 1989, legislation, policies, rules, and regulations were set in place to introduce free market mechanisms. Whether successful or not, Central European economic reforms were intended to reject the government's monopoly over economic decisions, increase productivity and living standards, increase economic transparency and the quality of products, and allow the market to take its course. These reforms were in direct contradiction to principles of state-run economies, were not uniform across the region, and did not always produce the intended results. Successful or not, these reforms were, however, decided in home capitals. Each country thought up their own approach to liberalizing the economy, some with better results than others. The Kremlin had no say in these decisions.

The Visegrad Group

Leading the trend of fundamental economic reforms in the region were the countries of the Visegrad Group.[35] Czechoslovakia (the Czech and the Slovak Republics), Hungary, and Poland adopted macro- and microeconomic strategies designed to decentralize, liberalize, and privatize the economy. Various schemes were adopted to sell off state assets, liberalize prices, create small- and medium-sized enterprises, increase competition, decrease net losses from the continued functioning of mammoth state-run enterprises, and increase the national GDP (gross domestic product).

Throughout the region, two main "philosophies" of macroeconomic reform were identified: a fast track and a go-slow approach to the speed and depth of reforms. Poland adopted a "shock therapy" approach with the Balcerowitz Plan, named after Finance Minister Lecek Balcerowitz who championed it under the advice of leading Western economists. The Czech Republic adopted a milder version of shock therapy, still considered a fast track type of transition. Hungary and the Slovak Republic adopted a go-slow approach that combined economic liberalization with measures to alleviate the impact of reforms on the population.

As a result of these efforts, after years of uncertainty about the effectiveness of either approach, by 2007 all the countries were recognized as "market economies" by international institutions such as the EU, the IMF, and the World Bank. Their economies continue to struggle to be competitive, increase growth, and yield opportunities across the social spectrum, with shortcomings registered throughout the process. Despite the difficulty of economic transition, none of these countries are interested to return to a state-run type of economy.

"Shock therapy" was promoted by economist Jeffrey Sachs and refers to a method of fast transitioning from a state-planned economy to a market economy through the sudden release of price controls, withdrawal of state subsidies from the economy, and immediate trade liberalization. Upon the advice of a team of Western experts of which Sachs was a member, then Polish minister of finance Lecek Balcerowitz designed an economic transition plan that included reduction of government spending and subsidies, stabilization of the exchange rate, wage restraint, common taxation for all companies (with no more exceptions for state-owned companies), and a framework for investments by foreign companies. The plan was presented to the public in October 1989, and in December, the Parliament (hereafter the Sejm) adopted it. The International Monetary Fund also approved of the plan, which was key to granting Poland a substantial loan to pay off the communist era debt that marred the economy at the time. Implementation started immediately. Within six months, these aggressive liberalization and stabilization measures helped increase domestic competition, led to the convertibility of the Polish currency, reduced the budget deficit, and boosted trade.[36]

In 1991, Poland started privatization of state assets. State companies that operated at a loss were liquidated. Further small- and medium-size privatization led to an increase in the share of GDP resulting from the private sector.[37] Political polarization eventually led to challenges to the Balcerowitz Plan. Despite occasional slowdown, successive finance ministers retained core principles of the Plan and secured the continuity of economic reform.

The Czech fast track transition to a market economy was conceived as a comprehensive market-oriented reform strategy and adopted in January 1991. The strategy envisioned rapid privatization and liberalization as part of a first stage of transition to a market economy. Symbols of the state-run economy such as the State Planning Commission were disbanded even before the first free elections in 1990. Small-scale privatization and price liberalization were launched as early as January 1991.[38] State assets were sold off in two waves of privatization and completed by mid-1993.[39] A third wave of privatization commenced in late 1995 and consisted primarily of consolidation of enterprise ownership. This wave was not nearly as successful, and by late 1996, after continued growth of GDP, the Czech Republic was entering a recession. By 1998, the imbalance between liberalization and privatization measures on one hand, and the incompleteness of institutional reforms on the other hand, led to a crisis of confidence in emerging markets across the region, according to European Bank's *Transition Report*.[40]

The "go-slow" approach to transition was championed by Mihaly Kupa the first postcommunist finance minister of Hungary. In his words,

> There are only two solutions: Either you focus on a very rapid transition to markets expecting that the profits generated by the private sector will then be distributed to those abandoned along the way, or you proceed more prudently, committing yourself not to exclude anyone from this process of transition. Since the actual state of our economy does not permit the first solution, we have adopted the second, placing priority attention on the social aspects of reform.[41]

The go-slow gradual transition advocated by the Hungarian government was characterized by a strict monetary policy, wage regulation to keep inflation under control, and subsidies to prices and industry, to prevent massive bankruptcies. Kupa defined 1991 as the year of privatization and definition of property rights, 1992 as the year when inflation would be lowered and the convertibility of the forint would be prepared, and 1993 as the year when growth would resume.[42] By 1993, growth did not resume (although it was in sight), the general public mood was characterized by political and social exhaustion and the appropriateness of the go-slow approach was questioned. As a result, the public voted the government of liberal parties out and the socialists back into power in mid-nineties. The subsequent measures introduced under the socialist government made Hungary look like the most promising market in Central Europe by the end of 1999, favored by foreign investors over Poland due to its higher stage of economic development.[43]

Slovakia used a transition approach more related to the centralized economy of the past. Between independence and 1998, economic policy was designed by the populist government of Vladimir Meciar who believed in more state involvement in the economy. Meciar's approach was perceived to be more in tune with Moscow's. During the first three years of Czechoslovak identity, market mechanisms had been triggered but as soon as the country split and Meciar took power, economic decisions made by the previous administration were reversed. Implementation of privatization was halted in 1994, a law regarding the state's interests in "strategic companies" was passed in 1995,[44] banks were added to the list of strategic companies that would not be privatized in 1996, and another law on the "Revitalization of Enterprises" through state subsidies was passed in 1997. Over 1,000 companies took advantage of the latter law and applied for state aid, inducing false expectations about the manner in which a market economy functioned.[45] With the change of political leadership in 1998, the government reenergized market economy mechanisms and caught up with the rest of the Visegrad countries. Privatization resumed, new investment incentives were enacted, fiscal discipline was introduced, jobs were created, and economic growth started.[46]

Bulgaria and Romania

In contrast to the Visegrad countries, Bulgaria and Romania took yet a third approach to the economic transition. For the first part of the nineties, neither country had clear strategies regarding the economic model they wanted to implement, and by 1996, Romania was entering a recession and Bulgaria experienced an economic crisis.

Like all the other former communist countries, Bulgaria and Romania were left with a poor economic legacy from the previous regime. A change was needed but post-1989 politicians argued for several years over what type of economic approach to use and enacted few, if any, changes.

At issue was the type of economic system politicians viewed as matching the countries' interests. In Bulgaria, the first postcommunist government was elected on a platform of change, yet politicians had little experience governing and a vague economic agenda. The Union of Democratic Forces was quickly voted out and former communists, self-styled as Socialists, were voted in power in two consecutive elections. The Bulgarian Socialist Party showed little intention to reform the state-planned economy and vetoed legislative initiatives conducive to a more open market. As a former presidential advisor summarized the situation in the country, Bulgaria had an "imitation of democracy, imitation of market economy and imitation of Western-oriented foreign policy."[47]

A somewhat similar situation occurred in Romania, where (charismatic) former communists self-styled as reformists also won two consecutive terms and enacted limited economic reforms. Their leader, former communist Ion Iliescu, campaigned and won on a platform of economic reforms that prioritized "the rights of the many" against an economic system he considered "unfair," that is the capitalist system.[48] Both Bulgarian and Romanian politicians clearly had a modest change of economic system in mind when they took power and their leadership took their countries into recession and crisis.

By 1996, both countries experienced consecutive years of negative economic growth, high levels of unemployment, hyperinflation, a degree of small- and medium-sized enterprise activity primarily in the service industry, and almost no large-scale privatization. Bulgaria defaulted on repayment of its IMF loan, Romania was still negotiating to get one. Angry masses of people in Sophia demanding economic reform and democratic practices forced the socialists out the back door of the government building. In Romania, mass demonstrations protesting the government's policies were frequent occurrences throughout the mid-nineties.

The third set of postcommunist elections brought more reform-oriented groups to power but by then, both countries had lost significant momentum and credibility with international lending institutions. The job of reforming Bulgarian and Romanian economies was therefore difficult, started late, and moved much more slowly than the Visegrad countries. Since 1997, Bulgarian and Romanian politicians introduced gradual but steady economic packages to transform their economies into viable open markets. While the transition is still in full swing, GDP growth has resumed. Corruption remains rampant and consolidation of accountable and competitive business practices is yet to occur but overall, both countries made progress toward an economic system that matches their national interests.[49]

Since the end of the Cold War, international research institutions designed indicators to measure commonalities and differences in the way countries of the world fare in specific categories. Economic freedom as a landmark of economic growth has been gauged by several institutions. For perspective, Appendix II offers a synopsis of ratings of economic freedom of the countries discussed in this book. The EFW (Economic Freedom of the World index) created by the Fraser Institute in Canada was designed to measure the extent to which governments are supportive of economic freedom policies in their countries.[50] EFW is based on thirty-eight components and subcomponents to construct a summary index that measures the degree of economic freedom in five areas: size of government, legal structure and protection of property rights, access to sound money, international exchange and regulation. The summary index is a rating on the 0 to 10 continuum, with zero the lowest and ten the highest rating of economic freedom. The annual report is published in cooperation with research institutes from seventy nations.[51]

EFW ratings in Appendix II confirm the economic trends discussed above. Poland started the transition from a comparatively poor situation (a 3.9 rating, well below a

5-point mid-level of economic freedom) and jump-started its economy with measures introduced in the early nineties. By 1995, the shock therapy policy helped the country's economic freedom rating over the 5-point mid-level (5.2). Continued liberalization of the economy brought Poland over the 6.0 level by 2004. Hungary started the transition from the best economic position (over 5.0 mid-level) and continued to liberalize bringing it close to the 7.0 level of economic freedom by the end of 2004. The Czech and the Slovak Republics underwent similar patterns of economic liberalization, with the Slovak Republic moving more slowly than the Czech Republic and catching up on par in 2004, when both countries were close to the 7.0 level (6.9 respectively). For comparison, in 1990, the economic freedom rating of the United States was 8.1 and in 2004 it was 8.2.

Romania showed clear regression in the early nineties, going from a 4.8 rating in 1990 to 3.8 in 1995, one full point regression in economic freedom during the first years of transition. By 2001, the reforms introduced after the 1996 elections brought the country to a modest but encouraging 5.1 mid-level rating, and helped improve its ratings to 5.7 by 2004.

Bulgaria showed little progress in the early nineties, with 4.3 rating in 1990 and a minimal rate increase to 4.6 in 1995. After the economic crisis of the mid-nineties, the country picked up speed and passed the 5.0 mid-level of economic freedom by 2000 and continued the trend in 2004.

All these countries passed the threshold of acceptability into the EU, based on their own decisions regarding the future of their economies. The help they received from international funding institutions such as the IMF and the World Bank was awarded because they asked for help, not because it was forced on them. Russia made no intervention in these decisions.

Civil Society Reforms and Liberties

The third major indicator of democratic reform is considered to be the growth of civil society exemplified by freedom of association and speech. The growth in the number of NGOs (nongovernmental organizations) and the degree of freedom of the media are generally agreed to be two minimum conditions for the thriving of civil society.

In the vanguard states, the expansion of freedom of association reflected in the number, scope, and activism of NGOs was steady after 1989. Across the region, new organizations sprang to life in advocacy, volunteerism, philanthropy, religion, social, research, and educational services. This was a new phenomenon for the region since in communist times, only organizations approved and designed by the communist party were legal.

The growth of NGOs in Central Europe was dependent on foreign aid and managerial know-how in the early nineties. In their initial stages, most NGOs were supported by international grants made available by the World Bank, the United States Agency for International Development (USAID), the EU, independent philanthropers such as George Soros, and various other foundations. In the long run, some NGOs survived and others disappeared. Those that were able to earn the continued confidence of granting institutions in their work and value-added to the growth of the sector secured long-term funding and continue to operate.

The variety and number of NGOs was remarkably high in a region that had little collective memory of civic outreach. In 1998, Freedom House reported approximately 150 civic associations in the Bulgarian capital alone, over 30,000 in the Czech Republic, over 55,000 in Hungary, 25,000 in Poland, approximately 500 functional NGOs in Romania (out of 23,000 registered), and 12,000 in the Slovak Republic.[52] These numbers do not account for specialized NGOs such as foundations, religious groups, charities, and services. Data are imprecise due to the speed with which some of these organizations registered, functioned for a short while, then disappeared, as well as to the diversity of methodology used to collect data. In the aftermath of the collapse of communism, Central Europe rejected the Soviet-inspired pioneers, youth organizations, and labor unions in favor of organizations that reflected their interests, sometimes chaotically and ineffectively.

Last but not least, freedom of the media from government control was one crucial indicator of the decisiveness of democratic reform in Central Europe. In communist times, the state controlled the information of all media channels, written or broadcast. This amounted to news and critical analysis filtered to fit the state propaganda of the superiority of the communist system. Public were offered the type and amount of information that governments approved, without accountability, oversight, or competition. There were virtually no independent media outlets. Starting in the second half of the eighties, due to satellite transmissions, some public were able to watch neighboring countries' shows and news, with no translation. For instance, Hungarians living close to the Western border were able to watch Austrian shows and news; Romanians living close to the Western border watched Serb and Hungarian shows. The Internet had not been introduced in the area and the only source of information about domestic and international affairs was the state-controlled channel. Radio Free Europe and Voice of America, two broadcast stations funded by Western agencies and operating in Germany, could occasionally be accessed by Central Europeans. In the eighties, this source of information was scarcely available as communist governments jammed the wavelengths.

After the fall of communist regimes, a battle for control of the channels of information was waged. Continuing past patterns of behavior, elected politicians tried to control the political message and offer one-sided views of "the country's best interest." Some countries moved toward allowing independent views in the mainstream of information faster than others. In the Visegrad and the Baltic countries, the information channels diversified faster than in former Soviet republics.

Western research institutes specialized in gauging media freedom around the world such as Freedom House and RwB (Reporters without Borders) followed events in the region to track the level of media independence from government interference. Both organizations find that Central Europe enjoys freedom of expression reflected in the adoption of legal frameworks to secure freedom of speech and private media channels, the variety of media outlets, the depth of analysis, and the legal protections for journalists.

Freedom House finds significant levels of media freedom in Central Europe. The institution uses a methodology with simplified ratings of "not free," "partly free," and "free." These three ratings are based on a composite gauge of several numerical and nonnumerical values such as whether legal protections for press freedom or penalties for libeling government officials exist, whether a proportion of media outlets are privatized and financially viable, whether the government seems to interfere in reporting and distribution channels, and whether access to the Internet is readily available. Based on these aggregate measurements, Freedom House found Central Europe "partly free" and "free" between 1990 and 1998, and "free" after 1998.[53]

RwB uses a different methodology to rank countries in the world with respect to the freedom that journalists and media outlets have and the governments' restraint in limiting those freedoms. RwB also finds that Central Europe ranks high in the degree of freedom that journalists and the media have in reporting the news relative to other countries that used to be in the Soviet sphere of influence. Of 139 countries whose media freedom was evaluated by the first Index of Press Freedom in 2002, RwB ranked Hungary 25th, Poland 30th, Bulgaria 38th, the Czech Republic 41st, and Romania 45th. For comparison, the United States ranked 17th and Russia 121st. Slovakia was not part of the 2002 study. Appendix III lists rankings for all the countries in this study from 2002 to 2006.

Appendix III also provides insights into trends of media freedom within each country. For instance, Romania and Poland seem to restrict media freedoms as they go along in their transition, with lower rankings in 2006 than in 2002 (in Romania, from 45th to 61st place, in Poland from 30th to 60th place). Wavering in their attitude toward freedom of the media are also Bulgaria, the Czech Republic, and Hungary. Between 2002 and 2006, all witnessed reversed trends in media freedom, ending up in better places in 2006 relative to 2002. The Slovak Republic steadily improved the legal framework for media freedom according to RwB, ranking among the top 10 most free countries among those in the study. The media, while initially focused on offering opinions versus information about candidates and their platforms, were by and large more informative than the previous state-run media.

Overall, in domestic policies Central Europe showed that it was determined to break with communist-style politics and to start anew by attaching the qualification of "free" to its new state and civil institutions. Each country developed free markets and free societies in their own image, asking for help (or inspiration) from Western institutions when they needed it, drawing inspiration from Eastern institutions when they wanted it, and transitioning to a new society at their own pace. They did so accepting the responsibility that open societies produce conflict as well as agreement. Public demonstrations in support of or against specific policies or issues were common place throughout the region. With few exceptions, these public protests were not silenced by security forces, even when they were not organized according to domestic legal frameworks. Public life became fervent with activity, controversy, speaking up, publishing one's own opinions and not being afraid to do so. Even as election results produced unclear majorities and stalemates in the new legislative bodies, the region was slowly learning the benefits, responsibilities, and downsides of a democratic process defined in the image of their national interests.

FOREIGN POLICY ASSERTIVENESS

In foreign policy, the region asserted its interests by renouncing membership in organizations not of their own choosing, such as the Warsaw Pact, establishing regional organizations with or without Russia such as the Visegrad Group, and pursuing membership in international organizations of their own choosing such as NATO and the EU. While the region's Euro-Atlantic choice irritated Russia, its assertiveness on select issues irritated its newest allies in the West as well. Overall, the conduct of foreign policy matched the conduct of domestic policy in the assertiveness with which countries pursued their interests and aspirations.

Self-Dissolution of the Warsaw Pact

The Warsaw Pact, officially titled the Treaty of Friendship, Co-operation and Mutual Assistance, was created in Warsaw, in May 1955 by the Soviet Union and the Central and East European communist states of Albania, Bulgaria, Czechoslovakia, East Germany, Hungary, Poland, and Romania. Prompted by the integration of then remilitarized Western Germany into NATO, the Pact was initially a mutual defense organization aimed to counter possible attacks from NATO. The founding treaty stated that relations among the signatories were based on total equality, mutual noninterference in internal affairs, and respect for national sovereignty and independence. It declared that the Warsaw Pact's function was collective self-defense of the member states against external aggression, as provided for in Article 51 of the United Nations Charter.[54]

Throughout its existence, the Pact served as a vehicle for the Kremlin to keep Central and East Europe in line with its political and communist ideology. Militarily, the Pact never confronted its nominal enemy but did intervene on the territory of its own members. Warsaw Pact military forces were used to quell the Hungarian Revolution of 1956 and the Czechoslovak Prague Spring in 1968.

As soon as communism fell, East Germany withdrew from the Pact in 1990. Other member countries started to demand the dissolution of the Pact's military structures and its transformation into a political consultative body. The Soviet military intervention in Lithuania's independence demonstrations in early 1990 was cause for alarm in Central Europe, where countries started to fear that the Kremlin would use the Pact as in the past, to quell sovereign aspirations. In January 1991, Czechoslovakia, Hungary, and Poland announced they would withdraw support for the Pact by July 1. Bulgaria followed suit in February. On July 1, at a meeting held in Prague, the Pact self-dissolved.[55] In Moscow, events were mounting toward the August coup and the Soviet authorities offered no forceful resistance against the dissolution of the Pact.

Establishing Regional Organizations with or without Russia

Central Europeans took various degrees of interest in and offered support for the transition to democratic political systems and free markets of neighboring former communist countries, even when their support irritated Moscow. They did so by establishing new groups and organizations that served common purposes, or by intensifying bilateral relations with countries considered strategic partners and allies. The Visegrad Group falls in the first category, and a host of bilateral and trilateral arrangements fall in the second category.

Established in February 1991 by Poland, Hungary, and Czechoslovakia, the Visegrad Group's mission was to support its members in pursuit of healthy relations among themselves and with their neighbors. The states resulting from the breakup of Czechoslovakia, the Czech and the Slovak Republics, joined in 1993. United in their aspirations to establish full sovereignty, democracy, and freedom, dismantle all the vestiges of the totalitarian regimes, build modern democracies based on the rule of law, respect for human rights and freedom, and build lasting relations with European institutions, the Visegrad Group continued to function even after its member countries became EU members.[56]

Visegrad members meet regularly among themselves and with other European groups to identify best practices and lessons learned from democratic and market transitions, to further common interests. They pursued Euro-Atlantic membership jointly, supporting one another even when one of them was left out of the 1999 round of NATO enlargement (the Slovak Republic). They coordinated their diplomatic efforts on issues of foreign policy, economic cooperation, cultural exchanges, and social policy, held joint military exercises, or formed joint battalions in support of specific missions, with and without NATO allies. They initiated the CEFTA (Central European Free Trade Area) to promote expansion of trade among members, promote fair competition, and remove barriers to trade. CEFTA grew to include other countries such as Bulgaria, Romania, and Slovenia.

They established a 4+1 formula of cooperation to aid Ukraine in its democratic transformation, or to coordinate with other countries including the United States, Israel, Austria, and Slovenia on specific issues of interest. Another type of cooperative arrangement involved Visegrad and other European countries based on specific projects of common interest, such as environmental degradation, transportation, and cross-border security. On occasion, they involved Russia in their talks in an arrangement called the hexagonal framework, with the four Visegrad countries, Russia, and the United States.[57]

The net result of the establishment of the Visegrad Group was an increased Central European identity, less zero-sum competition among member countries, and more cooperation on a broad set of issues. The Visegrad framework of cooperation helped countries learn to work with one another, reach compromises, and further common agendas. It has not been detrimental to any of the member countries and has not been anti-Russian.

Regional alliances sprang up in the region outside the Visegrad framework as well. Poland supported Ukraine on numerous occasions on issues of great sensitivity to Russia. In 2000, when Gazprom decided to change the route for a projected gas pipeline to Western Europe to avoid building on Ukrainian territory, Poland was adamantly in favor of a new pipeline but insisted that the project should not be carried out at Ukraine's expense. During the Orange Revolution of December 2004, the Polish president was a critical mediator between then Ukrainian president Leonid Kuchma and his challenger, Viktor Yushchenko. It was largely due to the efforts of the Polish and Lithuanian presidents, with help from the European Commission, that the outcome of the Orange Revolution was not violent.

Overall, regional cooperative arrangements in Central Europe championed with or without Russian participation led to more stability in the region. They brought a new sense of partnership and community among former communist countries and helped countries assert their interests as a function of the collective interest in security and stability.

Integration in Euro-Atlantic Institutions

Euro-Atlantic integration, defined as membership in NATO and the EU, was relentlessly pursued by Central Europe after 1990. The reason was simple: membership guaranteed the national security of individual countries.

NATO Membership

As the communist bloc crumbled, NATO members met in London in July 1990, to rethink security and the adaptation of their mission to the changing map of Europe. The London Declaration of the transformation of the Alliance was subsequently adopted, inviting the former communist countries to dialogue and cooperation.[58] One by one, each country took advantage of the London invitation. They redefined their foreign policy and defense strategies, initially to indicate that NATO was no longer an enemy, then to indicate that integration in NATO and the EU were in the countries' national interests. After intense and relentless diplomatic endeavors, the Czech Republic, Hungary, and Poland were accepted in NATO in 1999; Bulgaria, Romania, and the Slovak Republic were admitted in 2004.

The diplomatic activity in pursuit of membership went in lockstep with the redefinition of the countries' security and defense interests. In March 1991, ten days before the dissolution of the military structures of the Warsaw Pact, Poland's Foreign Minister Krzysztof Skubiszewski paid the first visit by a Polish official to NATO headquarters. In October of the same year, the presidents of Czechoslovakia, Hungary, and Poland met in Cracow and expressed their countries' interest to participate in NATO activities. In 1992, then president Lech Walesa was instrumental in defining Poland's postcommunist defense doctrine that stressed NATO membership as "Poland's strategic goal" for security reasons.[59] Walesa and other Polish politicians argued that the intention of the postcommunist government had been integration in NATO and Western structures all along, and that it had the full backing of the population.[60]

The Czechoslovak military doctrine adopted in March 1991 was based on the premise that the country would not join any more security structures.[61] After the break up of the country, Vaclav Havel changed course and pursued an active policy of Euro-Atlantic integration of the Czech Republic for the "protection of the country."[62] The Slovak government followed suit. It declared that NATO was the most effective European security guarantee and pursuit of membership was a top priority for national security reasons.[63] Slovak officials declared in Brussels that the country was preparing for full-fledged membership and claimed allegiance to NATO's strategic concept including that of nuclear weapons.[64]

In Hungary, then Prime Minister Gyula Horn declared that the decision to seek membership into NATO was Hungary's "sovereign decision" made by the National Assembly and the government.[65] Romanian President Ion Iliescu similarly argued that political parties agreed on the necessity of membership "as a guarantee of stability in the region" and Prime Minister Roman asked NATO to consider Romania's application at the same time as Hungary's.[66] Bulgaria designed its first postcommunist defense policy based on the premise that the country was not under external military threat.[67] The first elected postcommunist president changed course and strongly advocated the necessity to join NATO. In Zhelyu Zhelev's view, NATO membership was "the political ticket for entering the EU," a factor contributing to stability and security in the region.[68]

It is worth recalling that at the time of the collapse of communism in Central Europe, neither NATO nor the EU were institutionally or intellectually ready to admit former communist countries as members. Select member states were even against such approach. Members of a NATO delegation visiting Hungary in 1992 told the Parliamentary Committee on Defense and Foreign Policy that NATO membership was not a realistic option and that Hungary should seek security guarantees from other European institutions.[69] It was five years after the end of the Cold War, in 1995, that NATO published its long-awaited *Study on Enlargement* which enshrined the conditions for further enlargement; until that time, there was a lot of talk but no clear framework nor a road map to follow by prospective candidates.[70] The EU had a long and tenuous process of reevaluation of its institutional goals and enlargement to the east was under question for a decade after the collapse of communism.

In Russia, Central European calls for NATO membership were received with a great deal of negativity. From top-tier politicians to voters, Russians felt that with the Cold War over, both NATO and the Warsaw Pact should disappear as vestiges of the past. This argument gained particular strength after the dissolution of the Warsaw Pact.

A long period of diplomatic efforts to assuage Russian fears of a new division of Europe followed. Visiting Moscow in April 1996, Polish Defense Minister Stanisław Dobrzański argued that Polish foreign policy was not aimed at opposing or isolating Russia, rather that rapprochement with NATO was pursued simultaneously with closer (military) cooperation with Russia. "Poland won't be asking Russia for permission to join, but we are trying to establish the best possible relations with all of our neighbors, Russia included," said Dobrzański.[71] As Russia offered counterproposals for joint Russia-NATO security guarantees for the region, Poland and the other

Central Europeans remained concerned. Foreign Affairs Minister Dariusz Rosati told reporters in 1996:

> We are worried by some of the elements in the Russian thinking about the outside world. Among them is the vision of Russia's own "historic interests," implying "special responsibility" for certain regions. We have had some negative experiences with guarantees given by superpowers. We fear that such guarantees usually lead to objectifying the countries covered by the guarantee and turning them into vassals.[72]

Western diplomats also looked at various ways of assuaging Russian fears, and for a brief period in early nineties, even NATO membership for Russia was a topic of discussion. Numerous conferences, working seminars, and high-level diplomatic meetings were held to convince the Russians that NATO enlargement was not directed against them.

As of 2007, this remains true. Despite Russian qualms, NATO enlargement to nine former communist countries, including three former Soviet Republics (the Baltic countries discussed in chapter 3), produced no military conflict between the sides. Russia has its own permanent consultative arrangements with NATO and the EU.

Arguments pro and against NATO enlargement to the former communist countries were debated throughout the nineties. The main arguments in favor of the first round of NATO expansion made by Central Europeans and Western proponents of enlargement fall in the following categories:[73]

- Enlargement would fill the security vacuum after the collapse of the Warsaw Pact.
- Membership would increase domestic stability and speed up democratic structural reforms; it would secure continuous foreign investments.
- Security through military and economic integration is proven to work.
- Stability in Central Europe is in Russia's interest.
- Stability through NATO membership would serve as example to other countries interested in stability and democratic reforms.
- NATO changed its mission from fighting the Soviet Union to addressing out of area regional crises, it no longer has "offensive" potential (early nineties).
- NATO is an instrument to protect democracy, observe human rights, and prevent individual members from renationalizing their security interests.
- There is a (quiet) fear in Europe of the potential of a united Germany, an enlarged NATO would provide balance (early nineties).
- The continued fragmentation of the former Soviet Union could become another Balkan imbroglio (early to mid-nineties).
- Fears of a potential rebirth of an expansionist Soviet Union in the aftermath of Duma's decision to annul the dissolution of the Soviet Union in mid-nineties.
- Stabilizing CEE is necessary to involve the region in efforts to solve future European conflicts.

Opponents to NATO expansion made their own arguments:

- Russia would feel isolated and encircled.
- Russia would feel left out of the new European security map.
- Enlargement could be interpreted as the redrawing of spheres of influence, of new division lines in Europe.
- There is no current threat to Central European security (early nineties).
- Expansion of NATO's reach is motivated by anti-Russian feelings rather than genuine security concerns.
- NATO could position nuclear capabilities in Central Europe, which Russia opposes (mid-nineties).
- Russia and Western Europe could and should provide joint security guarantees to countries seeking NATO membership.

Despite these qualms, the first round of NATO enlargement to former communist countries occurred on the anniversary of the Alliance's fiftieth anniversary, in 1999. The process started with the PfP (Partnership for Peace) program, an intermediary step toward NATO membership. PfP was a test designed to show how ready Central Europeans were for membership. It asked candidate countries to observe international law, in particular to refrain from threats of force, observe existing borders, and solve all neighborly disputes peacefully. PfP also promoted a joint defense culture, democratic control over the army, openness in military planning, and discipline among the participating countries.

As soon as the first former communist countries joined NATO, they were asked to lend support to NATO's first ever military intervention, to push Serb troops out of Kosovo in the latter part of the Balkan wars. During the air campaign over Kosovo, Russia sided with the position of the Serb government in Belgrade on retaining Kosovo into the "Yugoslav Federation" against the will of the Albanian majority in Kosovo. Russian negotiators tried to convince NATO and Western leaders that the Belgrade position was acceptable, yet when NATO strikes were decided, Russian negotiators left negotiations in protest. The Kremlin decided to provide unilateral support to the administration in Belgrade via air power. It may never be known what would have happened if the Russian planes full of military troops sent by the Kremlin reached Pristina, the capital of Kosovo where a battle for positioning between Serb and Albanian forces was waged. Suffice it to say that the reason why the Russian planes never reached Pristina was the intervention of one new NATO member (Hungary) and two countries left out of the first round of NATO enlargement (Bulgaria and Romania). All three asserted their sovereignty by refusing to allow ground passage to convoys transporting supplies to Yugoslavia, and by blocking Russian planes from using their airspace to transport Russian troops going to the aid of Serb troops in Kosovo. The Pristina airport episode was described in detail by a direct participant in the events, General Wesley Clark who led the NATO campaign. In his words, "it would be the third night's test of the courage and steadfastness of Hungary, Romania and Bulgaria. . . [to] limit the scale of the Russian presence at the airfield." Bringing the Russians back to the negotiation table would "again depend on these three small countries."[74]

This episode alone shows how determined Central Europeans were to assert their sovereignty, even when it entailed going against the will of their former "big brother" Russia. It is fair to say that this episode also showed Russia that its influence over these countries' decisions could no longer be taken for granted. Yet not even this episode damaged the relations between Central Europe and Russia permanently. Kremlin leaders were slow to return to Central European capitals on diplomatic missions afterward but trade and diplomatic relations continued, and cooperation in the NATO-Russia framework resumed years later.

EU Membership

EU membership was achieved at high social, political, and financial costs for all the countries under discussion. Immediately after the collapse of the Berlin Wall, Central European leaders started to talk about "rejoining Europe," although it was not immediately clear that their economies, social safety networks, and political maturity were in line with European standards. Then EEC (European Economic Community) also understood that structurally and mission-wise, EEC was not prepared to admit new members, especially former communist states.

In Brussels, intense talks started about reshaping the organization. In December 1989, the PHARE program was set up to provide financial and technical assistance to Central Europe. In 1991, the Treaty of Maastricht was negotiated, setting benchmarks for future change. The EEC was renamed EC. The EU was created by adding new areas of intergovernmental cooperation to the existing Community work. Goals for monetary union by 1999, and new common policies such as a Common Security and Foreign Policy were also set. In 1995, three more European countries joined the EU (Austria, Finland, and Sweden). In 2000, the Lisbon Strategy was adopted to modernize the EU's economy and make it competitive worldwide. In 2002, the EU adopted the *euro* as a common currency. It also agreed to welcome ten of the former communist countries seeking membership.

The conditions for entry in the EU were tough for countries that were still in the process of radically changing the very foundation of their economies. Before accession, each candidate country had to adopt the entire body of EU laws called the *acquis communautaire*. The *acquis* amounted to approximately 26,000 pieces of legislation, for a total of 80,000 pages. Passing legislation was not sufficient, enacting legislation was also a requirement. Even with these tough requirements, Hungary and Poland were the first to apply for membership in 1994. They were followed by Bulgaria, Romania, and Slovakia in 1995, and by the Czech Republic in 1996.

In December 1997, the European Council decided to launch the enlargement process and in 1999, it confirmed that accession talks would be held with candidate countries. By December 2002, after long and tough negotiations, drastic changes to domestic economies, and numerous adjustments to domestic procedures, the EU and four of the six Central European countries reached agreement on enlargement. The date was set for May 1, 2004 and enlargement to the Czech Republic, Hungary, Poland, and Slovakia went ahead. In 2005, agreement was reached with Bulgaria and Romania and they subsequently joined in 2007.

Neither NATO nor EU membership for Central Europe was given at the end of the Cold War. Both had to be relentlessly pursued by candidate countries. Membership was not forced on candidates, nor was it part of a grand conspiracy to encircle Russia or isolate it. Membership was pursued by each country as a function of clearly defined national interests. It cost countries' politicians numerous elections, as the changes they had to introduce to comply with membership requirements took a toll on large populations. Overall, the Euro-Atlantic orientation was a sovereign choice that did not exclude Russia as a trade or diplomatic partner.

Assertiveness All Around

The net result of the patterns of transformation described in this chapter was that Russia started to think that Central European assertiveness was an anti-Russian phenomenon. While the Euro-Atlantic orientation of the region was clear, it did not amount to blind subservience, nor a go-along with all the decisions made in Washington and Brussels type of attitude. In fact, Central Europeans asserted themselves vis-à-vis American and Western European allies as well, causing consternation and strained relations within their new found Euro-Atlantic identity. Several examples illustrate this point.

First example: As soon as they joined NATO, Visegrad politicians had trouble facing their own domestic public as a result of the air strikes launched by the Alliance over Serbia and Kosovo. At the time, left-wing politicians and the public across the region viewed the air strikes negatively, while right-wing political groups united to demand that governments offer an immediate declaration of full support for the Alliance's actions. Czech politicians disappeared from public life, cancelled their appearances, and avoided reporters. Then Foreign Minister Jan Kavan said that he could not "imagine the Czech government agreeing to the Czech army's participation in any kind of ground force operation of NATO member states on the territory of Yugoslavia against the will of the Yugoslav government."[75] Hungarian officials expressed astonishment that an operation of this nature could take place so soon after NATO enlargement.[76] On the other hand, in Poland even the Catholic church rallied behind NATO. Noting that the church will never be in favor of military action to resolve a conflict, Bishop Tadeusz Pieronek recognized that "NATO is a blessing for Poland and the NATO operation in Yugoslavia protects the world against irresponsible individuals."[77] On the day the air strikes began, President Aleksander Kwaśniewski stated that "Poland deems NATO's intervention in Kosovo fully justified and hopes that this operation will make the Yugoslav government act reasonably."[78] The variety of responses by NATO's newest members was not lost on leaders in Washington and Brussels.

Second example: During negotiations for a draft EU Constitution, Poland held its ground in opposing select provisions of the draft, a fact which contributed to the collapse of the IGC (intergovernmental conference) of December 2003 that was supposed to approve the Constitution. The Constitution had been the subject of three years of negotiations by a commission of representatives from each EU member country and of candidate countries, chaired by a former French president, Valery Giscard d'Estaing.

At the last minute, the commission chairman proposed changes that were apparently not fully discussed with candidate countries, nor with all current members. The changes were incorporated in the final draft and presented as the product of "consensus" among all participants. Poland and Spain were among the countries that vocally opposed the draft. According to last minute changes, the EU could adopt motions according to a new, "double majority" system, where a motion carried if a majority of member states supported it, and if that majority represented 60 percent of the total population of the EU.

Under the double majority voting system, countries like Poland and Spain would lose voting power agreed at another EU summit in Nice, in 2000. The Treaty of Nice awarded both countries a generous number of votes in the enlarged EU Parliament. A referendum on EU membership had been held in Poland based on the agreements enshrined in the Treaty of Nice. Naturally, Poland rejected the draft Constitution and called on the EU to respect its own agreements.

The IGC went ahead as planned in December 2003, but failed to adopt the draft Constitution. Poland threatened a veto, prompting the German chancellor to fire back. "One cannot become a member of the European Union and start this membership with a veto," said Gerhard Schroeder.[79]

The Alternative Report to the draft Constitution, or Annex III called "The Europe of Democracies," stated reasons for which the draft Constitution was unacceptable to several participants. The Annex charged that the draft constitution was "never drafted through normal democratic methods," that "Giscard did not allow democracy and normal voting in the Convention," that "applicant countries were treated as observers and had no real say," that "only three political families were represented in the Presidium which drafted the tunnel vision text," and "the members were refused the right to have their amendments translated, distributed, discussed and voted upon." Therefore, "the draft constitution runs counter to all democratic principles."[80] Stunningly, the Annex was signed by only one representative of a vanguard state, the Czech Republic, and by eight "old Europe" members or alternative members of the European Parliament, the Parliaments of Denmark, Ireland, and the UK.

The Constitution was eventually adopted with amendments to the 2003 draft, but Poland made its case. The Constitution was voted down in two national referendums, in the Netherlands and France, leaving the Constitutional project on hold as of this writing. Poland revisited the controversy over the double majority voting procedure in 2007, with Prime Minister Kaczyński emphatically stating that Poland "was ready to die" to retain the Nice Treaty voting system already approved in referendum by Poles.[81] He was able to secure a ten-year delay in the introduction of the double majority voting system, which was adopted in June 2007.[82] His argument that Poland should have fairly equal voting power with Germany was grounded in his belief that Poland's population would be roughly the same as Germany's, but for Nazi Germany's responsibility for the loss of Polish population during WWII. "If Poland had not had to live through the years of 1939–1945 [when it was under Nazi occupation], Poland would be looking today at the demographics of a country of 66 million [twice as numerous as present-day]...We are only demanding that we get back what was taken from us," he stated boldly in Brussels.[83]

The compromise over the double majority voting system reached in June 2007 turned out to be insufficient. Later in the year, the Polish government announced that it would join the UK and opt out of the EU Charter of Fundamental Rights agreed in June, which was slated to replace the defunct EU Constitution. Poland would press for the inclusion of the Ioannina mechanisms in the treaty. These mechanisms allow for a temporary blocking of EU decisions when a small number of EU countries disagree. This blocking power would compensate Poland for the relative loss of voting influence under the double majority voting system.[84]

Third example: In the run-up to the Iraq war of 2002, NATO and EU allies disagreed on how to address the perceived threat that Saddam Hussein's regime posed. The U.S. administration favored an aggressive handling of Saddam Hussein believed to have or build weapons of mass destruction. European allies, particularly France and Germany, favored a moderate approach that allowed more time for UN inspections to work and ruled out a military strike against Iraq.

In the middle of this emerging trans-Atlantic rift over method and approach and before an emergency EU summit convened on February 17, 2003 to discuss the issues at stake, Central European candidates for EU membership signed two letters in support of the American approach. The letters called on Saddam Hussein to disarm and allow International Atomic Energy Agency inspectors back in the country, and warned that war was not inevitable. Several "older" EU members signed the letters, notably the UK, Spain, Portugal, Denmark, and Italy. Yet at the end of the February summit, French President Jacques Chirac had strong words of rebuke for the candidate countries who signed the letters endorsing the American position. Mr. Chirac called their behavior "childish" and warned that their support for the American position could impact their timetable of joining the EU. "They missed a great opportunity to shut up," he said, in a move that startled even founding EU members.[85]

Virtually all candidate countries fired back. "Poland...also has a right to decide what is in its own good, and France should in its turn consider it with respect," stated Polish Deputy Foreign Minister Adam Rotfeld. "Jacques Chirac should regret such expressions, which are not in the spirit of friendship and democratic relationships," said Romanian President Iliescu. "[W]e maintain the right of the Hungarian Republic to express a position which serves the country's interest. No-one can oblige us to be silent," said Istvan Szent-Ivanyi, chairman of Hungarian parliament's EU Integration Affairs Committee. Finally, Slovak Foreign Minister Eduard Kukan highlighted how Central Europeans were treated differentially (and disrespectfully) in this controversy. Picking up on the fact that other EU members signed the same letters supporting the American approach, Kukan said, "I do not comprehend why

Mr. Chirac is not criticizing Italy, Spain or Portugal. After all, they said exactly the same...I do not like it, and I do not think this way of marking us out is justified."[86] If Russia thinks that Central Europeans disagree only with the Kremlin, this exchange serves as an example that the vanguard states are not afraid to stand up to their new allies in the West either.

Fourth example: Poland's row with Germany over property restitutions for Germans expelled from Western Poland at the end of WWII provides yet another example of vanguard states' assertiveness toward countries other than Russia.

At the end of WWII, the Allies made a decision on borders that haunts European countries into the twenty-first century. At the Yalta Conference, Stalin argued that the Soviet Union had to be compensated with territory from Eastern Poland. The new Polish-Russian border follows what has become known as the Curzon line, cutting into eastern Poland. At a subsequent postwar conference in Potsdam, Stalin argued that Poland should be awarded parts of eastern Germany, on the rationale that "while on paper, these areas constitute German territory, for all practical purposes they were actually Polish since there was no German population left...all [nine million Germans] had fled westward" when the Red Army freed Poland.[87] It was eventually agreed that parts of eastern Germany would become integral part of Poland along what became known as the Oder-Neisse line, and the matter was not disputed until after the end of the Cold War.

In 2006, the Prussian Claims Society representing twenty-two Germans expelled from what is now Western Poland filed suit with the European Court of Human Rights in Strasbourg, seeking property compensation lost when parts of Germany became incorporated into Poland. Established in 2000, the Prussian Claims Society found no legal or political support for property compensation. Successive German governments argued that postwar payments made to millions of expellees settled the matter.

Yet the suit aggravated the Polish government and people. "The complaints against Poland may have a negative influence on Polish-German dialogue and disturb Polish-German relations in the long run," read a statement by the foreign ministry.[88] On several occasions, the president, Lech, and his twin brother, Prime Minister Jarosław Kaczyński, warned about strained bilateral relations arising from the dispute. "If German elites don't react firmly, the nation could again move in a direction that has already ended once in a great European tragedy," the prime minister was quoted, in an allusion to Germany's responsibility for the two World Wars. The "campaign of lies" against Poland, as the president called it, could lead to a change in the good-neighbor treaty signed by Poland and Germany in 1991. This possibility was raised as a newly founded Polish Claims Society asked the government to renegotiate the bilateral treaty. Established to assist Polish citizens who might seek reparations for harm and injustice done to them by the Third Reich, the Polish Claims Society wanted the government to introduce in the bilateral treaty the following sentence: "The parties to the treaty declare that German citizens' property claims with regard to Poland being the consequence of World War II are an internal issue of the Federal Republic of Germany."[89] As of this writing, Germany does not intend to change the bilateral treaty, the Prussian Claims Society continues with their suit, and the rhetoric between the countries soured relations.[90]

Controversy over historical outcomes is clearly not restricted to how and why the Soviet Union interfered in Central European affairs, it also surfaces regarding the role of Nazi Germany in Europe. Central Europeans are not shy to remind Germans of their responsibilities in waging two world wars, just as they are not shy to remind Russia of the consequences of communism that was imposed on them by the Kremlin.

Fifth example: In 2007, the Czech Republic opened formal negotiations with the United States to have a radar station built on its territory, as part of a new U.S. missile defense shield in Europe. Poland opened similar negotiations to have the actual missile placed on its territory.

In line with its previous attitudes toward any Western security instruments getting closer to its borders, Russia strongly opposed the positioning of the new system on territories of its former sphere of influence. Russian politicians argued that the United States justified the proposed missile shield based on an inexistent threat of medium-ranged missiles that Iran allegedly possessed. They argued that since Iran did not possess such weapons, the shield was in fact built "against us [Russia]." Finally, when rhetorical and diplomatic opposition proved ineffective, Russia threatened to redirect its weapons at European targets and started what appeared to be a new arms race. "If part of the U.S.' strategic nuclear arsenal is located in Europe and our military experts find that it poses a threat to Russia, we will have to take appropriate retaliatory steps," Putin said. "We will have new targets in Europe."[91]

Despite Russian opposition, the Czechs and the Poles moved ahead with negotiations. Then Czech Prime Minister Mirek Topolánek defended the decision as being in the Czech Republic's national interest to have the radar built on its territory. "We are convinced that the possible deployment of the radar station on our territory is in our interest," he told the Associated Press. "It will increase security in the Czech Republic and Europe."[92] The Polish prime minister was more direct in verbalizing a link between a U.S. missile defense shield on Polish territory and a potential Russian threat. "We are talking about the status of Poland and about Russia's hopes that Poland will once again come under its [Moscow's] sphere of influence...following the deployment of a missile defense base [in Poland], the chances of such undue influence arising will be greatly reduced for at least several decades," Jarosław Kaczyński said.[93]

Other Central European politicians had opposite positions and worried about the possibility of further antagonizing East–West relations. "The deployment of [missile] bases in the Czech Republic and Poland means that NATO military installations will move closer to the borders with Russia in violation of a verbal promise made by the United States to Gorbachev at talks ending the Cold War," former Slovak Prime Minister Jan Carnogursky said. "These actions could lead to a new 'cold war.'"[94] Former Polish Defense Minister Radoslaw Sikorski was more blunt in his warning that the new missile system could "provoke a spiral of misunderstanding, weaken NATO, deepen Russian paranoia and cost the United States some of its last friends on the continent." He was referring to losing the friendship of Poland in case the United States denied Polish request for additional gifts such as deploying batteries of Patriot missiles on Polish territory, to secure against a variety of possible attacks. Sikorski referred candidly to the American tendency of taking Poland for granted.

> Some genius at the State Department or the Pentagon sent the first official note describing possible placement of the [missile] facility with a draft reply attached—a reply that contained a long list of host countries' obligations and few corresponding U.S. commitments. Natives here tend to think they are capable of writing their own diplomatic correspondence. But in a region where goodwill toward the United States depends on the memory of its support in resisting Soviet colonialism, this was particularly crass. If the Bush administration expects Poles and Czechs to jump for joy and agree to whatever is proposed, it's going to face a mighty crash with reality.[95]

As of this writing, negotiations on the deployment of the missile defense shield continue, and American negotiators seem to have received Sikorski's message. These exchanges, however, indicate that Central Europeans show a spine toward both new allies of choice and their former "big brother" Russia.

Even as they assert their national interests toward east and west, it seems that Central Europeans tend to pick more political fights with the Russian government than with the Euro-Atlantic community, reinforcing the impression of Russian political circles that Central European post–Cold War attitudes are anti-Russian. This applies particularly to Poland–Russia relations, as the two countries share a difficult history.

For instance, in October 2005, Russia banned imports of Polish food, charging that Polish authorities forged health certificates. The government took measures to resolve the problem but Russia did not lift its embargo. In return, in November 2006, Poland blocked the start of negotiations between the EU and Russia on a new partnership and cooperation agreement. "If Russia wants to use economic sanctions against Poland, it means sanctions against the EU. Poland will never agree to be treated like a country that does not constitute a part of the European Union," said Prime Minister Jarosław Kaczyński.[96] President Kaczyński clarified that the veto was a function of Poland's national interest, "We simply stand up for our interests much more resolutely."[97] The foreign minister went as far as to refuse an invitation to speak with her counterpart in Moscow. "It is not a good moment for such an official event," Minister Anna Fotyga said. "It is hard to discuss things in a friendly manner when we are considered like a second-class country...there are two sides in this conflict: the EU and Russia. Poland isn't a third party...resorting to an embargo in trade relations is a kind of declaration of war. We don't understand why Russia is using this tool."[98] It took over two years for a breakthrough. In November 2007, Poland agreed to allow Russian veterinary experts to inspect its meat exports, in the framework of a trilateral agreement with the EU.[99]

In 2007, a bill to dismantle monuments glorifying the communist dictatorship was introduced in the Polish Parliament. Culture Minister Kazimierz Michał

Ujazdowski called on regional governors to "make reasonable decisions on this [law]...It's not about meticulous decommunization—that would be artificial and ridiculous. The goal is to remove the monuments that praise communist dictatorship," he said.

Understandably, Russia reacted angrily and complained that Poland was imitating Estonia in removing monuments of historical significance to the Russian people. "The bill is not aimed against Russia, and is not related to the recent developments in Estonia," Ujazdowski responded. "The law was not prepared with the Red Army in mind. It is intended to upgrade the Polish system of protection of national remembrance sites." Polish foreign ministry spokesman Robert Szaniawski reasserted the sovereign right of every country to make its own decisions about internal matters. "The law of the Russian Federation is in force in Russia, while Poland is a sovereign country and the only source of laws that are in force on its territory."[100]

Interestingly, statues in memory of Soviet-era events or personalities were removed or mocked elsewhere in Central Europe but Russia either did not have time to react, or the removal was performed under less public attention. In Bucharest, a larger than life statue of Lenin was removed in February 1990 from a public square, then taken "to the graveyard" in a symbolic burial of communism in the country.[101] In Prague, a statue of Lenin was installed after the collapse of communism and hovers over a central street in Old Town. Entitled "Hanging Out," the statue illustrates what Lenin might have looked like if hung and is a clear indictment of a historic figure that Czechs view as directly responsible for the birth of communism and its atrocities.[102]

It should also be noted that Central Europeans still fight the ghosts of communism whether they involve symbols of the past such as war monuments, or their own people. In virtually all Central European countries, laws were passed barring former communist-era nomenklatura from running for public office for long periods of time. The debates over such laws consumed a lot of energy among the public and the politicians alike. In Poland, laws were adopted to bar former collaborators with the communist regime from public office. In August 1997, the parliament passed the Screening Law, to verify past association with the communist secret services by high-level government officials.[103] A 1998 ruling of the Constitutional Court specified conditions that would prove that collaboration with communist agencies occurred. If evidence was provided that collaboration was secret, deliberate, and connected with the operational collection of information by the security services, or that contact was maintained between alleged collaborator and the secret services or that it led to concrete actions, then collaboration was established and punishable by law. In 2007, a new vetting law went much further and required a large segment of the population (including some who already filed based on the 1997 law) to file new documents asserting their innocence from collaboration. When the Supreme Court ruled that the vetting law was unconstitutional, the ruling party of the president and his twin brother prime minister voted to prepare a bill aiming for a "final and full opening of archives" held by the IPN (Institute for National Remembrance).[104] The IPN was established in the nineties with the purpose to gather secret police files from the communist era. These files presumably showed every deliberate affiliation with the communist regime and listed all the people who collaborated in crimes against communist resistance. An opening of all files would further pit segments of society against one another, yet Polish politicians considered it necessary in order to free society from the ghosts of communism.

Russian leaders may think that Central Europeans obsess over history, and they are right. Russian leaders also need to understand that Central Europeans obsess over history not solely with respect to Russia's role in the way the fate of their countries was hijacked in 1945, but as a matter of slow and painful coming to terms with half century of communist regime that transformed their personal and social lives and led some to collaboration with the regime. This is a collective burden that populations share, a burden that remains high on the agenda of self-reflection symposiums.

CONCLUSION

While Central Europe remains economically behind the level of complexity and competitiveness of its new Euro-Atlantic partners and is politically still struggling to consolidate democratic practices, it is fair to state that it has achieved a great deal of change in its domestic and foreign policies in a fairly short amount of time. It did so remaining on amicable terms with its former core of political influence, as it was moving further away from a Moscow-favored set of policy choices.

After fifty years of dominating the political decisions in the region, Russian leaders found themselves not consulted, nor being asked for approval regarding the countries' choices of domestic or foreign policies. This assertiveness did not sit well with many in the Russian political elite, who saw NATO enlargement as a direct security threat. Yet fifteen years and two rounds of enlargement later, an enlarged NATO works with Russia through various institutional arrangements that permit open consultations on security and military matters. Political rhetoric and occasional disagreements aside, the Euro-Atlantic community and Russia work together, trade, consult on a host of issues, and find ways to agree to disagree. When Russian politicians warn of new Cold Wars and arms races, they would be well advised to pay equal attention to all aspects of domestic and foreign policy in the vanguard states. If they were inclined to do so, they would have to admit that the respect and cooperation of Central Europeans needs to be earned, just as the Euro-Atlantic community has learned to accept.

The Vanguard Former Soviet Republics

The Baltic countries were the first former Soviet republics to assert their national interest in home capitals, in a manner that certainly did not conform to the traditional core-periphery approach. Starting in 1989 and before the August 1991 coup in Moscow, Estonia, Latvia, and Lithuania declared that the Soviet occupation never put an end to their countries' national identities, restored cooperative mechanisms that existed among themselves between 1920 and 1940 such as the Council of the Baltic Sea States, and declared that they would not sign the proposed Treaty of the Union intended to salvage the Soviet Union. They adopted declarations condemning the 1940 act of joining the Soviet Union, declared full independence, reestablished Estonian, Latvian, and Lithuanian as their respective official languages, and held referendums on independence. After the Soviet Union disintegrated, they pursued a domestic policy of democratization and liberalization of the market, and a foreign policy of decoupling from the former core and joining Euro-Atlantic institutions.

Domestically and in bilateral relations, the area of assertiveness that most aggravates Russia is the Baltic persistence to stick to their version of history according to which the Soviet Union annexed their countries at the end of WWII. Russia argues that the Baltic countries joined the Soviet Union as an act of self-determination. The Baltic countries argue that they were forced into an agreement that did not represent the will of the people, under difficult war circumstances.

In 1990, the Kremlin initially resisted their declarations of independence and reacted in its traditional forceful way—it sent military forces to intervene in Lithuania and Latvia. As the Soviet Union disintegrated, new Russian leaders recognized the independence of all three Baltic states. As of 2007, Russia continues to resent the Baltic Euro-Atlantic choice but works with all three countries in the format of NATO and EU-Russia mechanisms of cooperation. Relations have been on occasion tense, particularly in the run-up to the Baltic accession into NATO, but political dialogue and trade relations continue with each former republic.

HISTORICAL BACKGROUND

If Central Europeans consider Yalta the big injustice of WWII, the Baltic states point to two Yaltas in their history.

Historically, the territories currently occupied by Estonia, Latvia, and Lithuania had on and off been the battlefield between Germany, Poland, Sweden, and Russia. Prior to the twentieth century, Lithuania was the only one of the three Baltic countries that managed to establish its own state, as the Grand Duchy of Lithuania before 1252. In the eighteenth and nineteenth centuries, the three countries were part of the Russian Empire. In 1918, they all fought for independence against the Germans and the Russians. Their independence was recognized in 1920 but was short-lived. In 1940, the Red Army occupied the Baltic territories. This operation was part of the redrawing of the European map agreed in the Molotov-Ribbentrop secret protocol, which assigned the Baltic countries to the Soviet sphere of interest. The secret protocol qualifies as the first Yalta in the modern history of the Baltic states.

There were several stages of Soviet pressure on the Baltics before the occupation of 1940. First, in the framework of existing Treaties of Mutual Assistance between each of the Baltic countries and the Soviet Union, the Baltics were given ultimatums to accept Soviet military bases on their territories in September 1939. Following a display of Soviet air and naval military capabilities in the Baltic Sea violating Baltic air space and waters, and a buildup of Red Army troops along the Estonia-Latvia border, the Baltics signed the agreements which brought about the stationing of Soviet troops and a buildup of military capabilities on their territories.

In June 1940, the Soviet Union accused all three republics of conspiracy and demanded further concessions such as the installation of Soviet-friendly governments. The Baltics caved again hoping to avoid war, and pro-Moscow authorities were installed.[1] These authorities subsequently organized the 1940 elections, which were rigged to yield the victory of Moscow preapproved local communists. Only candidates on Kremlin-vetted lists were allowed to run. Andrey Vyshinsky, the same Kremlin envoy who would orchestrate the victory of the communist party in Romania in 1945, was instrumental in insuring the success of the communists in Latvia.[2]

Pro-Soviet governments were elected to power in all three countries and the new leaders applied to join the Soviet Union. In August 1940, the three Baltic countries were annexed based on their own applications. While Western countries formally protested the manner in which the elections were held and never recognized the annexation of the Baltic countries, they did little else to help the three countries. This qualifies as the second Yalta of the Baltic countries.

Current diplomatic tensions between the Baltic countries and Russia often flare up as a consequence of the fundamentally different ways in which the sides interpret the events of 1940. To Russia, the Baltic countries voluntarily applied for membership in the Soviet Union, therefore there was no "annexation" of the republics. Since the application was presented based on the laws in force at the time, there was no illegal action, and no apology or retribution is due. On the other hand, the Baltic countries argue that the Soviet Union pressured them into accepting elections with only pro-Soviet candidates allowed to run. The "application" to join the Soviet Union was in fact the result of an ultimatum of the Supreme Soviet, whose envoys demanded that the Baltics either join voluntarily or face occupation. As such, the coerced application to join the Soviet Union did not express the will of the Baltic peoples as stipulated by their Constitutions, but the will of Moscow operatives. The decision to cave to their demands was controversial in 1940 and remains so in the twenty-first century.[3]

The debate over what happened in 1940 is also a debate about the first Yalta of the Baltic countries: the secret Protocol between Nazi Germany and Soviet Russia according to which the Baltics were relegated to the Soviet sphere of influence. While current Russian politicians balk at suggestions of intentional occupation, historical evidence indicates that the Baltic states were indeed slated for annexation and the elections of 1940 were mere window dressing to make the occupation look legal. First, in the fall of 1939, the Red Army issued secret maps of the Baltic states identifying them as Soviet territories months before the actual takeover.[4] Second, the Soviet press service accidentally released the result of the 1940 elections in Latvia hours before polls closed. The results appeared in a London daily, showing a victory for the pro-Soviet communists.[5] The Baltic countries use these examples to make the point that the results of the elections could not have been known in advance unless those results were orchestrated by those who released the information, that is the authorities in Kremlin. As such, Russian politicians have yet to offer a clear explanation for their denial of a planned takeover of the three territories, and be more understanding of the strong feelings that the Baltic populations display every time this subject comes up in interstate affairs.

Between 1940 and 1941, the Soviet Union started to purge the intellectual elites in the Baltic states to avoid a resurgence of nationalism. Numerous Balts were deported to camps in Siberia and elsewhere. At the same time, a policy of Russification started, to populate all three Baltic states with Russian-speaking population. Numerous Balts died as a result of the first policy and many others lost their national identity as a result of the second.

In 1941, with the German betrayal of the Soviets, the Baltic states were conquered by Nazi Germany from the Soviet Union. During the German occupation, a Germanization policy was implemented, bringing scores of Germans to settle in the three countries. Further deportations of Jews and executions of the native Balts who opposed the new occupation occurred. Some of the local population initially welcomed the Nazi as "liberators" from the Soviet occupation, only to be deceived again by the abuses and crimes of the German occupiers. The Soviet Union reconquered the Baltic states from Germany in 1945 and the three states remained part of the Soviet Union until September 1991.

With the advent of *glasnost* and *perestroika,* the Baltic peoples saw an opportunity to claim back their statehood. Successive street demonstrations in 1986 and 1987 were disbanded by police. In 1989, one event, the Baltic Way, marked the beginning of large-scale pro-independence demonstrations. The Baltic Way was a 600 kilometer long human chain across all three Baltic states, symbolizing the shared fate of Soviet occupation and solidarity in search for full sovereignty. Approximately a million and a half people were involved in holding hands for fifteen minutes across all three Baltic republics, an event with large media reverberations in the Soviet Union and across the globe.[6]

In January–February 1990, street demonstrations in Vilnius, Lithuania prompted the Kremlin to its traditional response: it sent Soviet troops to squash demonstrations. Several people died in the conflict. International protests were filed against Gorbachev and his government's handling of the situation. Gorbachev eventually went to Lithuania in person, to try and convince people that staying part of the Soviet Union was to their benefit. According to eyewitnesses, he was totally surprised by the strength of nationalist feeling and the Baltic desire for sovereignty.[7] A few days later, he ordered the Soviet troops out. The following year, Russia recognized the independence and sovereignty of the Baltic countries and withdrawal of Soviet troops started.

Since gaining independence, the Baltic countries asserted their sovereign choices of domestic and foreign policies deemed beneficial to the national interest, to which we now turn.

DOMESTIC ASSERTIVENESS

Domestically, the Baltic countries chose to develop democratic institutions, introduce market economy mechanisms, and support civil society reforms and freedoms. In addition, they struggled to set straight the historical record of Soviet occupation, an enterprise that remains incomplete as of this writing. Although the Kremlin tried to interfere militarily before the countries gained independence, once sovereignty was restored, the core did not interfere in the countries' choice of internal policies. The Baltic countries chose democracy and market economy, and Russia stayed out of it. However, arguments over what exactly happened in 1940 continue, causing serious diplomatic tensions.

Development of Democratic Institutions

Democratic constitutions, free elections, and the introduction of a multiparty system were landmarks of democratic reforms in the Baltic countries as well. The primary focus of all three constitutions, however, was to establish the continuity of the Baltic states during occupation, thus implicitly denying a Soviet identity.

The preamble to Estonia's Constitution declares "the inextinguishable right to national self determination...proclaimed on February 24, 1918,"[8] in a reference to the continuity of the nation between 1940 and 1991. In the preamble to the Lithuanian Constitution, the language is even stronger. "Having established the state of Lithuania many centuries ago, having preserved its spirit, native language, writing and customs and having defended its freedom and independence for centuries," the 1992 Constitutional document proclaims the continuity of the Lithuanian identity.[9]

Latvia did not even wait to write a post-Soviet Constitution. In May 1990, the Supreme Council of the country passed a resolution declaring that the independence of Latvia recognized internationally in 1920 was *de jure* still in existence, and proclaimed the supremacy of the Latvian law over the Soviet law. The resolution reinstated Latvia's Constitution of February 1922 and charged the Soviet Union with violent interference in the country's internal affairs.

> Despite our endeavors to renew the independence of Latvia by peaceful, parliamentary means, to maintain friendly, neighborly relations and economic co-operation on an equal basis with the USSR and other republics, the population of Latvia and the lawfully elected Supreme Council is subjected to intense political, economic and military pressure and interference in the internal affairs of Latvia from the USSR...
>
> The Soviet Armed Forces and other Soviet Special Force Militia units stationed in Latvia are ever more aggressively interfering in the country's internal affairs and ignoring Constitutional requirements. They stormed the Supreme Council's building on May 15, 1990, and exploited any opportunity to demonstrate force and to ignore the laws of the legal government of Latvia...
>
> Regardless of the recent constitutionally guaranteed multi-party system in Latvia and in the USSR, separate subdivisions of the Soviet Armed Forces and divisions of the Soviet Special Force Militia from the USSR Ministry of Internal Affairs act as mercenaries of the Communist Party of Latvia. They not only hinder the implementation but also violate, laws, for example, assaulting court bailiffs and threatening them with weapons.[10]

Democratic reforms were important and were enshrined in the post-Soviet Constitutions adopted by 1992 in all three countries, but it is important to understand the difference in priorities between the Baltic countries and the Central European countries. While Central Europeans felt they were robbed of the opportunity to hold free elections and choose their own form of political system in 1945, the Baltic countries felt they had been robbed of their national identity in 1940 and made sure this was clearly spelled out in the preambles to their Constitutions.

Provisions for democracy, free elections, and a multiparty system were made in all the Baltic Constitutions. The language, however, prioritized a focus on "sovereignty." For instance, "Estonia is an independent and sovereign democratic republic... its independence and sovereignty is interminable and inalienable."[11] Or "[s]overeignty shall be vested in the people [of Lithuania]... no one may limit or restrict the sovereignty of the people or make claims to the sovereign powers of the people. The people and each citizen shall have the right to oppose anyone who encroaches on the independence, territorial integrity or constitutional order" of Lithuania.[12] While all Constitutions contain references to sovereignty and territorial integrity, the three Baltic countries were writing theirs during a historic time in which it was not clear that the Soviet Union was going to disintegrate, nor that the past tradition of military interventions in their affairs was going to stop. This constituted an act of remarkable political courage and assertiveness that the Kremlin did not oppose, nor tried to reverse once its course was set.

Landmark democratic values were also adopted. Personal freedom and the right to privacy, freedom of thought and expressing one's opinions in public, and freedom of movement and of assembly, as well as freedom to elect one's representatives through free elections, were all spelled out.[13]

Like their neighbors in Central Europe, the Baltic countries held free elections with broad popular participation. Appendix I offers voter turnout data in consecutive postcommunist elections relative to the total population of each Baltic country. The turnouts show a fairly consistent participation in the political process in all three countries.

The third basic element of a democratic system, political competition, was present in the political life of the Baltic countries as well. In Estonia, in 1992, seventeen parties competed for seats and nine entered parliament. In 1995, sixteen parties competed for seats and seven entered parliament. In 1999, thirteen parties competed for seats and seven entered parliament. In 2003 and 2007, six out twelve parties won representation in the parliament.[14] In Latvia, in 1993, eight out of twenty-three parties won representation in the parliament, nineteen competed in 1995 and nine won representation, twenty-one competed in 1998 and six won representation, six out of twenty parties entered parliament in 2002, and seven out of nineteen parties won representation in 2006 elections.[15] In Lithuania, in the 2000 parliamentary elections, thirteen parties and coalitions gained seats in the parliament out of twenty-eight parties and participating coalitions.[16] Twenty-two parties and coalitions competed in the 2004 elections and eight entered the parliament.[17]

In Lithuania, as of 1998, there were thirty-three registered parties and in Latvia, there were forty-one registered parties.[18] Like the Central European case, the sudden growth of political parties led sometimes to hard-fought political battles and insufficient consensus to push a political agenda forward. As such, governments in the early nineties were fairly unstable and political scandals caused several governments to fall. Yet the effervescence of political activity was markedly different from the previous Soviet rule, when political life was limited in choices and outcomes to whatever the Kremlin approved.

Introduction of Market Economy Mechanisms

The second strong indicator of domestic assertiveness in the Baltic countries was the rejection of the state-run economy in favor of a market economy. The Baltic countries were even faster than their Central European neighbors to introduce small- and large-scale privatization, introduce liberalization policies, and adopt competition practices to replace the state-planned economy. By 1991, all three Baltic countries started either small-scale privatization or piecemeal privatization of state enterprises. As was the case across the region, the introduction of free market mechanisms was not always smooth, nor always successful as evidenced by a significant banking crisis in mid-nineties. Yet all three countries moved forward, motivated by the resumption of economic growth and the prospect of becoming EU members. Each country adopted its own approaches to liberalizing the economy, some with better results than others. The Kremlin did not interfere in their choices.

The transition to market economy mechanisms in the Baltic countries did not proceed along the Polish "shock therapy" lines but it was fast-paced. Small-scale privatization started in Estonia and Latvia in 1991, and a voucher privatization of all state enterprises was introduced in Lithuania. The voucher scheme was not sufficiently attractive and did not produce the desired revenues. Like Central Europe, the voucher schemes were designed to permit workers and managers to own shares in the enterprises in which they were working. Yet this scheme did not produce the necessary cash revenue for the government since shares were offered to the enterprise managers at preferential prices. Nor did it produce a genuine privatization. Some managers turned the privatized enterprises into closed corporations to prevent takeover bids; few of these corporations became productive and competitive. Others formed manager-controlled investment companies that participated in the tenders for the remaining share in the enterprises in which they already owned shares. Known as "insider ownership," this scheme also brought little revenue to the government budget, and little competition for better management. In 1997, Lithuania opened up the privatization of a dozen strategic enterprises to foreign investment and revenue started flowing. Privatization was also accompanied by restructuring of enterprises and by 1998, all three countries witnessed economic growth from the private sector.[19]

Liberalization of prices occurred in early 1991 and 1992. National currencies were pegged initially to the Deutschmark, then transferred to the Euro, tariffs were abolished by mid-nineties, and tight fiscal policies were introduced to control inflationary pressures. A spillover effect of the crisis in the Russian banking system in mid-nineties was felt among Baltic banks with strong business connections to Russia. Central banks reacted quickly to tighten regulations regarding regional exposure.

The high rate of economic growth experienced as a result of these combined market measures put the Baltic countries ahead even of Central Europe in terms of ratings of economic freedom. The Fraser Institute Index of Economic Freedom (Appendix II) finds the Baltic countries more advanced toward free markets than Central Europe. As of 1995, Estonia was ahead of all the Central European vanguard states except the Czech Republic and Hungary, with a rating of 5.6 (slightly above midpoint level of economic freedom). Latvia and Lithuania were ahead only of Bulgaria and Romania with 5.1 and 4.9 ratings, respectively. By 2000, Estonia was ahead of all Central European countries in economic freedom, with a rating of 7.1, and retained that front-runner position into 2004 (7.7 rating, well above the midpoint). Latvia was almost on par with the Czech Republic and Hungary in 2000 (6.6 versus 6.7 for Central Europeans), caught up in 2001, and then surpassed Central European ratings through 2004 (from 6.8 to 7.1 rating). Lithuania also caught up in economic freedom ratings, moving from 6.6 in 2000 to 7.0 in 2004. All three Baltic countries were rated as having higher levels of economic freedom than Central European countries in 2004.

The Baltic countries' sovereign decisions turned them into growing market economies and earned them EU membership based on compatibility with EU markets and Western values. Russia did not interfere in this process. If Russia had an influence on domestic developments, that was due to the unintended spillover effect of Russia's own economic crisis of the mid-nineties, not to the traditional political interference of "the core."

Civil Society Reforms and Freedoms

The growth of NGOs and freedom of speech, two landmark signs of a vibrant civil society, were evident characteristics of Baltic civil society since the late eighties.

In the Baltic states, the expansion of freedom of association reflected in the number, scope, and activism of NGOs was initially associated with the growth of organizations aiming to restore the countries' independence. The Estonian Students Society publicly displayed the national flag at a time when the Soviet Union still existed and its troops were stationed in the country in 1988.[20] The Latvian Environmental Protection Club founded in 1987 to protest a planned Soviet power plant on the country's largest river quickly turned to political advocacy and demanded the restoration of sovereignty.[21] The Lithuanian Green Movement initiated a public campaign against the Soviet troops stationed in the country in 1989.[22]

Popular movements rising in late eighties and early nineties were aimed at de-Sovietization, restitution, and sovereign modernization. Soviet-type of organizations began to dismantle, such as the case of two major sports associations in Estonia, Spartak and Dynamo. Pre-1940 voluntary organizations such as the Estonian Students Society were being restored, to emphasize the element of national continuity. Modernization of the sector was possible due to international grants made available to the Baltic countries by the United States, the World Bank, and the EU. From technical assistance to know-how, the Baltic countries benefited from sustained international support for the growth of civil society.

The variety and number of NGOs were high although the citizens of the three countries displayed different levels of interest in civil organizations. Partly due to a rollover from Soviet times, when civic organizations were tools in the hands of the communist party, Lithuanians remained suspicious and relatively uninvolved in volunteerism or civil activities despite the existence of over 3,000 NGOs as of 1997.[23] Estonians and Latvians were more proactive. The Latvian Ministry of Foreign Affairs estimated that 1993 had been the year with the highest rate of growth of NGOs (almost 1,000); and the Registry for Enterprises found that the steady growth of NGOs since 1993 was a manifestation of increased civic interest and participation. As of 2001, the Registry found over 6,000 NGOs in the country.[24] In Estonia, over 5,700 NGOs had been documented by the Institute of International and Social Studies as of 1997, although the viability and continued existence of all of them could not be fully assessed.[25]

In the Baltic countries, as in Central Europe, NGOs were involved in a wide variety of activities, from political activism to environmental and health issues. More importantly, NGOs set up by the Russian minorities in each of the three countries enjoyed equal rights before the law and competed for grants on par with Baltic organizations. When the Russian government shows anxiety about the well-being of the Russian minorities that found themselves in a different country in 1991, it rarely admits that Russian groups are proactive within the legal framework of each Baltic country.

Lastly, freedom of the media from government control was implemented quickly in the Baltic countries, faster than in Central Europe. Freedom House ranked the

Baltic countries "partly free" before 1993 and "free" afterward, five years sooner than Central Europe.[26]

The first time the Baltic countries were included in the RwB Index of Press Freedom in 2003, they ranked eleventh (Latvia), thirteenth (Estonia), and eighteenth (Lithuania) among 166 countries included in the study, ahead of established democracies such as France (twenty-sixth), the UK (twenty-seventh), and the United States (thirty-second). Appendix III shows that Latvia was ahead of all the Central European countries in terms of media freedom, Estonia was ahead of all but one (the Czech Republic), and Lithuania was ahead of all but two (Czech and Slovak Republics) in 2003. The better ranking for the Baltic countries relative to their Central European neighbors was maintained through 2006.

Rewriting the Historical Record of Soviet Occupation

The element of Baltic domestic assertiveness that remains the most problematic for Russia is the attempt to reestablish the record of the countries' past and spell out "Soviet occupation" in history textbooks. Some of the most acrimonious diplomatic exchanges between the Baltic countries and Russia occurred regarding this topic. All three countries had instances of reaffirming the continuity of their national identity through strong symbolism that ranged from diplomatic rhetoric and gestures, to resolving issues of citizenship, language, and borders. While Russia continues to call the incorporation of the Baltic countries in the Soviet Union a "request" or an "application" by the 1940 Baltic authorities to join the Soviet Union, the position of the Baltic states can be best summarized by a Baltic editorial.

> The desperate Russians, who have lost faith in democracy, worship their past, including the victory in the Great Patriotic War, because they have no other ideals. They often do not want to acknowledge unpleasant historical facts of the past world war...Psychologically, Moscow draws some comfort from the belief that the Soviet Union's revival is still possible. It wants to control former Soviet republics economically, politically, and morally. It cannot accept that its neighbors are independent countries with their own interests and affairs.[27]

Throughout the post-Soviet years, calls by the Baltic states for Russia to apologize for the occupation of their countries found strong opposition among the Russian public and politicians alike. Core-periphery relations with the Baltic countries have been much more problematic than relations with Central Europe precisely because of a distinctive interpretation of historic events in the region. Russia believes that it liberated Central Europe and the Baltic countries from Nazi Germany and that without the sacrifice of the Red Army, there would have been no freedom to speak of, nor any sovereign independence. In the words of Russian Foreign Minister Sergei Ivanov, "When some people discuss the alleged Soviet occupation, I want to ask them: what would have happened to you, would anyone of your people have survived, if we had not defeated Nazism?"[28]

The Baltic countries think that Russia owes them a sincere apology for forty-five years of occupation. A 2005 Russian foreign policy commentary clarified that it did not consider "occupation" to be the appropriate legal term describing the situation in the Baltic countries in the late thirties because

> ...[i]n accordance with the international legal doctrine of the mid-20th century, "occupation" meant the acquisition by a state of uninhabited territory that did not previously belong to any state by establishing effective control over it with intent to spread its sovereignty to it. In addition, the term meant temporary occupation during the course of an armed conflict by the army of one of the warring states of the territory (or part of the territory) of another state...[yet] there was no state of war between the USSR and the Baltic states and no military actions were being conducted, and the troops were introduced on the basis of an agreement and with the express consent of the authorities that existed in these republics at the time—whatever one may think of them.[29]

Correspondingly, the ministry believed that "any claims, including demands for material compensation for alleged damage which, as some think, was the result of what happened in 1940, are without grounds."[30]

The Latvian ambassador to the Russian Federation Andris Teikmanis disagreed. "Our positions are at variance here...Few people in Latvia will share the opinion that in the 1940s the Baltic countries voluntarily, in free elections voted for voluntary accession to the USSR," the ambassador stated in an interview.[31]

The War of Monuments

The war of words was accompanied by a war of monuments. In 2002, the city of Parnu erected, then removed a memorial statue to recognize and honor the Estonians who fought for the liberation of the country in WWII. The Parnu memorial originally featured an Estonian soldier dressed in SS uniform, pointing a gun east, toward Russia. The uniform represented the local population picking up arms to fight alongside the German army when it was believed that the intention of the Germans was to liberate them from the Soviet occupation. The SS symbols were afterward removed from the memorial plaque. The inscription on the monument, "To all Estonian soldiers who died in the second war for the liberation of the fatherland and a free Europe in 1940–1945," is self-explanatory for the type of debate and anger such events elicit. It sparked serious opposition in Russia and was criticized by Estonian authorities as well.

Another monument whose symbolism was hotly debated was the so-called Bronze Soldier. Erected by an Estonian sculptor in Tonismagi Square in Tallinn, at the burial place of Soviet soldiers fighting for Estonia against Nazi invaders in 1945, the statue was a symbol of occupation to many Estonians. The original inscription on the monument read, "To the Soviet liberators fallen during the Great Patriotic War." In 1995, that was changed to read, "To the fallen of the Second World War."

Numerous frictions occurred regarding this monument. On the night of May 20–21, 2006, the Bronze Soldier was stained with white and blue paint, the colors of the

Estonian national flag. On May 30, two Russian servicemen of the Estonian Armed Forces were punished by their commanders "for unauthorized abandoning of their military unit" in order to lay flowers at the controversial monument.[32]

Estonian Prime Minister Andrus Ansip stated that the presence of such monument "exasperates him personally. I consider it to be an occupation symbol, and not as a monument to war victims, and the sooner the monument is moved away from Tonismagi [the central square], the better."[33] President Toomas Hendrik Ilves called the statue an insult to Estonians and "a monument to mass murder." "In our minds, this soldier stands for deportations and murders, the destruction of our country, not liberation," he said in an interview in February 2007.[34]

In late 2006, Estonia's State Assembly passed a bill on the demolition of Soviet war memorials on first reading.[35] The law was approved by the country's president in January 2007. In February 2007, the parliament passed another law entitled "On dismantling prohibited constructions" which stated that "any construction that glorifies occupation of the Estonian Republic or mass repressions in it, which can threaten life, health or property of people, inflames discord or can result in disorderly conduct" was prohibited.[36]

These laws paved the way for the relocation of the Bronze Soldier monument and other monuments in memory of Soviet soldiers. In a move widely seen as anti-Russian and even pro-Nazi by Russian politicians, Prime Minister Andrus Ansip stated, "[M]emorials should unite people. But this specific monument in this specific place divides society, and I am convinced it should not be there."[37]

In April 2007, the Bronze Soldier was moved from the center of Tallinn, in the middle of the night, after intense street riots between supporters and opponents of the removal of the statue.

In Russia, strong words of rebuke and protest demonstrations for the removal of the statue followed. The Estonian embassy in Moscow was picketed, and signatures were collected by the youth movement Nashi to "dismantle the fascist Estonian embassy." A photo gallery by a leading Russian publication showed Russian demonstrators ready to picket the embassy until the "Estonian government asks the Russian people for forgiveness."[38]

In Estonia, the war of words continued. "It is beyond my comprehension why Russia, which calls itself a democracy, is unable to face squarely the history of the Soviet Union," President Ilves said in an interview with the Russian government newspaper *Rossiiskaya Gazeta*. "Russia, unfortunately, is still playing blind man's bluff with the past."[39]

A more damaging, indirect effect of the relocation of the Bronze Soldier came in the form of Internet attacks on Estonia's government sites, news organizations, political parties, and several banks. Known as Distributed Denial of Service, the attacks consisted of flooding Web sites with tens of thousands of messages that overcrowded and jammed the bandwidths of the servers running the sites. Coming from all over the world, the origin of attacks could not be proven, but the Estonian government accused the Kremlin of direct involvement. "Internet protocol addresses have helped to identify that the cyber attacks against the internet pages of Estonian government agencies and of the office of the president have originated from specific computers and persons in Russian government agencies, including the administration of the President of the Russian Federation," charged the Estonian minister of foreign affairs. As the first cyber attacks were launched immediately after the relocation of the Bronze Soldier, it was hard to believe that anyone other than Russia had a motif in launching the attacks, although definitive proof could not be secured. NATO dispatched specialists to help Estonia, but never accused Russia directly of conducting these attacks. Neither the EU nor American authorities pointed fingers but all sides expressed concern and a renewed commitment to safeguard against "cyber wars."[40]

In May 2007, demonstrations recreating a smaller scale Baltic Way occurred in all three Baltic countries, in support of Estonia's right to manage its own affairs, in the aftermath of riots in Russia provoked by the removal of the statue, the cyber attacks, and a Russian blockade of cargo vehicles crossing the Estonian-Russian border.[41] The Russian Ambassador to Estonia was summoned by the Estonian foreign ministry to offer explanations for the blockade and he stated that he was "unaware" of orders for a blockade. The cargo trying to cross the Narva river was, nevertheless, delayed at the border crossing for weeks after the removal of the statue, prompting analysts to speculate that this was a retaliatory gesture.[42]

Symbolism remains highly important in these countries and monuments are symbols. In a parallel move to restore the symbolism of the country's continuity during occupation, Latvia raised private money to restore the Freedom Monument, built in 1935 in Riga. After three years of restoration work, the monument was unveiled in a central place in the country's capital in 2001, in the presence of the president. Vaira Vike-Freiberga stressed in her address that the monument was a "symbol of the soul and freedom of the Latvian people," and that its survival during forty-five years of occupation is a symbol of the survival of the Latvian people.[43]

Civic organizations such as the TB/LNNK (Latvian Fatherland and Freedom/ Latvian National Independence Movement) initiated further legislative movements to criminalize the denial of the country's occupation. ". . . Such understanding of history that deny occupation of Latvia by the USSR is shared by many people, who in their time were actively fighting against restoring Latvia's independence. The government should not let them propagate their ideology that influences the views of the youth with impunity," TB/LNNK Chair Maris Grinblats said in 2007.[44]

Yet another symbolic gesture that the Baltic countries were not going to get along with whatever the Kremlin asked—or invited—them to do came when two of the three Baltic countries refused to honor an invitation by Vladimir Putin to attend the sixtieth anniversary of the victory of WWII in Moscow. When Russian Minister Lavrov reminded his Lithuanian counterpart about President Putin's invitation, Minister Valionis reminded Ivanov that May 9 had ambiguous meanings in his country. "To Lithuania, it indicates not only victory against fascism but also beginning of new occupation."[45] Neither the Lithuanian nor the Estonia presidents attended the ceremonies in Moscow in 2005, in a symbolic move that further aggravated the Kremlin.

Borders

Agreement on borders is yet another symbol of the tug of war between Baltic resistance to the Soviet past and of Russian determination to stick to its view of history. All the Baltic countries lost territory as a result of the Soviet occupation. The Soviet Union chipped away at the eastern borders of all three countries, particularly but not solely in areas of dense Russian population. Of the three countries, Lithuania never raised any territorial claims or border issues with Russia and signed bilateral border agreements with Poland and Belarus, accepting existing borders. Latvia and Estonia negotiated border agreements with Russia and eventually reached consensus in the late nineties. The final agreements were supposed to be signed and ratified in 2005 but both processes experienced further delays associated with Baltic amendments to the initial agreements.

The border treaty between Russia and Latvia was agreed in 1997. While ratifying the treaty, the Latvian parliament enclosed a preamble that referred to the Tartu Peace Treaty of 1920. Article III of the Tartu Peace Treaty outlined the borders of the country according to which the Jaunlatgale/Abrene district (now Pytalovo District in Russia's Pskov Region) was part of the territory of Latvia. By making such reference, the Russian Foreign Ministry considered that the preamble could become a ground for territorial claims to the Russian Federation. This prompted Putin's widely circulated remark that Latvia will likely "receive the dead donkey's ears" rather than the Pytalovo District.[46] As one could expect, Russia withdrew its signature from the bill rejecting the add-on Estonian preamble. In a foreign ministry commentary, Russia stated, "...the text of the declaration does indeed mean the bringing forward of territorial claims against Russia...Russia will be ready to sign the treaty as soon as Latvia disavows its unacceptable declaration." To underscore how the sides talked past each other, the Latvian response a day later was, "[T]he declaration approved by the government does not present territorial claims against Russia."[47]

In early 2007, the country's parliament approved the 1997 agreement and rejected four supplements to the border bill that could have been interpreted as leaving the door open for territorial claims. Two-thirds of the country's deputies supported the bill on its first reading in January 2007. President Vaira Vike-Freiberga called on the parliament to "demonstrate political courage and statesmanship" by taking "the right step at the right moment" and approve the treaty.[48] On February 8, 2007, the parliament promulgated the law and eleven days later, the president followed in its footsteps, authorizing the government to sign the border agreement with Russia.[49] In March 2007, the border treaty was finally signed by both sides in Moscow.[50] It was expected to be ratified by Russian parliament in July 2007.

The Russia–Estonia border agreement was also negotiated for years, with an agreement on final wording reached in 1996. Afterward, Russia delayed the final signature on the treaty, prompting analysts to speculate that the Russian government hoped to delay or completely stall the country's accession to NATO. "Russia once hoped that stalling the border question would slow the entry of the Baltic states into NATO and the European Union. This did not happen. The lever that Russia thought it had in hand did not prove efficient," commented Dimitri Trenin, foreign policy expert at the Carnegie Center in Moscow.[51]

On May 18, 2005 Russia and Estonia signed the border treaty. Two days later, the Estonian parliament ratified the treaty but added an introduction that made references to the 1920 Tartu Treaty and to the country's "annexation" by the Soviet Union in 1940. Consequently, Russia withdrew from the agreement.[52] Since the preamble was appended to the border treaty and Russia refused to sign it, Estonian politicians sent mixed signals about a resolution of the situation. Then Foreign Minister Urmas Paet was resolute that "Estonia will not renounce the preamble to the bill on ratification of the sea and land border treaty with Russia."[53] As of June 2007, the status of the border agreement between the two countries remains unresolved.

Language and Citizenship

Another issue of contention between the Baltics and Russia is that of language and citizenship. As a result of Stalin's Russification program, thousands of Soviet citizens were relocated on the territories of the Baltic states when they were incorporated in the Soviet Union. These people retained their Russian identity and spoke the Russian language. They had little, if any, incentive to learn the language of the local population, especially since at that time, they lived in a country called the Soviet Union. When the Baltic states regained their independence, these Russians and their children found themselves in a different country, Lithuania, Latvia, and Estonia respectively. Each of the Baltic countries restored their languages, making Russian a "foreign" language.

Each country dealt with the language and citizenship issue differently, but all had a common goal: to restore the national identity through the wide use of the native language and cultural heritage. This posed a problem for the Russian population who became nervous and felt estranged. It also led to significant opposition to the "integration" of the Russian population in the culture of their new countries. This was especially difficult in conditions of segregated education, where the Soviet-style of education was maintained. When the Baltic countries were part of the Soviet Union, Russians had their own schools where instruction was held exclusively in Russian. By comparison, natives had schools where instruction was held in the native language.

Latvia, for instance, passed a law on citizenship in 1994 according to which all Russian inhabitants had an opportunity to apply for Latvian citizenship. A Naturalization Board was set up, and a language and history test was designed. All those who passed the test could become citizens. Older Russians had difficulty learning the native language, so the government set up a language training program in 1996. The rate of learning Latvian remained slow among older and younger generations alike, in part due to the maintenance of the exclusively Russian-language schools which perpetuated the instructional system set up in Soviet times. As such, the naturalization of the Russian population proceeded slowly.

A new law on education was passed in 1998, to introduce bilingual instruction in "minority schools," that is schools where instruction was held in the language of eight national minorities, including Russian. The intent of the law was to enable national minorities to retain their culture and language while learning the language of the country in which they resided. Bilingual curricula were introduced in elementary schools in 2002, in the framework of an eight-year plan of bilingual instruction that would enable students to gradually transition to fully bilingual education. If successful, the program would gradually lead to the naturalization of younger generations of Russians.

Beginning in 2003, public opposition to the bilingual instruction program started to grow. From radical parliamentary groups to adult activities, the Russian-speaking population protested the program and demanded that Russian-only schools maintain the *status quo*. The Russian government expressed its disapproval of the bilingual education program as well, which further fueled public protests in Latvia. President Putin called the naturalization programs "discriminatory violations of the rights of the Russian-speaking population...unworthy of Europe," and called on the EU to back the Russian position.[54] Protests were conducted to demand changes to the language and citizenship law. Yet the EU and the Council of Europe considered that the law was in keeping with the general framework of Euro-Atlantic institutions and supported Latvia's position.

In Estonia, Refugees International found approximately 160,000 Russian natives living in a state of "statelessness" in 2004, carrying alien passports and facing all the restrictions on rights and privileges associated with the lack of citizenship.[55] Like Latvia, Estonia's citizenship law requires a language test that the country's Russian population still struggles with. "If I had time, I would go off to a village for six months and learn the language, but I have to work...," said a Russian living in Estonia in an interview with the *BBC* in 2007. The country's population affairs minister offered her government's vantage point, "If we give just anyone citizenship, there is very often no motivation to learn the language."[56] Between these two positions, about 10 percent of the country's total population remains stateless, particularly in the eastern parts that tend to have a higher concentration of Russian population. In Lithuania, the citizenship law allowed for automatic citizenship for all residents and such issues do not apply. The Russian government has expressed numerous concerns and offered official protests to the citizenship requirements of Estonia and Latvia in European courts. As of 2007, these issues remain contentious and a source of friction between the sides.

A final note on the assertiveness of the Baltic countries toward the former core should include the issue of past ghosts of communism and occupation. As is the case in neighboring Central Europe, the Baltic struggle with past ghosts is using up a lot of national energy. For instance, seven years after independence, in 1998, the Latvian government set up a History Commission to research the Soviet and Nazi occupation. The Commission's specific goals were to identify crimes against humanity committed in the territory of Latvia during the 1940–41 Soviet occupation, the Holocaust between 1941 and 1944, and the 1944–56 Soviet occupation. The commission periodically reported findings to the country's leadership and the general public and its initial mandate was extended by the government.[57] The Commission's work helped the country commemorate events such as the 1941 deportations and killings of Latvian officers. Documentary movies, a Museum of Occupation, and a dedicated date on the calendar (June 14) are all designed to remember, commemorate, and possibly heal the wounds of the past.[58]

Commissions of this nature exist in one form or another across the region and they are testimony to the open wounds that some of these countries still experience regarding their past. It is probably these psychological wounds that provoke such strong reactions in bilateral relations and occasionally harden positions on contested issues. Russia's refusal to acknowledge a role in causing these historic wounds leads to further bleeding of anger and frustration in the Baltic countries.

FOREIGN POLICY ASSERTIVENESS

Baltic assertiveness in foreign policy translated into decoupling from the core-periphery format of relations with Russia, seeking Euro-Atlantic membership and taking firm positions on various issues, irrespective of where Russia or the Euro-Atlantic community stood. As the record shows, the Baltic countries proved as outspoken and assertive about their national interests as the Central Europeans in their relations with their new Euro-Atlantic community.

Decoupling from the Core and Resisting Russian "Pressure"

Demanding the withdrawal of Soviet troops from all three Baltic countries was one of the first instances of Baltic refusal to continue the core-periphery format of relations with Russia. An estimated 130,000 Soviet troops resided on the territories of Estonia, Latvia, and Lithuania at the time of their independence in 1991. All three countries wanted the troops withdrawn immediately and petitioned the Kremlin to that effect.

In early 1992, negotiations led to an initial agreement for troop withdrawal. In August 1993, all Soviet troops were withdrawn from Lithuania. In August 1994, withdrawal of troops from Estonia and Latvia was completed.[59]

The negotiations on troop withdrawals were not easy. They involved linkage between Western support for Russia, and the withdrawal of troops from Central Europe and the Baltic countries. Several aid packages were offered by Western countries and the United States.[60] With each new round of negotiations, the Russian side asked the Baltics to accept additional agreements before the withdrawal would move forward. From seeking financial compensation for the expenses incurred by withdrawal of troops, to demanding the right of Russian military to become citizens of the countries in which they were stationed, to asking the Baltics to defray the cost of new apartments that had to be built to accommodate the returning troops, Russian representatives from the ministry of defense returned to the negotiating table with renewed demands over a period of two years. At the 1992 G7 summer conference, Mr. Yeltsin said the following about the withdrawal process: "We cannot simply withdraw 100,000 soldiers to an empty field. In that case they would be our enemies. These are former soldiers of the Soviet Union who were and are stationed on its territory but have been transferred to Russian jurisdiction because they cannot belong to no one. They should fall under someone's jurisdiction so they can be financed accordingly."[61] While the Kremlin's argument made sense from the Russian point of view, the delays created tensions among the Baltic governments who feared that the Russians were not genuine about withdrawing, and stalled to gain time. The Russian pressure for more time was balanced by foreign assistance and increased cooperation, and eventually the Russian troops left the Baltic territory.

Core-periphery pressure sometimes resembled a game of chicken. Whenever Russia became aggravated with a Baltic position or policy, it seemed to use economic leverage to force an outcome of its liking. If the Baltics stuck to their position and Russia did not achieve what it wanted, it applied further pressure usually in the form of economic leverage.

For instance, in the spring of 2006, the Lithuanian government announced plans to sell the only crude oil refinery in the Baltic, Mazeikiu Nafta, to a Polish company. The Russian government long favored a Russian firm takeover. In summer, Lithuanian officials underscored that the sale to a Polish company "increased Lithuania's energy security."[62]

At the end of the summer, oil supplies from Russia to the refinery through the Druzhba pipeline were halted because of reported damage to the pipeline. Coming months before the expected sale to the Polish company, the interruption of oil supplies was perceived as political pressure on the Lithuanians to sell to the Russian firm. In December 2006, the sale of the refinery to a Polish company went through, with PKN Orlen acquiring a majority share in the refinery.[63]

Russia continued to delay repairing the Druzhba pipeline that fed the refinery, prompting the Baltic countries to bring the matter to the EU's attention. Lithuanian authorities warned that if Russia would not resume oil deliveries, they would block negotiations on a new EU-Russia partnership agreement in 2007.[64] Estonian foreign minister underscored that negotiations on a new partnership agreement would be "premature," in light of Russia's perceived economic pressure on the Baltic countries.[65] Latvia's European Energy Commissioner also underscored that "[t]he Russians insist it's an accident and they are losing money [by not reopening oil deliveries through the pipeline]. Although Mazeiku Nafta could be fed by other ways, we consider it is also important that the pipeline works and if there is a problem, that it is repaired and maintained...from our side, we believe [the oil] was cut off not exactly for a technical issue" as the Russian side claimed.[66] This represented an indirect way of telling the Russians that the Balts would not tolerate economic pressure for political ends.

One year after the disruption of oil deliveries and some $39 million in losses to the refinery, Russian Minister of Energy and Industry Viktor Khristenko said that repairs to the pipeline proved to be economically not reasonable. Instead, oil deliveries would be resumed via a more expensive route, by sea. Underscoring that not repairing the pipeline would not threaten Lithuania's energy security, the minister did not give a precise date when deliveries would resume.[67]

Another instance of apparent economic pressure was Russia's ban on Latvian canned fish products. On October 20, 2006, Russia imposed a temporary ban on deliveries of canned fish produced by two factories in Latvia, Brivais Vilnis and Gamma-A. The Russian Agriculture Ministry blamed the ban on high levels of a dangerous substance, benzopyrene, allegedly detected in the Latvian products. While the Latvian factories denied the allegations, they also pointed out that Russia's standards of acceptable levels of benzopyrene are five times more drastic than the EU's and that the Latvian products account for 30 percent of the Russian canned food market. "Heightened interest in our products has been motivated by competition," not by health concerns claimed Arnolds Babris, board chairman of Brivais Vilnis.[68] Whether the Russian worries over the quality of fish products from Latvia was legitimate or not was a point lost in the rhetoric over politically motivated trade bans. It did not help that Russia refused to offer documentation to the EU, to substantiate its claims of health safety concern over the banned products. As such, Russia left the impression that it used economic levers to punish countries that no longer checked in first with the Kremlin before they made significant economic or political decisions.

Euro-Atlantic Membership

Probably the most significant strategy of assertiveness in foreign policy was the Baltic choice to apply for membership in NATO and the EU, thus reorienting the countries' loyalties, security and defense policies, and future political direction.

By far the strongest Russian opposition to the Baltic states' integration into Euro-Atlantic institutions involved NATO membership. Throughout the nineties, Russia steadily and strongly opposed Baltic membership into NATO and succeeded in thwarting it for the first round of postcommunist enlargement. At the 1997 Helsinki summit, Russian President Boris Yeltsin tried to secure a "gentleman's agreement" from Clinton that the Baltic countries will never be admitted in NATO. President Clinton refused.[69] When Poland, Hungary, and the Czech Republic were invited to join in 1999, the Baltic countries were put on hold despite the fact that readiness-wise, they were on par with the vanguard Central European states.

Since the events of 1990, Russia has continued to view NATO membership for countries that used to be Soviet republics as a grave and unjustified interference in an area of Russian "traditional national interest." At the height of strong debates about NATO enlargement in 1997, then Russian Foreign Minister Primakov restated that the "U.S. and Russian points of view on issues concerning the Baltic states are different." He warned that Moscow's protests regarding the Baltic states' NATO membership would not change but that the particular historical context was adequate for the creation of a new security system in which both the West and Russia could and should provide security guarantees to countries who desired it. "Right now, there is a need to create a system that would guarantee the Baltic states their security, independence, and sovereignty." The system could be supported by Russian guarantees or by two-way guarantees provided by Russia and the West, Primakov offered.[70]

In response, Baltic countries distinguished between "enlargement" and "expansion," the latter of which was often construed by Russian politicians as a hidden, Western agenda of reimposing dividing lines in Europe. Baltic countries emphasized the difference in terminology vis-à-vis NATO enlargement, a point that was critical in semantics but mostly in intentions. In a 2001 article, Estonian deputy undersecretary of the Ministry of Foreign Affairs captured the meaning of enlargement to the Baltic states.

> ...we are dealing with a process of NATO expansion that is a result of enlargement, not with a process of enlargement that is a result of expansion—otherwise reference is made to NATO as the active side that intends to gain new territories. In fact, the opposite is true. The aspiring members are the ones who want to join; that is also why we should perceive the process as the free choice of sovereign nations, not as the aggressive design of a political-military alliance...The argument that NATO enlargement will draw new lines in Europe can easily be dismissed...In all previous rounds [of enlargement], applicants have been on the active side of the process. This can hardly be characterized as "drawing lines." The only lines that exist in today's Europe are those that are resulting from the free choices of various states. European nations are not choosing sides; they are choosing a certain set of values they prefer to identify themselves with...Estonia, Latvia and Lithuania are not striving to become members of NATO against anyone. Rather, we seek to join the alliance in order to restore our natural place within the trans-Atlantic family of nations...
>
> For us, NATO membership is one of two main foreign policy goals, and is on par with our aspirations toward membership of the European Union. These two organizations are complementary, not contradictory, and that's why we cannot accept the argument that membership in the EU would be sufficient for us. The "EU-only" option, would, in fact, boil down to creating a "Gray zone" in our region...When discussing our future membership in the alliance, the issue of Russia inevitably arises. Membership will bring clarity not only to our relations with Russia; it will also enhance dialogue between the three Baltic countries and Moscow and, in the long run, will enhance cooperation between Russia and NATO as well...When Russian President Vladimir Putin spelled out the options of Russia-NATO relations, he pretty well revealed Moscow's bottom line: according to Putin's argument, either Russia should be a member or there should be no NATO at all. In other words, if Russia is not in, others should not enjoy the right of membership either.[71]

An official statement by the ministers of foreign affairs of countries left out of the first round of postcommunist enlargement similarly underlined the distinction between enlargement of an institution due to the lawful application of aspiring candidates and "expansion" of an institution against the countries' wills. The ministers pointed out that "the Alliance is not in the process of expansion, but enlargement, based on a unity of values and the free expression of the will of people of democratic nations...this process is in everyone's interest and not directed against any nation."[72]

The Estonian prime minister reflected on the European heritage of all the Baltic countries and on Euro-Atlantic membership as an act of historic rectification.

After the First World War, we fought our way to independence, but lost it two decades later. Together with our Baltic brothers and sisters we helped dismantle the former Soviet Union and, as a result, regained our independence after five decades of Soviet occupation. But we understand that in order to remain independent, we must participate actively in European and trans-Atlantic structures of like-minded democratic nations. That's why we've made a choice with a very clear goal—to anchor ourselves where we belong, in Europe. For us, achieving this goal would imply that the Cold War has ended. It would also imply that finally, we would have a Europe whole and free.[73]

Further aggravating relations with Russia was the Baltic countries' consistent support of Euro-Atlantic integration for other former Soviet republics. To the extent that other republics expressed an interest in Euro-Atlantic membership, "Lithuania [would] further support the path of democracy and reform which Ukraine is following and the goals which Ukraine has, that is, the European path, the European-Atlantic path," President Valdas Adamkus said during a joint news conference with his Ukrainian counterpart, Viktor Yushchenko, in November 2006.[74] Lithuanian Prime Minister Gediminas Kirkilas also pledged support for Georgia's aspirations to join NATO and offered to share the experience Lithuania had gained in the process of accession.[75]

The Baltic countries' thorough decoupling from the core occurred with the admission of all three countries in both NATO and the EU in 2004. Decoupling from the core-periphery relationship with Russia, however, did not translate into blindly coupling with a new center of power. As the next and final section of this chapter shows, the Baltic countries took their Euro-Atlantic membership seriously both regarding their responsibilities and their constructive critique.

Assertiveness All Around

Even before joining NATO, the three Baltic countries asserted their national interests in foreign and domestic policies in a manner that often times ran counter to what Russia or their newest Euro-Atlantic allies would have preferred. Since at the time, these countries were not under any security umbrella, their assertiveness must have taken great courage and determination. For instance, when NATO strikes over Kosovo started, all three countries voiced their support for the alliance's actions. "Lithuania supports NATO's decision to initiate air operations in Yugoslavia as a means to prevent [the] spreading of [a] military conflict and humanitarian catastrophe in the Balkan region," a Lithuanian Foreign Ministry statement said. "If NATO requested it, Estonia [would be] ready to send troops to Kosovo," said Estonian Defense Ministry Vice-Chancellor Margus Kolga. "Latvia understands NATO action against military objectives in Yugoslavia. This was the only remaining option," Latvian foreign ministry press spokesman Toms Baumanis underscored as well.[76] The Baltic countries knew that their position ran counter to Russia's pro-Serb, pro-Milosevic policy in Kosovo, and yet stuck to their guns and supported NATO's military intervention.

On the other hand, the Baltics showed a spine in their relations with West Europeans as well. During the spat between European allies and the United States over the handling of Iraq, the Baltic countries sided with the United States in opposition to the Brussels position on the war, which created much aggravation among EU members. When Baltic leaders signed letters of support for the American position toward an invasion of Iraq and the French president blasted them for "missing an opportunity to shut up," the Baltics took the opportunity to assert themselves. "Our country and other countries have a right to express [their] opinions," said Estonian spokeswoman Tiina Maiberg.[77] Much like Central Europeans, none of the Baltic governments appreciated Chirac's scolding and made their position clear in Brussels and elsewhere.

The Baltic countries also stepped into Central Europe's footsteps regarding the promotion of regional cooperative arrangements that increased regional stability and cooperation. Participation in security and non-security structures involved establishing a multinational peacekeeping battalion in 1994 (BALTBAT), developing regional qualified defense officers (BALTDEFCOL), establishing combined air-surveillance networks in 1996 (BALTNET) and a navy squadron in 1997 (BALTRON), establishing a combined battalion between Poland and Lithuania (LITPOLBAT), and establishing a consultative arrangement with Ukraine and the UK (Estonia-UK-Ukraine trilateral). New initiatives in the sphere of infrastructure development (Via Baltica) and political support for Euro-Atlantic membership in 2000 (the Vilnius Group) brought about new levels of regional cooperation and integration never reached under the Soviet system.[78] Regional security and defense integration was enhanced to the point where Poland took over from the United States the duties of policing the air space of the three Baltic countries in 2005.[79] These activities were undertaken without asking for Russia's approval and displayed political courage, initiative, determination, and regional leadership. None of these cooperative arrangements were detrimental to Russia, yet they embodied the pursuit of national interests defined in Tallinn, Riga, and Vilnius.

In the same assertive vein, the Baltic countries actively supported the rights of neighboring countries to choose the democratic system of government and the allies they wanted. "As Europe gains new neighbors through [Baltic] accession and becomes more united, more complete, we too acquire new neighbors through Europe...We are ready and open to share our experience with the nations that are yet to pursue the road of Euro-Atlantic integration such as Ukraine, South Caucasus, and the Balkan states," said the Lithuanian minister of foreign affairs a year before his country's accession into the EU.[80]

As Lithuania made a conscious decision to become "the centre of regional partnerships and international initiatives," Vilnius hosted meetings and conferences intended to enhance cooperation not only with its newest allies in the West but also with its neighbors to the east and south. Cooperation and extending a hand to Ukraine, the Caucasus, and even Belarus were the focus of intense talks. As a result, a 3+3 format of cooperation between the three Baltic countries and the three Caucasus countries emerged in 2005. "In efforts to consolidate our position as the centre of regional co-operation, we must enhance our relations with neighboring countries, warmly respond to the changes taking place in these countries and, if required, offer a friendly hand," the Lithuanian foreign minister further stated.[81]

Enhanced levels of regional cooperation helped diffuse political tensions in neighboring countries experiencing a crisis, as was the case of Ukraine during the presidential election of December 2004. Together with Poland, Lithuanian leaders were invited by then Ukrainian President Leonid Kuchma to help mediate a difficult stalemate between contenders for the presidency, Viktor Yushchenko and Viktor Yanukovych. While the result of elections appeared to favor Yanukovych, who was the Moscow- and Kuchma-backed candidate, large numbers of Ukrainians favored the Euro-Atlantic-oriented Yushchenko, and started what became known as the Orange Revolution. Elections were widely regarded as rigged by the Kuchma administration, to insure the success of the pro-Moscow candidate. Yushchenko and his political allies demanded a new election and accused the government of electoral fraud. The stalemate lasted several weeks, with inconclusive domestic negotiations among contenders and the sitting administration.

Eventually, the Polish and Lithuanian presidents, backed by the authorities in Brussels, were invited to help end the crisis—and they did. They brought the parties together and helped them reach a compromise that all could live with. "Conclusions adopted by the Council [of the EU] confirm European Union's confidence in Lithuanian and Polish presidents who, settling Ukrainian crisis, represent the whole European Union. The fact that [the] Ukrainian President directly invited Lithuanian and Polish leaders to mediate the complex talks indicates Ukrainians' trust in the presidents of these EU states. It is also recognition of Lithuania's ability to solve problems arising in the region," the Lithuanian minister of foreign affairs underscored.[82]

When the Baltic countries felt that Russia was not taking an adequate position vis-à-vis the sovereign rights of neighboring countries, they called on the Kremlin to respect those rights. For instance, Lithuania praised Russia for the withdrawal of its military forces from Georgia, but reminded it to respect its obligations to withdraw military forces from Moldova as well.[83]

Alternatively, when the Baltic countries felt that Russia made progress in a direction that they could endorse, they spoke up to recognize such progress and support Russia. In 2002, the same Lithuanian foreign minister, who would later call on Russia to respect its agreements, praised it for progress in democratic reforms and underscored that "...Lithuania would support Russia in the Council of Europe and the European Union when support would be sought [by the Russian side] for the implementation of co-operation programs..."[84] Even as he declined Putin's invitation to attend the fiftieth anniversary of the end of WWII in Moscow, Valionis emphasized that the relationship with Russia remained complex but not inimical. "...our relations with Russia remained substantially constructive and we have been engaged in the professional solution of a number of specific issues relevant to our business, tourism and cultural exchange sectors. The incident of a Russian military plane crashing in Lithuania was also settled without any infringement of either international law or sovereign national interests."[85]

It is therefore an incomplete venture to assess the relationship between Russia and the Baltic states either as a Russian attempt to pressure the Baltics into a renewed political subservience to the Kremlin or as a Euro-Atlantic plot to take over the Baltics. As we shall see next, the Baltic countries were not shy to tell the Euro-Atlantic allies what they thought about specific policies either.

The Baltic countries asserted themselves vis-à-vis their Euro-Atlantic allies even before they were allies. Baltic disappointment over the perceived condescending attitude of "the West" toward EU candidates was high in the nineties. All three countries had a sense that double standards were being applied in the East–West relationship by the powers in Brussels. In a speech to the Swedish Institute for International Affairs, then Estonian Minister of Foreign Affairs Toomas Hendrik Ilves highlighted Western preconceptions about his country. He gave an example of a 1997 meeting of the Council of Europe, when an Estonian diplomat asked why rules of the Council seemed to apply only to the former communist countries. An ambassador of a "major European country" dismissed the charge but without realizing, underscored the double standards that the Estonian minister was complaining about by stating that the Council of Europe rules "[did] not apply to real countries." Ilves further highlighted the negative clichés that the West attached to the former communist countries as necessarily backward and corrupt. He charged that the Estonian minister of social affairs was berated and insulted on account of the country's insufficient female representation in high-level government positions. Yet, he pointed out, Estonia had more women ambassadors than a "real country" such as the UK at the time of the gender-bias charge. He complained that the meetings of the Stockholm Group, a group of ten countries calling themselves "the Friends of the Balts," were typically held to discuss the situation in the Baltic countries without inviting any of them to the discussions. "To discuss us without inviting us is simply bound to recall us the past," he said, in an indirect reference to the manner in which the fate of his country was decided in WWII.[86]

Negotiations for EU membership also illustrate the condescending attitude of the West toward the three Baltic states. Negotiations were long and arduous, prompting the Lithuanian minister of foreign affairs to remark that "not all original member states of the EU were ready for enlargement and some of them were inclined to view us, the new member states with superiority...or disregard us entirely."[87] Underscoring that the Baltics were not asleep at the wheel, Valionis argued that "there should not be two different regional policies—one for the old EU members, another for the new ones."[88] He later called on the EU to be honest toward candidate countries by demanding "that the enlarged European Union [be] responsive to and equitable with its smaller member states."[89] Such diplomatic rhetoric occurred before Baltic accession into the EU and NATO, prefacing the sovereign assertiveness that was yet to come.

Once admitted in the EU, the Baltic countries stood up for their interests and disagreed vigorously with a 2005 proposed budget that involved substantial subsidy cuts to the new members. Lithuania was one of the countries that voiced clear opposition to UK's budget proposal to cut the financial support for incoming EU members.

"The proposal should be substantially revised," Lithuanian foreign minister emphasized. "We need a proposal based upon fundamental principles of equality and solidarity in Europe," Minister Valionis stated. "We disagree with such attitude of the Presidency and it does not bring us closer to the agreement on the budget. The agreement must not put the least economically developed Member States at [a] disadvantage," Valionis said.[90] The budget proposal was eventually revised, but the Baltics, like the Central Europeans, made their case: They were no pushovers and their positions should not be taken for granted.

CONCLUSION

Whether relations between Russia and the vanguard Baltic countries will ever be characterized by trust and mutually beneficial cooperation remains to be seen. The evidence provided in this chapter shows that the Baltic countries do not take *only* anti-Russian positions, they take domestic and foreign policy positions that reflect the national interest of each country, defined by elected presidents and parliaments, rather than by outside powers who happen to be their allies—or not. Even a Russian ambassador to a Baltic country had to agree that relations between the two countries, strained as they may sometimes be, were not inimical, nor aggressive. Asked whether relations between Russia and Estonia were "icy," the Russian Ambassador to Estonia had this to say in a 2004 interview:

> . . .neither [my Ambassador] position nor my personal opinion can be characterized by the word "icy." Yes, there are numerous problems and friction in our relations, but if one looks at foreign trade figures then these are increasing and transit has not decreased. I am not in favor of magnifying political and diplomatic differences of opinion. I would not say that relations have deteriorated over the three-four years I have spent here [in Tallinn] . . . Russia and Estonia are at the start of a new and long path. There can be friction and misunderstanding along the path. This does not mean, however, that our relations can be called "icy." Naturally, [they are] not excellent, either. The correct wording [to describe relations] would be "adequately normal."[91]

As the Russian ambassador underscored, the relationship between Russia and its former Baltic republics is evolving, with the ups and downs inherent in any relationship. The fact that trade and commerce, cultural exchanges, and sometimes even non-contentious high-level meetings can occur speaks of the potential for future normal relations. Again, it is incumbent on both Russia, to drop the core-periphery mentality in approaching these countries, and the Baltics, to continue to assert their sovereign interests in a principled manner. The future of relations will involve working together toward meeting global challenges that can only be met if, as a Lithuanian minister recently highlighted, "leaders of the Russia-NATO Council. . .refrain from the Cold War stereotypes and not use them in their internal political struggle."[92] The question is: What type of relationship with these countries will Russia choose? As the following chapters show, the jury is still out on this question.

4

The Late-Bloomer Republics

The late-bloomer Soviet former republics of Central Asia had a much harder time decoupling from Russia's big brother influence than the vanguard Central European and the Baltic states. In the post-Soviet period, even some late-bloomer governments considered themselves Russia's traditional sphere of interest. These Central Asian republics had long been the battlefield between expanding Russian influence in the region and the British Empire's interests in the Indian subcontinent and its surrounding lands in the nineteenth century. Known as the "Great Game" for influence in Central Asia, the balancing of interests between Imperial Russia and colonial Britain led to the Central Asian territories falling under the influence of Imperial Russia. Hence, post-Soviet Russia harbors a sense of entitlement to call this area a traditional sphere of national interest.

The former Soviet republics of Armenia, Azerbaijan, Belarus, Georgia, Kazakhstan, Kyrgyzstan, Moldova, Tajikistan, Turkmenistan, Ukraine, and Uzbekistan each took different approaches to their postcommunist, post-Soviet national identity. Armenia, Georgia, and Moldova joined the Baltic states to boycott the New Union Treaty in 1991, designed to salvage the Soviet Union. In their choices of both domestic and foreign policies, these former republics retained elements of the past or introduced reforms that seemed right to the national governments. Sometimes that meant retaining fairly obsolete, Soviet-style authoritarian leaders such as Niyazov in Turkmenistan and Lukashenko in Belarus. Sometimes it meant more substantial change in the direction of democratic reforms and moving toward a market economy, as was the case in Georgia. None of the late-bloomer former Soviet republics had an easy transition to a postcommunist system of their choosing, and some did not even start a transition. Some maintained a Soviet-type of hierarchy and leadership style, as remains the case in Belarus, Turkmenistan, and Uzbekistan. Some started their post-Soviet identity with a "Russia first" foreign policy, only to move toward rapprochement with the Euro-Atlantic community in the twenty-first century, as was the case in Moldova. Some went through color revolutions that overthrew corrupt domestic regimes, and made Russian politicians nervous about the prospect of similar developments within their own borders. Sixteen years after gaining independence, each country has a distinct sovereign identity and its own style of dealing with Russia. Overall, Russia was more involved in their domestic affairs, although it still refrained from its traditional mode of operation. To Russia's credit, when developments did not go the Kremlin's way, it did not send military troops to intervene in the affairs of these countries.

HISTORICAL BACKGROUND

The countries under discussion in this chapter share one thing in common: they were all incorporated into the Russian Empire in the nineteenth century, and then in the Soviet Union in the twentieth century against their will. Apart from that, each has its culture, unique national identity, aspirations, and its share of interethnic tensions. This section provides a brief historical background of developments in each country, listed alphabetically. The historical background provides the context in which some of these countries were able to assert a degree of sovereignty vis-à-vis Moscow, while others were not.

Armenia

Armenia is one of the three Caucasus countries. Located in the southern part of the Caucasus mountains, Armenia was incorporated into the Soviet Union in 1920, and gained its independence in 1991. Traditionally at odds with Turkey as a result of atrocities committed when the country was under Ottoman rule, Armenia had a short-lived statehood from 1918 to 1920. In 1920, it was invaded and annexed by Bolshevik Russia. In 1922, it became an integral part in the TSFSR (Transcaucasian Soviet Federative Socialist Republic) together with Azerbaijan and Georgia. In 1991, it gained its independence from the Soviet Union and has been a sovereign country since.

Sovereign Armenia started its post-Soviet journey against the backdrop of full-scale war with its neighbor, Azerbaijan. At issue was the status of the heavily Armenian-populated enclave of Nagorno-Karabakh, located inside Azerbaijan, that wanted to secede and join Armenia. War lasted until 1994, but a cease-fire agreement was not accompanied by a political solution and as of 2007, Armenia and Azerbaijan have not found common ground on the status of the enclave. Karabakh Armenians control the enclave and a portion of Azeri territory surrounding it. Armenia supports this *status quo* despite several UN resolutions which called on the government to return the enclave to Azerbaijan.

Marred by war, the beginnings of Armenian statehood were difficult and often times tentative. The country held relatively free elections, introduced limited economic reforms, and allowed some freedom of the press and association.

In foreign and defense policy, Armenia maintained a Russian military base at Gyumri, became member of the Russian-dominated CIS in 1991, of PfP in 1994, joined the Council of Europe in 2001, and strengthened relations with both Russia and the Euro-Atlantic community. The country is also a member of the BSEC

(Black Sea Economic Cooperation Organization). In 2005, it signed an IPAP (Individual Partnership Action Plan) with NATO.[1]

The only two exceptions to these overall good external relations are Turkey and Azerbaijan. The borders between Armenia and these countries remain closed and diplomatic relations strained. Economically, Armenia has become a market economy and despite dependence on Russia for its gas consumption, it diversified its energy resources in recent years. Armenia banned media censorship in 2004 but prison terms for journalists who defame the government remained legal. Journalists have been jailed for criticizing the government, an issue that was highlighted by international human rights watchdog institutions such as Human Rights and Freedom House. Politicians have recently called for a reorientation of the country's foreign policy, toward closer ties with the EU and NATO but as of this writing, Russia continues to provide security guarantees through its existing military base and border patrols that operate in the country.

Azerbaijan

Rich in oil and gas, Azerbaijan is the largest of the three Caucasus countries. Like Armenia, after World War I, it had a short-lived period of independence between 1918 and 1920, only to be occupied again by Bolshevik Russia. In 1922, it became part of TSFSR in the newly established Soviet Union. In early 1990, as a result of *glasnost*, Azeris demanded independence from the Soviet Union and demonstrated in the streets of Baku for a free and sovereign Azerbaijan.

Compounding the situation were the ongoing armed conflict with Armenia over the enclave of Nagorno-Karabakh and Azeri–Armenian violence inside the country. Anti-Armenian pogroms occurred in the capital city of Baku in January 1990. Soviet troops were sent to suppress mass demonstrations in support of independence in what has been called Black January. The troops rounded up civilians, beat them, and imprisoned them. The Kremlin defended the military intervention as a means to protect the Armenian minority population against the Azeris but according to Human Rights Watch, the Soviet military intervention was planned before pogroms against the Armenian minority took place.[2] Moscow was increasingly worried about the nationalist movements across the Soviet Union and was trying to suppress local anti-Soviet leaders who sought independence. In October 1991, the country declared independence while still part of the Soviet Union. A national referendum in December confirmed the people's will for self-determination, and accelerated the collapse of the Soviet Union.

Before the 1994 cease-fire agreement with neighboring Armenia, the country witnessed unstable governments, elections fraught with fraud, limited media freedom, and general corruption. Several unlawful overturns of the government brought back to power a former Soviet communist leader, Heydar Aliyev, who was perceived inside and outside the country as autocratic, pro-Moscow, and against reforms that would have made the government more accountable to its people. Aliyev ruled Azerbaijan until 2003 when, in ill-health, he stepped down and nominated his son as the sole presidential candidate of the ruling party in the upcoming elections. Ilham Aliyev won the elections, but like his father, suffered from charges of electoral fraud, media intimidation, and corruption. Anti-Aliyev demonstrators were beaten and imprisoned, and journalists were persecuted if their coverage was anti-Aliyev. While freedom of speech and the media are guaranteed by the constitution, in practice, intimidation of media outlets critical of the government still occurs, and journalists are sometimes murdered.

Economically, the country should be doing very well, given its vast natural resources. However, the national wealth was not used to boost other sectors of the economy. In 1994, the country signed an investment contract with a Western consortium worth $7.4 billion, for the construction of the first non-Russian oil pipeline from the Caspian to Western markets. The BTC (Baku-Tbilisi-Ceyhan pipeline) was built across three countries—Azerbaijan, Georgia, and Turkey—and started providing non-Russian oil for Western markets in 2006.

In foreign policy, the country has been a member of CIS since 1993, of PfP since 1994, of the Council of Europe since 2001, and cofounded a regional organization named GUAM in 1997.[3] It is a member of BSEC. In 2005, it furthered its relationship with NATO by signing an IPAP.

Belarus

Belarus is one of the least reform-oriented countries under analysis. With a tumultuous history of being occupied by various European powers throughout centuries, Belarus had a short-lived period of independence from 1918 until 1919, when it was occupied by the Bolshevik troops and became the Belarusian Soviet Socialist Republic. During WWII, it was occupied by Germany, then reoccupied by the Soviet Union at the end of the war.

There are similarities between the experience of the three Baltic states and Belarus with respect to Moscow's policy of Sovietization and Russification at the end of the war. Stalin deported thousands of local leaders and installed Soviet bureaucrats in the most critical government positions of Soviet Belarus, to avoid a surge of nationalist and secessionist feelings, and to create what was called a *cordon sanitaire* between Russia and the Western world. Deportations led to a depletion of local population levels, particularly among the Jewish community. The Belarusian language was deliberately and forcefully replaced with the Russian language; by the end of the Soviet era, there were no public schools teaching in Belarusian, in Minsk. This policy intensified after 1959, when Nikita Khrushchev declared in the Belarusian capital of Minsk that "the sooner we all start speaking Russian, the faster we shall build communism."[4] Culturally, Belarus had gradually lost some of its identity by the time of *perestroika*.

In 1986, the nuclear accident at Chernobyl gave Belarus the most significant blow in loss of human lives and long-term effects on the health of the population of all the Soviet republics. By the end of the year, a group of twenty-eight Belarusian intellectuals sent Gorbachev a grievance letter that coined the term "cultural Chernobyl."

They complained that the cultural identity of Belarus had been gradually undermined and was in peril of extinction, unless the Belarusian language was reintroduced in all spheres of life.[5] Without a positive response from Moscow, Belarusians started demonstrating for the restructuring of the country, particularly after the 1988 discovery of mass graves of presumed Belarusian victims of Stalin's purges. Demonstrations were violently dispersed by police. In 1991, a series of strikes for higher wages and economic opportunities erupted. In August 1991, Belarus declared its independence.

Between 1991 and 1994, the country went through a period of turbulent politics, with attempts to revise the constitution and establish a new direction. A new constitution was agreed upon in 1994 and elections were held. The pro-Russia candidate, Alexander Lukashenko, won the presidential elections and has governed the country ever since. Constitutionally, the country is a democracy, but in reality freedom of speech and of the media are restricted, freedom of association is severely limited, no "Western-style" economic reforms have been implemented, and the government has asserted an increasing role in a form of planned economy similar to the Soviet one. Belarus is largely dependent on Russia for oil and gas, but is also a transit country for Russian oil and gas to Western markets.

In foreign policy, Belarus is the country that maintained the closest ties with Russia. In 1991, it signed the birth document of the CIS. Lukashenko sought closer ties with Russia to the point of endorsing a Russia-Belarus union that has yet to materialize. In 1995, Belarus joined PfP but never joined the Council of Europe unlike other former Soviet republics. Its ties with Euro-Atlantic members are strained as a result of Lukashenko's openly anti-West attitude. Numerous European institutions and organizations called for more individual freedom for the citizens of Belarus on account of increasingly totalitarian policies of the president.

Georgia

The third Caucasus country, Georgia, shares a similar history with the other two: It enjoyed a period of brief statehood followed by Red Army occupation and transformation into a Soviet Republic. It was independent from 1918 until 1921, when it was occupied by the Soviet Union. Stalin ordered deportations of Georgian nationalists, in the name of cleaning the country of antirevolutionary elements. Georgia was thus stripped of born-and-bred leaders and remained part of the Soviet Union until 1991, when it declared independence. In 1989, peaceful street demonstrations in Tbilisi were violently suppressed by the Soviet army, which precipitated demands for independence under *glasnost* and *perestroika*.

In 1992, a popular uprising against Zviad Gamsakhurdia, the first post-Soviet president of Georgia, brought to power Gorbachev's former minister of foreign affairs, Eduard Shevardnadze. Gamsakhurdia was perceived as corrupt, in favor of a union with Russia, and increasingly totalitarian. He fled to Western Georgia and instigated a counter-rebellion. South Ossetian and Abkhazian forces revolted and declared independence, seeking a reunion with Russia. The legal status of these

Georgian provinces remains unresolved, with South Ossetia seeking unification with North Ossetia, which is an integral part of Russia.

During his eleven years in office, Shevardnadze presided over a deteriorating economy, high poverty, increasingly corrupt government practices, and separatist movements in the breakaway republics of South Ossetia and Abkhazia. With Russian help, a cease-fire was negotiated in the breakaway republics in 1994, but the situation remains volatile. While some political and economic reforms were introduced, they were incomplete, unfocused, and marred by corruption.

The 2003 parliamentary elections were perceived as flawed by international and Georgian election standards. A popular revolt followed, the government was overthrown, Shevardnadze resigned, and new leaders took power. This was the first domestic overthrow of a post-Soviet administration through a popular revolution. It became known as the Rose Revolution, because street protesters were waving and offering roses to the police sent to suppress their movement. Mikhail Saakashvili emerged as the leader of the Rose Revolution and was thereafter elected to the presidency. He ran on a platform of increasing ties with the Euro-Atlantic community, and bringing South Ossetia and Abkhazia breakaway republics into the fold.

Under the Saakashvili administration, Georgia became increasingly assertive toward Russia, demanding troop withdrawal from the four military bases Russia retained on its territory, and warning against Russian support for breakaway republics. Heavily dependent on Russia for energy resources, Georgia's assertiveness in domestic and foreign policy provoked tit-for-tat reactions in Moscow. In 2006, Russia's state-owned Gazprom doubled the price of gas to Georgia, then doubled it again. Georgia started to look for alternative energy sources, particularly from its neighbor Azerbaijan. In the aftermath of the Georgian parliament's resolution to demand Russian troop withdrawal by 2008, Russia banned Georgian wine imports, imposed a postal blockade, and cracked down on Georgian immigrants.

In foreign policy, Georgia joined CIS in 1993, PfP in 1994, the Council of Europe in 1999, was a founding member of GUAM, the Caucasian Group of Four, and BSEC. Under Saakashvili, it made strides in a rapprochement with NATO and the EU, and in 2004, it was the first late-bloomer republic to submit an IPAP to NATO. This moved the country to a second stage of Euro-Atlantic integration, a move that left the Kremlin very concerned about the advance of the West in its area of traditional interest.

In 2005, Georgia was a founding member of the CDC (Community of Democratic Choice), together with Ukraine and Moldova, the Baltic countries, Romania, Slovenia, and the Republic of Macedonia. Conceived as a regional alliance to promote democratic ties among members, the organization saw itself as a vehicle to "remove the remaining divisions in the Baltic-Black Sea region...[and promote] political, security and economic rapprochement between the Western and the Eastern part of the European continent." Vladimir Putin was invited to participate but he declined. A former Kremlin advisor called the organization "an antechamber [for participating countries] to join NATO," while the Russian media warned that the "Unfriendly Community" was a new CIS without Russia, rising in Russia's backyard.[6]

Kazakhstan

Natural resource-rich Kazakhstan is the largest Central Asian former Soviet republic. The territory of present-day Kazakhstan was a fault line for the battle for preeminence in Central Asia between Tsarist Russia and colonial England, with Russia occupying it and exploiting its resources. The first significant uprising of the local Kazakh population against Russian occupiers occurred in the early twentieth century. Despite a Russian colonization of the territory, famine in the twenties, and loss of many Kazakh lives in the armed struggle against Russia, the local population retained its identity and language. In 1936, the Kazakh republic became a Soviet republic and retained this status until full independence in 1991.

Like the other former republics, Kazakhstan suffered its share of deportations, labor camps, famine, and Russification at the hands of successive Soviet administrations. In 1986, Soviet interference in local Kazakh politics and the Kremlin's replacement of a Kazakh leader with a Russian bureaucrat led to the first modern protests against Soviet rule. Soviet troops quelled the protest through armed intervention and many Kazakhs were jailed. Discontent against Soviet rule continued and in 1990, Kazakhstan declared its sovereignty as an autonomous republic within the Soviet Union. In 1991, after the dissolution of the Soviet Union, it declared its independence.

The Kazakh population had few opportunities to develop its homegrown leaders and leadership style during centuries of Russian and Soviet occupation. Independence in 1991 was followed by elections won by the former chief of the Kazakh Communist Party, Nursultan Nazarbayev. He won second and third terms in elections considered rigged and unfair by Western observers, and remains in power as of this writing. His leadership style blends totalitarian tendencies of the communist times, with more liberal measures in the economy. His successive administrations have relied on tight rules regarding human rights and freedom of speech. Nobody has a right to criticize the president. His family's assets are secrets of state. The president retains broad, unchecked powers. Progress toward establishing a democratic society has been assessed negatively by outside observers.

On the other hand, the economy has grown rapidly, attracting foreign investment due to the country's large oil, gas, and mineral resources. The U.S. Congress and the EU recognized a "market economy" status for the country, although both remain critical of its sluggish democratic reforms. Natural gas and oil production largely account for the economy's rapid growth. Kazakhstan is estimated to have vast reserves of both, and the development of new gas and oil fields is being planned. This vast national resource has not, however, translated into higher standards of living for the population. Poverty remains rampant. Like many countries run by powerful and unaccountable leaders, the national energy resources benefit only the top tiers of the administration.

In foreign policy, Kazakhstan has developed good relations with all its neighbors and pursues a policy of cultivating good relations with Russia and the United States, China and Western Europe. These relations led to a large infusion of direct foreign investment in the development of the country's resources extraction. Kazakhstan is a member of CIS, the EEC (Eurasian Economic Community), the SES (Single Economic Space), the CSTO (Collective Security Treaty Organization), the SCO (Shanghai Cooperation Organization), and the CACO (Central Asian Cooperation Organization). In 1994, it joined PfP, and in 2006, it signed an IPAP with NATO. In 1999, it applied for observer status in the Council of Europe. The Assembly of the Council responded that Kazakhstan was eligible to apply for full membership but that would not be granted, due to its poor human rights record.

After the September 11, 2001 attacks on the United States, Kazakh authorities offered critical support to the military operations led by the United States in Afghanistan. Air corridors were open to American airplanes transporting military equipment and personnel, and intelligence information was shared about possible movements of known terrorist organizations operating in northern Afghanistan. Speculations abounded about Kazakh offers of domestic air bases for the use of the U.S. military but as of 2007, the United States does not use Kazakh bases.[7]

Kyrgyzstan

The country was occupied by the Russian Empire in the nineteenth century and massive popular revolts led to violent Russian suppression of Kyrgyz nationalism. Soviet influence was established early in the twentieth century and in 1936, Kyrgyzstan was turned into a Soviet Republic. Stalin suppressed the Kyrgyz national identity and domestic tensions remained high throughout the Soviet years.

With the *glasnost* era, domestic organizations initiated political movements for change and elections were held in 1990, while still under Soviet rule. The elections brought to power the liberal president of the Kyrgyz Academy of Sciences, Askar Akayev. He appointed reform-oriented politicians to critical government jobs. Despite what appeared to be strong support for an independent Kyrgyzstan, the March 1991 referendum held on the question of preserving the Soviet Union showed strong popular support for the preservation of a "renewed federation" of willing, autonomous states. The failure of the August Moscow coup was followed by a declaration of independence in Bishkek, the capital of the country. Akayev ran for president and won by a large margin. He ruled the country from 1991 until 2005, when he was ousted by a popular revolt that became known as the Tulip Revolution.[8]

Akayev was initially embraced by the Kyrgyz as a good domestic alternative to Soviet authorities. Despite the fact that the country is rich in natural resources, the Akayev administration used the returns on those resources primarily for personal gain. The president elected by 95 percent of the popular vote in 1991 became increasingly authoritarian, lacking transparency of governance, promoting family and relatives to key government jobs, and building a reputation of corrupt management of the economy. The Tulip Revolution was a grassroots rejection of his administration, in the aftermath of rigged parliamentary elections. The president was accused of rigging the elections and thousands of demonstrators flooded the streets of the capital and several other cities in the country. In the face of anti-Akayev popular demonstrations, the president and some of his family fled the country and sought refuge in Russia.

Post-Akayev Kyrgyzstan held new, transparent elections and Kurmanbek Bakiyev was elected to the president's office. He ran on a platform of rooting out corruption but the efforts of his administration have so far fallen short of achieving visible progress. Domestic unrest remains, particularly in the poorer parts of the country and in areas with large Uzbek populations. Although post-Akayev Kyrgyzstan enjoys more credibility with international institutions, the country has a long way to go to achieve political stability.

In foreign policy, the country is a member of CIS, the EEC, the CSTO, the SCO, and CACO. It joined PfP in 1994. After the September 11, 2001 attacks on the United States, the country allowed the use of one of its airports as a base of operations for U.S. forces fighting against terrorist groups in Afghanistan and beyond. While the United States used the Manas airport in Bishkek, Russia received permission to use the Kant airport for the same type of antiterrorist operations. The two airports are located within 30 kilometers of each other (approximately 15 miles). Kyrgyzstan has a balanced approach to its relations with Russia and the Euro-Atlantic community.

Moldova

The territory of present-day Moldova was occupied by Tsarist Russia in the nineteenth century but, unlike other countries under discussion, it proclaimed independence after the Russian Revolution in 1917, and immediately united with Romania. Ethnically, Moldovans and Romanians have close cultural and language ties and share common ancestry.

Moldova's current territory is made up of two distinct areas, divided by the Dniester River. The territory west of the river used to be called Bessarabia and was part of Romania until 1940, when the Soviet Union occupied it as a result of the Molotov-Ribbentrop Secret Protocol. The area east of the river was an autonomous region within Ukraine until 1940, when the Soviet Union combined it with Bessarabia to form the Socialist Republic of Moldova. The territory that used to be part of Romania is heavily inhabited by people of Romanian descent; the territory that used to be part of Ukraine is primarily inhabited by people of Ukrainian and Russian descent.

During Soviet rule, Moldova underwent Russification and deliberate uprooting of any Moldovan leaders advocating for reunification with Romania. Immediately after WWII, it witnessed famine, deportations, anticommunist protests, and mass resistance to Soviet rule.

During *glasnost,* the Moldovan parliament adopted a language law that established Moldovan as the state language, and replaced the Soviet-imposed Cyrillic alphabet with the Latin alphabet. In 1990, it held the first free elections for the parliament while still part of the Soviet Union. In August 1991, it declared independence.

In 1992, after the collapse of the Soviet Union and increasing calls in Romania to reestablish the pre-1940 "greater Romania," the Trans-Dniester population east of the river felt threatened and unilaterally declared independence from Moldova. Fighting broke out and only came to an end with the introduction of Russian peace-keepers. Ever since, the separatist region continues to claim independent status, and organized a referendum on the question of reunification with Russia in 2006. Neither independence nor the validity of the referendum was recognized by the Moldovan government or the international community. Russia continues to support a political solution to the status of breakaway Trans-Dniester that is mutually agree-able but that solution has yet to materialize. Moldova resents Moscow's continued military presence in a territory it considers its own and relations have been strained.

Despite expectations of reunification with Romania, the results of a 1994 referen-dum overwhelmingly supported continued sovereignty. The first post-Soviet govern-ments tried to introduce reforms but were largely ineffective and were voted out of power. In 2001, the Communist Party of Moldova scored overwhelming electoral success and observers expected a return to a more pro-Russia foreign policy. Instead, Vladimir Voronin, the new president, tried to secure the withdrawal of Russian troops from Trans-Dniester, a development which led to a deterioration in relations with Moscow. Voronin and his party won reelections in 2005 and contrary to expect-ations, started to talk about Euro-Atlantic rapprochement, EU membership, and in the long run, a closer relation with NATO.

Moldova is heavily dependent on Russia for energy supplies. When Gazprom doubled the price of gas in 2006, Moldova refused to pay and Russia cut off supplies. A temporary agreement was reached for a price increase, with further price hikes expected in 2007. The cutting off of gas supplies to Moldova, and as we shall see to Ukraine as well, was not well received by the Euro-Atlantic community, who started to doubt Russia's reliability as an energy supplier. Whether Russia believed that it was acting appropriately or not, the long-term result of mixing energy with politics reflected negatively on the Kremlin.

In foreign policy, Moldova is a member of CIS, CDC, BSEC, GUAM, and is an observer in EEC. It joined PfP in 1994, and signed an IPAP in 2006. It signed a PCA (Partnership and Cooperation Agreement) with the EU in 1998, conducive to an institutional framework for bilateral relations; and a European Neighborhood Policy Action Plan in 2004. It also receives assistance from the EU through the TACIS program.

Tajikistan

"The land of the Tajiks" or Tajikistan was another Central Asian territory that suffered from the Russian expansion of the nineteenth century. A Soviet Socialist Republic since 1929, the country witnessed little to no notable resistance to Soviet occupation. It declared its independence after the dissolution of the Soviet Union in 1991, and almost immediately collapsed into civil war.

The civil war between 1992 and 1997 is mostly known for the complicated mix of warring factions, over 50,000 casualties, and hundreds of thousands of displaced civilians. Like other Central Asian countries, Tajikistan is composed of a mix of ethnic groups, with Tajiks, Uzbeks, and Russians being predominant. The country also has considerable numbers of Islamic groups. Fighting broke out between disenfranchised groups from the northern part of the country and supporters of the president elected in 1991 elections, Emomali Rakhmonov, from the south of the country. Several disenfranchised groups known as the UTO (United Tajik Opposition) took to the streets in 1991 to protest the result of the elections and demanded representation in the country's political process. By 1992, armed militias were mobilized and fighting broke out. Rakhmonov's side enjoyed military and political support from Russia and was able to prevail. In the process, ethnic cleansing was reported in the southern parts of the country, with many people fleeing in the face of ethnic persecution and atrocities.[9]

A cease-fire was brokered by the United Nations in 1994 and was backed by Russia, who was a party to the negotiations. The peace agreement took two more years to negotiate, partly because Russia backed Rakhmonov in his refusal to accept that UTO should have as much political representation as it demanded. The takeover of Kabul by the Islamic Taliban in neighboring Afghanistan in 1996 was cause for concern in many countries, including Russia. UTO organized and operated militias from bases in the northern parts of Afghanistan and the prospect of having the Taliban putting its weight behind Islamic groups in Tajikistan was perceived as a threat to Central Asia. Russia convinced Rakhmonov to accept UTO's demands and a peace agreement was signed in 1997, giving UTO the 30 percent representation in the country's government positions that it demanded.[10]

The civil war left the country in a state of ruin, with the economy barely functioning, and people living off food provided by international aid agencies. There were serious concerns that the population would starve in the absence of concerted international aid. Political tensions remained, with UTO militias not fully disarmed, and continuing occasional armed squabbles among rival groups. High-level political assassinations became common, underscoring the low level of trust among those fighting for power. Elections held in 1994, 1999, 2000, and 2005 returned Rakhmonov's party to power but were considered rigged and marred by irregularities by outside observers. President Rakhmonov has considerable power and does not tolerate dissent. The country's media management is dominated by the government and few dissident voices make their way to the population at large. Overall, Tajikistan is considered one of the least democratized former Soviet republics and, in the aftermath of the civil war, one of the poorest and least reform-oriented. It is also considered the first stopping point of drug-traffickers from Afghanistan toward Western markets, and drug money appears to influence the political process as well.

In foreign policy, Tajikistan is a member of CIS, the EEC, CSTO, SCO, and CACO. It joined PfP in 2002. In 2001, after the terrorist attacks on the United States, the country became strategically important to the countries fighting against terrorist groups in Afghanistan. In 2004, Russia opened a military base at Dushanbe, also to strengthen the antiterrorism campaign. Tajikistan has unresolved border disputes with Uzbekistan and Kyrgyzstan. Overall, it has developed good relations with both Russia and the Euro-Atlantic community.

Turkmenistan

Turkmen groups fought the hardest against expanding Russian influence in Central Asia but were ultimately defeated. By the end of the nineteenth century, Turkmenistan was incorporated into the Russian Empire and in 1924, it became a Soviet republic. Nationalist groups were scarce and the Turkmenistan Soviet Socialist Republic was one of the few who voted to retain a reformed version of the Soviet Union in the 1991 referendum. When the Soviet Union collapsed, the country declared independence.

Post-Soviet Turkmenistan was vastly influenced by the leadership of Saparmurat Niyazov, the chief of the Communist Party since 1985. He was elected to the presidency of sovereign Turkmenistan in 1991, and ruled with an iron fist, an unprecedented cult of personality, and thorough control of the media. He influenced the parliament to offer him a "president for life" status in 1999, called himself the "father of the Turkmen," reinvented the country's history and culture, and mandated the teaching of a book he wrote, *Rukhnama* or *Book of the Soul*. *Rukhnama* was marketed as the sole truth of Turkmen history and ethics.

Niyazov used the country's vast gas and oil revenues to build huge statues of himself throughout the country and kept the population relatively uneducated. His administration also created jobs and offered substantial social benefits to all countrymen. No political opposition was permitted and no free media outlets were known to exist. The security apparatus was strong, repressing any signs of popular or political opposition. Upon his sudden death in 2006, the government quickly selected an acting president and announced that the country would remain committed to the political course set by Saparmurat Turkmenbashi. As of 2007, Turkmenistan remains the former Soviet republic with the least progress in democracy and human rights, and one of the poorest populations in spite of its large natural gas and oil resources.[11]

In foreign policy, Turkmenistan joined CIS in 1991. In 1995, it adopted a policy of permanent neutrality and in 2005, it withdrew its full membership from the CIS, but retained an associate member status. The country joined PfP in 1994. In line with its permanent neutrality policy, the country politically isolated itself but retained diplomatic and trade relations with the region, and with countries further to the West. By the nature of its underdeveloped infrastructure and geographic position, it sells most of its natural resources to Russia. New pipelines may be built to connect Turkmenistan directly to its Western markets but such projects remain under discussion as of this writing.

Ukraine

The territory of present-day Ukraine was occupied at various times in history by nomadic Mongol and Tatar tribes, the Polish-Lithuanian Commonwealth, and the Austro-Hungarian and the Russian Empires. It enjoyed a brief period of independence after the Bolshevik Revolution, from 1917 to 1921. In 1922, Ukraine was partitioned between Poland and the Soviet Union, with the former occupying the western part of Ukraine and the latter taking its eastern part. Present-day Ukraine tends to mirror these hundred-year old influences, with western Ukraine showing more interest in ties with the Euro-Atlantic community, and eastern Ukraine favoring a pro-Russia identity.

Russification, purges of the Ukrainian elite, ambitious industrialization plans, and the collectivization of agriculture had lasting and devastating effects on Ukraine. During the second five-year plan of the socialist economy, Stalin's industrialization program required increased amounts of agricultural products to feed the industrial machine. Known as "the bread basket of Europe," Ukraine was the ideal place to produce the necessary food for the Soviet needs. Independent Ukrainian farmers were forced into collectives. At harvest time, they had grain quotas to deliver to the Soviet authorities. If the quotas were not met, the peasants would not receive their rations of food. This punitive practice, coupled with communist zealotry, led to the starvation of millions of Ukrainians in what is known as the Great Famine, or the *Holodomor*. Elite purges further deprived the Soviet republic of its best and brightest Ukrainians.

During WWII, a scenario much like the one in the Baltic countries occurred, with German troops occupying western Ukraine from the Soviet Union and being received as "liberators" by the local population. Nazi Germany pursued its own plan of persecution and deportations of Jewish and Ukrainian populations, and prepared the territory for Germanization. As the war changed course against the Axis powers, Ukraine was liberated, then occupied by the Red Army. The war left the country devastated, without its elites, and with a decimated rural population.

During *glasnost,* nationalist tendencies were tempered by strong, pro-Soviet Union party communists. In January 1990, in a move similar to the Baltic Way, over 300,000 Ukrainians demonstrated in support of national unity by holding hands in the streets. In July, the parliament adopted the Declaration of State Sovereignty of Ukraine and ruled that Ukrainian law was paramount over Soviet law. The Act of Independence from the Soviet Union was adopted immediately after the August coup in Moscow, and submitted to a referendum in December. Ukrainians turned out in large numbers to vote for independence and elect a homebred president. Leonid Kravchuk became the first president of independent Ukraine.

Post-Soviet Ukraine went through uneven and incomplete political and economic reforms, increasing corruption at the highest levels of consecutive administrations, and predatory practices in the privatization of state assets. Dissatisfied, Ukrainians voted Kravchuk out and Leonid Kuchma in. He served for two terms and during his time in office, the level of corruption among state officials reached new peaks. He cracked down on independent media and on civil liberties. During his tenure, notorious crimes against journalists took place, some of which drew the attention of the international community due to their level of violence. Heorhyi Gongadze, an investigative journalist known for his criticism of the president's office, was found beheaded in 2000. Tapes apparently recorded in Kuchma's office and smuggled out of the country by one of his former bodyguards seemed to indicate that the president had been involved in planning Gongadze's abduction and execution.[12] Relations between Ukraine and the Euro-Atlantic community, particularly the United States, became very strained in the aftermath of this affair.

In 2004, presidential elections pitted Kuchma's favorite, his premier Viktor Yanukovyich, and former Prime Minister Viktor Yushchenko. The Central Election Commission declared victory for Yanukovyich and Vladimir Putin congratulated him for his win. Yanukovyich was considered a pro-Russia politician whose election guaranteed that Ukraine would remain in the Kremlin's orbit of influence.

In Kyiv, however, thousands of demonstrators wearing Yushchenko's electoral color, orange, blocked the center of the city, accused the administration of electoral fraud, and demanded new elections. Yushchenko and his political allies took to the streets, and were joined by increasing numbers of dissatisfied citizens in what has become known as the Orange Revolution. After weeks of impasse, Lithuania, Poland, and the EU stepped in and helped the parties reach an agreement. New elections were held and Yushchenko was declared the winner. Eastern Ukraine voted primarily for Yanukovyich; western Ukraine voted overwhelmingly for Yushchenko, known for his Euro-Atlantic sympathies.

Yushchenko had difficulty implementing a program of domestic economic and political reforms and his initial coalition of Orange political allies broke down within a year. He had to accept his political rival, Yanukovyich, as prime minister but political consensus was still not reached. While he restated Ukraine's ambition to join Euro-Atlantic institutions, the domestic political stalemate slowed down the country's rapprochement with the Euro-Atlantic community. As of this writing, Ukraine remains in a political impasse.

In foreign policy, Ukraine is a member of CIS, founding member of CDC, SES, GUAM, and BSEC. It joined PfP in 1994. Despite political rhetoric regarding closer ties with NATO, Ukraine does not have an IPAP agreement. In its relations with Russia, it witnessed several crises over gas supplies and a host of diplomatic rows about history. Russia is strongly opposed to Ukraine's overtures to join NATO, although Ukraine does not have an actual Membership Action Plan toward membership.

Uzbekistan

Considered the poorest Central Asian former Soviet republic, Uzbekistan was also incorporated in the Soviet Union in the early twentieth century. Opposition to Soviet rule was occasional and ineffective, and was eventually eliminated by the Soviet authorities. In 1991, Uzbekistan declared independence from the Soviet Union and became a charter member of the CIS.

Since independence, the country's elected leaders promised gradual reform to a market economy and a democratic system but *de facto* consolidated authority in the hands of a few. The economic power of the country remains firmly in the hands of the government. Foreign investment and private enterprises are scarce. The political system resembles the Soviet past: while the government is a step above the level of authoritarianism of Turkmenistan, it is fairly close ideologically. The institutions of the past merely changed names, not substance. Such cosmetic changes are symbolized by the so-called transformation of the Communist Party into the People's Democratic Party. Islam Karimov, the president of the country before 1991, has remained at the helm of the government.

Karimov and his authoritarian system were able to survive using a combination of repression of liberties and fear. Freedom of speech and association were severely curtailed. Promising alternative political parties were either declared illegal or banned from running for parliament based on technicalities. Party and independent activists were jailed or persecuted. Independent media does not exist, therefore alternative voices are not heard. As a result, no effective political opposition exists in the country.

In addition, countrymen were warned that too much freedom would lead to the rise of an Islamic threat and the country could sink into civil war, as was the case in Tajikistan. Mass protests and demonstrations were suppressed; a 2005 revolt in Andijan, against the repressive nature of the government, was violently put down in the name of defending the country against the Islamic threat. Outside human rights organizations and several Western countries condemned the crackdown on political opposition figures, the censorship of the media, and the general lack of individual freedoms.

In foreign policy, Uzbekistan is a member of CIS, CSTO, EEC, GUUAM (from 1999 until 2005), and SCO. It joined PfP in 1994. In the aftermath of the September 11 attacks in the United States, Uzbek authorities permitted the American military to use a domestic base in the south of the country, with access to the Afghan border. After the violent repression of the 2005 Andijan domestic riots, the United States called for an investigation of the administration's brutal handling of this domestic uprising. In response, the Uzbek parliament voted to ask the United States to leave its military base in the south. Soon afterward, the country signed a bilateral treaty with Russia for closer military cooperation.

All the countries under discussion in this chapter have been heavily influenced by the Soviet past in shaping their own statehood and sovereign aspirations. Having been an integral part of the Soviet Union, their models of governance sometimes resemble the communist hierarchy and mode of operation. In the absence of alternative political models, one should remember the starting point of these countries in their transition from non-sovereign republics to fully independent countries and be mindful of cultural complexities. By the nature of the historic relationship established between the core in the Kremlin and the periphery in each of these countries' capitals, "big brother" Russia will continue to have an important role to play in the evolution of Central Asian sovereign and assertive states. Yet even little brothers eventually get tired of being lectured by big brothers and run away from home. As the remainder of the chapter suggests, some of them are already at the door.

DOMESTIC POLICY ASSERTIVENESS

Late-blooming republics displayed variable degrees of domestic assertiveness vis-à-vis Russia and other centers of power in almost reverse priority order from the vanguard Central European and the Baltic states. For late bloomers, the main threat to sovereignty was energy security. Most of them depend on Russia for gas and oil supplies, and most of them experienced some form of economic pressure from Russia since becoming independent. Setting the historical record straight and not yielding to further pressure from the Kremlin was an erratic priority, not nearly as systematically implemented as it was in the Baltic countries. Finally, developing democratic institutions and a free market were long-term goals for some but not for others, and several countries chose a more authoritarian type of governance. The evidence suggests that Russia tried to interfere more often in the affairs of late-blooming sovereign neighbors and openly supported domestic leaders with a pro-Russia orientation. Nevertheless, each country seemed to define priorities in their home capitals. As Putin's agenda for a strong Russia became more evident, the late-bloomer republics did not automatically adopt pro-Kremlin policies. Instead, they asserted their national identities as a function of a "don't take us for granted" approach, even when they knew that a coalition with Russia was in their best interest.

Attempts to Reduce Dependence on Russian Energy Resources

The following former Soviet republics depend on Russian energy supplies: Armenia, Belarus, Georgia, Moldova, and Ukraine. The following countries bordering on the Caspian Sea extract oil and gas from the seabed (a shared seabed-exploration formula has not been finalized): Azerbaijan, Kazakhstan, Russia, Turkmenistan (and Iran, outside the scope of this book).[13] Kyrgyzstan depends mostly on Uzbekistan for its energy needs. Uzbekistan can be energy self-sufficient, when resources are properly managed. Tajikistan still struggles to turn a large electricity-producing plant into a self-sufficient, electricity-exporter resource. To date, the country has witnessed years of unstable electricity supplies, with no government explanation for erratic plant closures. When shortages occur, Tajikistan relies on its neighbors, Turkmenistan, Uzbekistan, and to a small extent, Russia for electricity.

An interdependence exists between Russia and late-blooming republics regarding supply, demand, and transit of energy resources. Russia holds the monopoly over resource extraction and refining. Some late-bloomer republics own transmission networks. They need oil and gas for domestic and industrial consumption, while Russia needs to place its oil and gas with dependable consumers.

Russia delivers approximately a third of its oil exports to Europe through a 1960 Soviet-era pipeline system called Druzhba. The main pipeline originates in Russia and branches off in three directions from Belarus. One branch goes northward to Lithuania and Latvia, another westward to Poland and Germany, and another branch goes across western Ukraine to Hungary, Slovakia, and the Czech Republic. Oil pipelines are owned and operated by Russian state-controlled Transneft company.

The Yamal Peninsula at the Kara Sea in Siberia holds the world's largest known natural gas reserve and is owned by Russia. The Yamal-Europe pipeline links European consumers to Russian gas via Belarus. State-owned and controlled Gazprom is the Russian gas company with the exclusive right to export natural gas out of Russia.[14]

Due to increased worldwide demand for energy supplies, aging Russian extraction and refining technology, and insufficient Russian investment in new transmission networks, Russia is sometimes dependent on Central Asian gas to meet its supply obligations toward European consumers. On occasion, when European demand is higher than Gazprom's production capacity, Russia imports low-priced gas from Turkmenistan and Uzbekistan for domestic consumers, and uses its domestic gas production to fulfill its contractual obligations toward European consumers. Russia also owns the pipelines linking it to Central Asian gas from Turkmenistan and Kazakhstan; therefore, these countries cannot sell directly to European or other consumers.

Countries such as Belarus and Ukraine (used to) own the distribution networks that transport Russian gas and oil to Europe. After gaining independence, they made a barter arrangement with Russia: they provided access to the gas and oil transit services in exchange for gas and oil for domestic use. If their domestic demand was higher than the quota provided by the barter system, they bought further gas and oil from Russia at prices significantly lower than what Russia charged its Western European clients. This arrangement came to an end in the second Putin administration.

Whether due to increasing worldwide oil and gas prices, or to the increasing assertiveness of some late-bloomer republics in decoupling from the Kremlin, or due to Russia's awareness that energy was a significant source of political leverage, the barter system was changed in 2006. Vladimir Putin decided that since some countries chose to go their own way, Russia should not feel obligated to subsidize their energy needs. He instructed Gazprom to recalibrate gas prices to former republics compatible to the prices it charged its European consumers.[15] Appendix IV offers a snapshot of the evolution of Gazprom fees for select European and Central Asian consumers. While precise information about gas prices is elusive, Appendix IV indicates that at the time European consumers were charged over $200 per thousand cubic meters of gas per year, the former republics paid a fourth, or less, of the Western prices for the same amount of gas. As Austria was paying $221, Germany $217, and Turkey $243, former republics were paying between $50 and $80 for the same amount of gas. The Russian decision to raise prices needs to be viewed in proper perspective.

While Russia had a right to sell its products at whatever prices it wanted, it was the manner in which the higher prices were imposed that indicated political, rather than market-related, reasons behind the Kremlin's decision. Countries were caught by surprise by drastic price increases only a few months before winter started. In some cases, late-bloomer countries had long-term agreements for deliveries of Russian gas or oil. Gazprom unilaterally decided to renegotiate those agreements, and tripled or quadrupled the price. As winter approached, and as domestic budgets did not provide for spending at the new price levels, governments found themselves in a situation of either spending money they did not budget for, or letting their populations freeze. Some countries negotiated to lower the new prices. Others tried to leverage their transit facilities and threatened a tit-for-tat price hike for transit fees. Finding themselves at the end of the supply–transit chain, European consumers became nervous and accused Russia of being an unreliable energy supplier. Russia retorted that the supply was not in question, the transit through former republics was. As of 2007, Russia continues to increase the price of gas. Late-blooming republics have therefore started looking for alternative sources of energy, further decoupling from their former core of political influence.

Armenia

The country started looking for alternative sources of energy as early as 1992, when it signed an agreement with Iran for the construction of a natural gas pipeline that would transport Iranian gas directly to Armenia. After the initial agreement, however, the deal did not move forward for various political and economic reasons. At the time, Armenia was paying $50 per thousand cubic meters of gas from Russia (see Appendix IV) and was considered a pro-Russian former republic.

Construction of the Iran-Armenia pipeline started twelve years later, in 2004. In March 2007, Armenian and Iranian presidents opened the first section of the pipeline. Iranian gas offered an alternative source to Armenia, and reduced its over-reliance on Russian gas, supplied almost entirely by Gazprom until the opening of the Iranian-Armenian pipeline.[16] In anticipation of the opening of this pipeline, Russia decided to raise the price of gas it sold to Armenia. In 2006, Gazprom more than doubled the price of gas for Armenia, to $110 per thousand cubic meters, in what was largely viewed as retribution for the country's diversification of resources from non-Russian suppliers.

In addition, Armenia's foreign minister articulated the country's interest to participate in a planned Transcaspian gas pipeline from eastern Turkmenistan via the Caspian Sea, through Azerbaijan and Georgia. "It will be a second step after construction of the Iran-Armenia pipeline aimed at diversification of gas supply to Armenia," Minister Vardan Oskanyan said.[17] Armenia is not fully independent of Russia for its energy supplies but diversification allows it a bargaining position that makes it less vulnerable to drastic price increases.

Azerbaijan

Direct access to Caspian resources makes Azerbaijan much less vulnerable to Russian price fluctuations than most late-bloomer republics. In addition to being able to extract as much oil as it needs for domestic consumption, Azerbaijan can also sell it to its neighbors. Immediately after the collapse of communism, in the early nineties, development of Caspian Sea transmission networks became an international endeavor of high priority, given the vast energy resources estimated to lie beneath the seabed. This eventually led to the construction of the BTC, after over a decade of negotiations, despite strong Russian objections against any pipeline that would not cross its territory or its dedicated area of the seabed.

The BTC represents the most significant source of non-Russian oil in Central Asia, and the likely reason for decreasing dependence on Russian oil by several late-blooming countries. Considered the second longest oil pipeline in the world, BTC originates in the Azeri oil shores of the Caspian Sea, passes through the capital, Baku, northwest through Georgia's capital, Tbilisi, and then southwest through Turkey to the port of Ceyhan. Discussions about bringing Caspian oil to the Mediterranean, avoiding the congested Bosphorus Straits in the Black Sea, started in the early nineties. Russia was initially part of the discussions but insisted on a route that would cross Russian territory. When negotiations indicated that Russia would not get what it asked for, it withdrew from planning and execution. The final route was agreed upon in 1999, construction started in 2002, and the pipeline was completed in 2005. The first oil was pumped out of the Caspian in May 2005 and reached Ceyhan a year later. The pipeline is 1,778 kilometers long (approximately 1,100 miles).[18]

The AIOC (Azerbaijan International Operating Company) ships Azeri oil through BTC to European markets. Before the BTC was operational, AIOC was using a Russian pipeline to the Black Sea port of Novorossiysk for its exports. In 2007, Azerbaijan stopped using the Baku-Novorossiysk pipeline and exported its oil exclusively through BTC.[19] This is by far the most significant level of independence from Russian energy supplies or transmission networks among late-blooming republics.

In addition to being self-sufficient in the production and export of oil, Azerbaijan made itself self-sufficient in its domestic need for gas, and in the process, short-circuited its supplies of oil to Russia. This represents a unique situation between Russia and a former republic, with Azerbaijan giving Russia a taste of its own medicine.

Gas prices are critical for Azerbaijan because almost all the electricity-generating capacities in Azerbaijan operate on gas, a total domestic need of approximately 10–11 billion cubic meters per year. The country generates 5 billion cubic meters from its own reserves and (used to) import the rest from Russia. The price that Gazprom charged Azerbaijan was $110 per thousand cubic meters of gas.

In 2006, Gazprom proposed to more than double the price of gas to $235 for 2007. Believed to be a Russian reaction to Azerbaijan's increasing energy independence, the Azeri leadership refused the offer and labeled it "commercial blackmail." President Ilham Aliyev told the media that he could not "allow that to happen. Azerbaijan is no longer the kind of state that can be forced into anything."[20] Instead, the country looked for alternative energy resources from Iran. Initial talks looked promising but the two sides could not agree on a price by the end of 2006.

At the end of 2006, the Azeri government decided not to accept the Gazprom price hike and stopped importing Russian gas. In order to make up for the gas it imported from Russia, the country redirected a portion of its crude oil production from exports to refining and used the more expensive fuel oil to make up for the gas it needed for domestic consumption. In order to do so, Azerbaijan stopped crude oil supplies to a Russian Black Sea terminal in January 2007, saying it needed more oil to produce electricity domestically. President Aliyev said Azerbaijan had no other way to ensure its electricity security but to reduce the volume of oil it exported to Russia via the Baku-Novorossiysk pipeline.[21]

Much like other countries whose gas prices were doubled overnight by Gazprom, Azerbaijan showed that it would not stand for price increases it considered politically motivated. Azerbaijan, however, is in a comparatively strong position due to its proximity to the Caspian Sea; as we shall see, other former republics are not that fortunate and have little leverage over Russia.

Belarus

Belarus depends entirely on Russian gas for domestic consumption. Russia depends on Belarus for transit of its oil and gas to Europe.

Russia transports about a fifth of its total of oil exports (approximately a million barrels per year) via Belarus through the Druzhba and Yamal pipelines. Oil supplies from Russia were free of export duties until 2006. Under a bilateral arrangement, Russian companies refined low-quality crude oil in Belarus. Belarus in turn exported the refined products to Europe at market prices, with high profit margins for the Russian suppliers and the Belarus refineries. Belarus charged export duties on the refined products, earning good revenues for the state budget.

In 2006, Gazprom proposed to raise the price of gas from $47, well below the market price, to $180 per thousand cubic meters. The Belarusian administration was outraged by the threefold price hike and started looking for alternative sources of energy. Belarus could not identify other sources of gas before the Gazprom dead-line and accepted a more than doubling of the gas price for 2007. Two minutes before the end of 2006, Belarus signed the new contract with Gazprom, which envisioned a price increase from $47 to $100 per thousand cubic meters. Even after signing the new contract, Belarus continued to pay the old price, accumulating a debt of $460 million by mid-2007. Under Gazprom's threat of diminished gas flow, the country agreed to pay the debt from its national reserves.[22]

In addition to the price increase, Belarus agreed to sell Gazprom the remaining 50 percent of Belarusian gas pipeline operator Beltransgaz shares. This was by far the last Belarusian bargaining chip in its relations with Russia, so the authorities decided to make the best of a difficult situation and charged a higher price than Gazprom was prepared to offer. Gazprom was ready to buy out Beltransgaz for $1.65 billion, but Belarus asked and received $2.5 billion.

Lastly, Russia also imposed an oil export duty of $180.7 per metric tone on Bela-rus. In what was widely regarded as a tit-for-tat move, the Belarusian government announced a raise in the transit fee for Russian oil to $45 per tone, an equally outra-geous increase from the $.41 per metric tone of oil that Russia paid since 1996.[23] Announcing the tax, President Alexander Lukashenko accused Moscow of taking "extremely unfriendly steps" toward its neighbor. "If Russia, choking on this influx of petrodollars...is still willing to make a scapegoat of Belarus...then let's ask the Russian Federation—so huge and so rich—to pay us in full for our services," he said announcing the new transit tax on Russian oil.[24] "The introduction of the duty is a reciprocal measure of the Belarusian side following the Russian government's earlier decision to use export duties on oil brought into the [Belarusian] republic," a spokes-man for the Ministry of Foreign Affairs said.[25]

When Russian oil company Transneft refused to pay the new transit fee on the first oil shipment of the year, Belarus took the Russian company to court and halted oil supplies via the Druzhba pipeline to Poland, Germany, and Ukraine.[26] After ten days of halted supplies, high-level negotiations in Moscow, and phone conversations between presidents Putin and Lukashenko, the dispute was resolved and oil supplies restored. Belarus dropped the transit fee on Russian oil and negotiated down the new export duty on oil, from $180 to $53 per metric ton. The two sides also agreed that Russia would receive 70 percent compensation from Belarus's exports of refined Russian oil in 2007, 80 percent in 2008, and 85 percent in 2009, according to Russia's Prime Minister Mikhail Fradkov.[27]

The Belarusian government went further in asserting itself. During a January 2007 meeting, a decision was reached to demand Russia to pay rent for the land under the pipelines. Alexander Lukashenko was quoted as saying, "Without fuss or ambitions, we will take corresponding measures in line with international law, and will demand that they pay us."[28] In addition, Lukashenko issued a statement and instructed his government to look into the issue of Russian property being stationed on Belarusian territory, to make Russia pay for services. This was regarded as further fallout from the dispute on the doubling of Russian gas price to Belarus.[29]

Even if the sum total of these developments indicates a net long-term gain for Russia in terms of energy leverage, it is worth noting that Belarus stopped behaving like a pushover. Considered by many analysts as the former Soviet republic most likely to cave to pressure and eventually reunite with Russia, Belarus showed surprising self-determination and gave Russia a fight for the Belarusian resources it eventually captured. This feisty position is new for Belarus, but due to the authoritarian nature of its government, it is not clear if it indicates increased sovereign assertiveness or Lukashenko's wounded pride.

Georgia

Georgia's strategy to lower its energy dependence on Russia focused on securing bilateral agreements with gas- and oil-rich neighboring countries, consequently reducing the amount of energy resources it needed from Russia.

Georgia has transit agreements with Azerbaijan and Iran, and purchases gas and oil from both, in addition to Russia. The BTC provides the Georgian government with oil for internal consumption as well as revenue from the transit fees.

As far as gas consumption, the situation became precarious, particularly in the aftermath of the Georgian government's 2005 resolution that Russian military bases on its territory be closed down and troops sent home. After months of negotiations in which the Georgians did not back down and did not accept alternative Russian proposals for a lengthier period of troop withdrawal, signs of Kremlin political pressure were felt. A diplomatic row over Georgia's arrest of four Russians on spying charges did not make the bilateral relation any easier.

In November 2006, Gazprom informally aired the possibility that it might ask Georgia to double the price it paid for gas, from $110 to $230 per thousand cubic meters of gas. President Saakashvili articulated that Georgia would not be bullied into such agreement. He made his case in the court of public opinion, at the European Parliament in Strasbourg. He illustrated the political undertones of the Kremlin-orchestrated price pressure by highlighting that Georgia's neighbors were paying $65 and $110 for the same amount of gas.[30] The Georgian government underscored that it was determined to seek higher energy independence from Russia by purchasing gas from other countries such as Iran, Azerbaijan, and Turkey.

Months of negotiations with neighboring countries followed. During negotiations, the Georgian Energy Minister said that Gazprom would remain Georgia's major gas supplier, but that the country would "strengthen [its] energy security and be ready for any possible surprises," in an indirect reference to the gas crisis that Ukraine experienced the previous winter. Bilateral and trilateral negotiations with Azerbaijan, Iran, and Turkey secured barter agreements that involved swapping electricity, with no cash payment on either side.[31]

In November 2006, Azerbaijan announced that unexpected technical problems at their Shah Deniz field, slated to meet a portion of the Georgian need for gas in winter, prevented the country from providing Georgia with the gas it thought it had available. The State Oil Company of Azerbaijan announced that gas production from the first well at Shah Deniz had been suspended for technical reasons.[32] Georgia found itself without the alternative source of gas it counted on.

In December 2006, Gazprom formally announced that it would raise the price of gas for Georgia to $235 per thousand cubic meters and asked the government to determine how much gas it wanted to purchase.[33]

At the end of December 2006, both Saakashvili and Prime Minister Nogaideli announced that they fully expected to start importing gas from Azerbaijan as soon as repairs at the Shah Deniz pipeline were completed, in April 2007.[34] In late December, an agreement on exports of Azeri gas to Georgia at $120 per thousand cubic meters was signed. The gas would be pumped via the Gadzhigabul-Gazakh pipeline, but it would only meet a small portion of the domestic need.[35] Gas pumped through the South Caucasian Gas Pipeline from Baku, through Tbilisi and Erzerum (from Azerbaijan to Turkey, via Georgia) also provided some non-Russian gas to Georgian consumers in 2006. The pipeline parallels BTC and provides Georgia with another portion of the gas it needs for domestic consumption.[36] Prolonged repairs at the Azeri Shah Deniz well forced Georgia to sign an agreement with Gazprom in December for the supply of an additional 1.1 billion cubic meters of gas at $235 per thousand cubic meters, to meet remaining domestic needs in 2007.

Georgia was more successful in securing electric energy from non-Russian sources. In October 2006, Energy Minister Nika Gilauri signed a long-term barter agreement with Iran for supplies of electric energy, and underscored that his country had "done everything possible to diversify electricity supply routes...Agreements on electricity imports, whether under barter schemes or through parallel operations of energy systems, have been signed with all neighboring countries—Russia, Armenia, Azerbaijan, Turkey and Iran."[37] Under the agreement, Georgia would import electricity from Iran during the winter and would return it to Iran in summer, when the country produced electricity in excess of its needs.

While Georgia caved to Gazprom's pressure for discriminatory gas prices, it also was able to secure partial diversification of its energy suppliers. In the long-term, there is no reason why Georgia could not free itself from Gazprom-Kremlin pressure as long as it continues on the path of supply diversification.

Kazakhstan

Kazakhstan is rich in natural energy resources and has the potential to become a major factor in the world energy market. Until recently, the country's dependency on Russian distribution networks limited its ability to assume a more prominent role among the world's energy giants. Yet, as Kazakhstan realized that it had the ability to supply increasing resources to a variety of consumers and make a good profit, it started to look for ways to reduce its overreliance on Russian distribution networks and diversify its customers.

Kazakh oil from the Tengiz field on the Caspian Sea is of superior quality to the oil that Russia pumps from its share of the Caspian seabed. Yet, Kazakhstan was constrained in the transportation of this oil to westward markets by its geographic location on the east side of the Caspian, with the sea and Russia between its resources and potential consumers. The only pipeline available to transport Kazakh oil was the Russian-dominated CPC (Caspian Pipeline Consortium), through southern Russia to the Black Sea port of Novorossiysk. Kazakhstan has thus a double dependency on Russia, both for land and for sea transit and transport.

While trying to maintain a good relationship with Russia and not create the impression that it competed for Gazprom's or Transneft's customers, Kazakh authorities nevertheless decided to become more assertive in world energy markets. In 2005, they adopted a long-term strategy to turn their country into one of the top fifty most competitive economies, and to do so by implementing an ambitious energy development program. The plan stipulated that Kazakhstan would produce 150 million tones of oil per year by 2015 and thus become one of the top ten oil producers in the world.[38]

A country may adopt plans and strategies but unless it has the means to implement them, plans do not become reality. Even if Kazakhstan could increase production from the Tengiz field and open additional oil fields, the question remained as to how to export it and to whom. The CPC provided one transit route but its capacity was limited. An alternative was transporting oil in tankers across the Caspian to Baku, then westward through the BTC. Azerbaijan's Aliyev held numerous talks with Kazakh authorities and made his hopes for a bilateral agreement public. "Kazakhstan's participation in the BTC project would meet the interests of both Kazakhstan and Azerbaijan, and bolster regional security on the whole...For our part, we are ready to create all conditions for Kazakh oil to be transported by BTC pipeline," Aliyev said visiting Astana in 2004.[39] Kazakh authorities evaluated the BTC option as a valuable alternative transit route and eventually reached an agreement with Azerbaijan in 2006.[40]

It appears that the two years of negotiations had to do with appeasing Russian opposition against Kazakhstan's use of a non-Russian route for the sale of its resources. Russian pressure against the use of BTC was applied on Astana, and threats of punitive tariffs for Kazakh goods shipped via Russia were reported.[41] Yet Kazakh authorities made sovereign decisions that made best sense for the country, and committed to exporting the country's resources via both non-Russian and Russian routes. A 2007 agreement for a new Caspian pipeline to carry Turkmen natural gas to Europe via Russia and Kazakhstan underscored that Kazakh authorities remained committed to Russian routes as well.[42]

In line with the ambition to become a world energy supplier, Kazakhstan also explored the possibility of exporting its resources eastward, toward the oil- and gas-hungry market in China. China is a major investor in Kazakhstan's oil industry. In 2005, the two countries agreed to build a 2,900 kilometer oil pipeline, jointly-owned and designed to supply China with oil directly from Kazakhstan.[43] This became known as the Atasu-Alashankou pipeline, and became operational in 2006. An additional line is planned from Atasu to the Kazakh new oil field of Kashagan, to link China directly to Caspian deposits by 2009.[44] The Atasu-Alashankou pipeline opened eastbound distribution routes for Central Asian, non-Russian oil, coming in direct competition with Russia's ambitions for the eastward markets.

Kazakhstan also showed signs of increasing assertiveness toward Russia itself. At issue was the fee that Russia paid for the transit of 50 billion cubic meters of gas it imported from Turkmenistan and Uzbekistan, using Kazakh pipelines. In 2006, Kazakhstan initiated talks with Gazprom on raising the transit fee. The Kazakh energy minister offered to raise the fee by 45 percent, from $1.10 to $1.60 per thousand cubic meters per 100 kilometers.[45] The Kazakh authorities justified the raise as a function of the price of gas, rather than political pressure on Russia. No announcement on an agreement for the new fee has been made as of this writing. However, if presidential speeches are clues, as of March 2007, Russia had not agreed to the new fee. In his 2007 State of the Union Address, the Kazakh president identified "bureaucratic and protectionist barriers to imports and exports" as an area of further negotiations with "regional neighbors...for a more favorable business climate in Central Asia which will allow Kazakh companies to freely invest in neighboring countries."[46] It appears that Gazprom and the Russian government assume the right to set prices of their choosing on energy supplies but do not recognize that the same right applies to former republics. Understandably, the visible application of double standards increased European customers' nervousness about overreliance on Russian supplies and alienated some of the Russian-leaning republics such as Kazakhstan and, as we shall see further, Turkmenistan.

Moldova and Ukraine

Both countries depend on Russian gas for domestic consumption. Both started their post-Soviet political life with a pro-Russia orientation and enjoyed low Russian gas prices and barter agreements. Both reoriented their foreign policy toward the Euro-Atlantic community and faced political pressure from Moscow. Both were asked to pay much higher prices for gas in 2006 and initially refused. The lack of alternative sources of gas made them concede to Moscow's demands. Moldova relied on Ukraine for support when it found itself in a gas shortage crisis, and both countries currently seek to diversify their supply sources.

Like other former republics considered "friendly" and politically close to Russia, Moldova enjoyed low gas prices until 2005, when it received a Gazprom offer to double the price. Justified as part of the Russian government's realignment of prices in conformity with global markets, the price increase came as the Moldovan government refused a Russia-sponsored final settlement in the breakaway Trans-Dniester republic. Moreover, Moldova not only talked about Euro-Atlantic integration, it actually applied for EU membership.

The Moldovan government refused to pay the new price and Gazprom cut off gas supplies on January 1, 2006. Intense diplomacy and nervousness in European countries affected by the interruption of supply flows led to a resumption of the gas on January 4. A provisional agreement was reached for Moldova to pay $110 per thousand cubic meters of gas for the first four months of the year, and further negotiations to be resumed for a long-term agreement. Eventually, Moldova had to accept a price of $160 per thousand cubic meters of gas and agreed to sell 65 percent of the shares in the Moldovan distribution network to Russia. Between January 1 and 4, Ukraine helped Moldova with gas from its reserves.

A similar situation occurred in Ukraine. Russia decided to triple the price of gas in 2005, three months after the country's Orange Revolution. Negotiations started in March and initially envisioned a price increase from $50 to $150 per thousand cubic meters of gas. Ukrainian authorities naturally opposed the increase and for a few months, they talked tough about defending "Ukraine's national interests" in opposing any new deal that did not take those interests into account. First Deputy Minister of Fuel and Energy and Chief Executive of Ukraine's main natural gas company, Naftogas, spoke on the record about Ukraine's right to agree to a deal that will meet "Ukraine's national interest. [any]thing else [was] unacceptable." He called on Gazprom to honor previous bilateral agreements, which guaranteed gas at a lower price through 2013.[47] Gazprom invoked the need for additional Intergovernmental Protocols to be signed before the amount and price of natural gas transit were set.[48] In December, Kremlin officials announced that the price they calculated based on the market value of natural gas was $230 per thousand cubic meters of gas, and that Ukraine should be prepared to pay it starting the following month.

Russia justified the increase in light of market prices and a decision to do away with the barter system.[49] In addition, President Putin and his government articulated their belief that Ukraine could handle a price increase of such proportions, and that continuing at the $50 level was a financial burden to the Russian people. In Putin's words, Ukraine could afford to pay more for gas because it had received "billions of dollars...through privatizations, [and] credits from Western financial institutions for energy projects." Moreover, Russia had switched from barter to cash payment of transit taxes and the resulting "direct transfer" of Russian money into Ukraine's budget added up to one billion dollars, a "heavy burden for the Russian budget." Such a burden could not continue since "consumers in Ukraine [were] getting gas for [a] much lower price than Russian citizens [paid] in their own country," Putin said.[50]

While trying to cast the price increase as an economic decision with no political undertones, Putin inadvertently acknowledged that comparative political calculations informed the Kremlin's decision. The billions of dollars earned from privatizations that Putin referred to were for the sale of Ukraine's largest steel mill, Kryvorizhstal, to a Western company for $4.8 billion.[51] The fact that the Russian leadership looked at Ukraine's revenues from "billions of dollars in privatization" earned in 2005 and decided that Ukraine could afford "to pay more for gas" did not reflect a market price calculation, but a political calculation as to what Ukraine should do with the money it made on the sale of its assets.

An additional indication that political and not economic rationales informed the sudden and severe price increase was Putin's notion that Ukrainians should pay more for gas because Russians paid comparatively higher prices. Such rationale was inconsistent with reality. The actual price that Russians paid in 2005 was $45 per thousand cubic meters of gas, lower than the $50 rate for gas Russia charged Ukraine. It was only in 2006 that the Russian government started to talk seriously about price increases for its own domestic consumers, with industrial clients estimated to be charged prices close to Western prices, while domestic consumers were allowed ten years to get used to gradual increases.[52]

As one could expect, the Ukrainian government rejected a sudden price raise of such proportions and asked that the country be given a few years to budget accordingly. Gazprom therefore cut off supplies on January 1, assuring its European partners that this would not affect their supplies. The gas flow to Europe was, however, affected, with reductions in gas pressure witnessed in several countries. Gazprom accused Ukraine of siphoning off gas destined for European markets. Ukraine denied any wrongdoing. Later it admitted withholding gas, but only as much as it contractually had a right to withhold.[53] On January 4, gas supplies were restored after a compromise was reached.

Critics charged that the Kremlin was "punishing" Ukraine for the result of the Orange Revolution, and choosing a president with a Euro-Atlantic orientation. Others speculated that the threat of having past business dealings looked into was too high for the Kremlin to leave the Orange administration unchallenged. Even if one takes the Russian government's position at face value, the instances of Kremlin pressure on sovereign-minded governments in late-blooming republics are too numerous to be discarded as mere coincidences. At any rate, the pressure of the core on its periphery produced very different results than what the Kremlin counted on. Georgia, Ukraine, and Moldova's subsequent search for alternative sources of energy to replace their dependency on Russian resources are examples of how core-periphery pressure backfired.

Three months after the energy crisis, on March 15, 2006 the Ukrainian parliament approved the country's new energy strategy. The document set three main goals: reduction of energy consumption in the economy, greater energy independence, and stable energy supplies to customers. Presenting the national energy strategy up to 2030 to the parliament, Viktor Yushchenko restated the country's need for alternative sources of energy. "It is time to reassess the coal industry in the Ukrainian energy sector, and look into the future of nuclear energy from a different perspective," the president said.[54]

In Moldova, a similar energy strategy was adopted through 2020. Raising the efficiency of the energy sector, wider use of renewable resources, energy market restructuring and privatization, with attractive incentives for foreign investors, were pillars of the strategy but fell short of securing the country's independence from Russian resources. Energy cooperation with Ukraine and Romania was the only indication of an "alternative supply plan," although neither is fully independent of Russian resources either. Work started in January 2007 to build high-tension electricity lines to insure interconnections with Romania's and Ukraine's electric and energy systems, should supplies be abruptly interrupted again.[55]

Ukraine also tried to secure gas from non-Russian sources. In October 2006, Dmytro Marunich, spokesman for Ukraine's state-owned gas company Naftogaz, announced that in the future, Ukraine would stop purchasing Russian gas. An agreement to purchase 57.5 billion cubic meters of gas needed for internal consumption had been reached with Turkmenistan, Uzbekistan, and Kazakhstan. Ukraine would pay these three countries the same price for gas it paid Russia, in a determined move to gain energy independence from the Kremlin. "There is no need to buy from anybody else," Marunich told the *Associated Press.*[56]

Domestic political reversals of fortunes, so often experienced in vanguard Central European countries, started to occur in late-blooming republics such as Ukraine as well. Later in 2006, a political realignment in Ukraine brought Yushchenko's political opponent into the prime minister's seat. Pro-Moscow politician Viktor Yanukovych came to power promising a long-term agreement on gas supplies with Gazprom that would be acceptable to Ukraine. In February 2007, after several visits to Moscow for further negotiations on a final gas contract, Yanukovych proposed to yield a portion of the gas transmission network to Russia. Ukraine's parliament defeated his proposal and passed a new law to insure that the distribution network would not fall into foreign hands. Previous legislation banned privatization of the pipeline network but the new law went further. It closed remaining legal loopholes, such as management and concession rights, through which the network could be ceded to foreign enterprises. The new law also precluded potential manipulations, including renting, leasing, or mortgaging to foreign enterprises, and prevented Naftogaz from being liquidated under bankruptcy legislation. In proposing the new legislation, Yulia Tymoshenko likened the Yanukovych proposal to "selling off the family silver to an overbearing relative who seeks wider control of the family estate," in a transparent reference to Moscow's attempts to capture the energy distribution networks.[57]

Like Belarus, while Ukraine agreed to pay a higher price for gas in 2007, by October it had accumulated debt on gas payments. Early elections for the country's parliament were predicted to return to power the Russia-friendly political group of Viktor Yanukovych. Prior to elections, Gazprom did not exert pressure on Ukraine to settle the debt. When the popular vote returned Yulia Tymoshenko's and Viktor Yushchenko's parties to power, Gazprom immediately announced that gas supplies would be cut off if Ukraine did not settle the debt in October. During the campaign, Tymoshenko promised that her premiership would reopen the gas agreement with Gazprom and renegotiate it in more favorable terms for Ukraine. Gazprom's announcement came as soon as it became apparent that Tymoshenko was going to be the next prime minister. This was widely perceived as political pressure to motivate the victors of the elections into including Yanukovych in the government. "We regard [the Gazprom ultimatum] as a certain political pressure on Ukraine in this complicated moment of forming a new government in our state," a presidential administration chief said.[58] A member of the Rada's fuel and energy committee stated his belief that Gazprom "recommenced the hard-line policy towards Ukraine," and that new negotiations would follow the difficult path of the 2005–6 energy negotiations.[59] As of this writing, a long-term gas contract is yet to be negotiated and Ukraine continues its search for energy independence from Russia.

Turkmenistan

Turkmenistan sits on the second largest reserves of natural gas in Central Asia. Consequently, it does not depend on Russia for energy resources. Its geographic location makes it dependent on its neighbors to the north, Kazakhstan and Russia, for the export of its rich natural resources, and particularly on the latter as Gazprom owns the transit pipelines. The country's refusal to agree on a shared formula for the exploration of the Caspian seabed proposed by Russia and Kazakhstan limits its choices for the development of undersea pipelines to Azerbaijan. During the authoritarian government of Saparmurat Niyazov, the country followed an isolationist approach toward the rest of the world. Since Niyazov's death, the country has been reasserting itself as an energy provider for world markets and is pursuing a policy of diversification of business and trade ties.

Until Niyazov's death, Russia was one of only three countries that the government used to do business with; the other two were Uzbekistan and Iran. Business ties were not smooth and Turkmenistan stood its ground on several occasions, demanding that Russia pay higher prices for gas. Transit of Uzbek and Turkmen gas via Kazakhstan to Russia totals 45–50 billion cubic meters annually. In 1997, Turkmenistan cut off gas supplies to Russia, charging that former republics benefiting from Turkmen gas owed them back payments in the range of hundreds of millions of dollars. In 1999, the government reached an agreement with Gazprom for the resumption of Turkmen gas supplies. Turkmenistan tried to raise the price of gas to $42 per thousand cubic meters, and Gazprom agreed to pay $36.[60] By 2005, Turkmenistan was able to further raise the price to $66 per thousand cubic meters and in 2006, it insisted and obtained a further increase to $100. Russia reexports most of the Turkmen gas at much higher prices, making good profits that Turkmenistan is aware of.

Although Turkmenistan did not always receive what it was hoping for from Gazprom, it fought hard to set gas prices of its own choosing. The severing of gas supplies when Gazprom refused to pay new Turkmen prices showed Russia that the former republic could no longer be taken for granted.

Under the leadership of Gurbanguly Berdymukhammedov, the Turkmen government indicated an interest to open up to foreign investment and develop business ties with the United States and China. It also agreed to develop new transit corridors north, through Kazakhstan and Russia. In May 2007, Berdymukhamme-dov invited the U.S. oil company Chevron to work in Turkmenistan's side of the Caspian bed.[61] Speculations abounded that the new Turkmen leader might endorse a new U.S.-backed Caspian pipeline that would bypass Russia. Less than ten days later, he agreed to a new Caspian pipeline to transport its gas to European consumers via Kazakhstan and Russia, in what was largely seen as a defeat of the American project. In August, Turkmenistan further signed a thirty-year agreement to supply China with 17 billion cubic meters of gas annually.[62] The gas would reach China via a new, yet to be built gas pipeline across Kazakhstan, and would transport the gas from Turkmenistan to the financial center in Shanghai and beyond.

Finally, speaking in New York, on his first official visit to the United States, Berdy-mukhammedov indicated that his country's "international energy strategy [was] aimed at developing a multiple pipelines system to bring Turkmen energy resources to the international markets on a stable and long-term basis...not dependent on either political circumstances or any kind of ideological biases."[63] He was also quoted as saying that his country "gave primary importance to developing relations with the United States, particularly in oil and gas,"[64] and that even as a new pipeline going north through Russia had been agreed, plans for a U.S.-backed pipeline that would bypass Russia were "not completely dropped."[65]

Turkmenistan thus remains energy self-sufficient, retains huge potential for further exploration, and is not to be taken for granted either by Russia, China, or the Euro-Atlantic community. The new Turkmen leader's pronouncements indicate that his country will select the infrastructure projects that make the best sense for his country, while trying to maintain good, yet neutral relations with all the parties involved. This position may be politically unpredictable, but it is a choice made by the country's leaders, not by other centers of power.

Overall, the late-blooming republics that depend on Russia for energy resources have found creative ways to assert a level of independence from the core, even if some of them remain heavily dependent on Gazprom. The Kremlin continues to set the tone for resource extraction in Central Asia, and has locked in a number of deals that secure its primacy as the region's energy provider. However, it is not clear that this position will remain uncontested much longer. Azerbaijan, Kazakhstan, and Turkmenistan pose direct global challenges to Russia's primacy. The Kremlin's distinctive use of energy resources for political means, to pressure former republics into agreements and arrangements of its choosing, is the weak link in the Russian approach to its energy policy. If and when Russia understands that economic deci-sions are different from political decisions, and allows the market to set the price of oil and gas, the landscape of exploration, extraction, and distribution of oil and gas in Central Asia will change.

History-Related Disputes

Of all the countries under discussion in this book, Ukraine was the most assertive regarding the historical record of Soviet occupation. From resolving the status of the Black Sea Fleet and associated territorial claims, to blaming the Soviet Union for genocide against the Ukrainian people during the Great Famine, and for displacements and deportations of Ukrainians at the end of WWII, Ukraine has been at odds with the Kremlin since the early nineties. In the case of deportations, Ukraine was able to find common ground with Poland, whose Soviet-installed authorities encouraged and performed systematic displacements of Ukrainians to Polish territories. In the case of coming to terms on the historic record with Russia, Ukraine received much of the same lack of recognition of any wrongdoing from the Kremlin as the vanguard Baltic and Central European countries did. While acknowledging past mistakes helped Ukraine and Poland start the process of healing, refusing responsibility for the crimes of the Soviet authorities merely aggravated bilateral relations with Russia.

The Black Sea Fleet and Associated Territorial Issues

The status of the Black Sea Fleet and of the Crimean peninsula provided post-Soviet Russian authorities with an early opportunity to articulate their position on the status of Ukraine. It also highlighted the deep divisions regarding the common history of the two countries and the fundamentally different ways in which Russia and Ukraine viewed their post-Soviet coexistence.

The Fleet has historically been stationed in the port of Sevastopol on the Crimean peninsula. The Fleet was founded by Russian Prince Potemkin in the eighteenth century, and played an important role in Russia's strategic outreach ever since, in the Black Sea and beyond. In 1954, Soviet leader Nikita Khrushchev transferred the Crimean peninsula to the Ukrainian SSR (Soviet Socialist Republic) in a gesture of good will, to mend relations after the years of Stalinist atrocities. To Russians, the Fleet is an important symbol of greatness, military power, and geopolitical positioning.

At the end of the Cold War, the Crimean peninsula became an issue of territorial contention between Ukraine and Russia, with ramifications related to the ownership of the Fleet and its continued location in Sevastopol. Crimea is inhabited by a large Russian population (67%), a Ukrainian population (25%), and remnants of Crimean Tartars that had been deported by Stalin at the end of WWII. During the 1991 referendum on retaining the Soviet Union, Crimeans voted for autonomy within Ukraine, and for independence a year later. Negotiations with Kyiv authorities eventually brought about an arrangement acceptable to both sides, in which Crimea remained an integral part of Ukraine but retained a significant degree of autonomy. Negotiations with Russia for the status of the Fleet were much lengthier and contentious, and tensions remain to this day.

In 1994, Ukraine, Russia, and the United States signed a trilateral agreement in which Ukraine's territorial integrity was guaranteed in exchange for its nuclear disarmament. Russia continued to delay a ratification of the bilateral treaty of friendship with Ukraine, despite this trilateral agreement.

At stake was the fact that many Russian politicians considered Crimea (and Ukraine) a birth right of the Russian Federation. Transferring Crimea to the jurisdiction of Ukraine was viewed as a "gift" bestowed in specific historic circumstances by Khrushchev, as a gesture of good will and friendship, at a time when it was believed that Ukraine and Russia would be one and the same country for ever. Select Russian politicians argued that Crimea had nothing to do with Ukrainian culture and history, therefore the peninsula's population should not be forced to be part of a culture that was not its own. Such arguments were raised as early as 1990, even before the breakup of the Soviet Union. In 1992, the Russian chairman of the parliamentary committee on foreign affairs, Vladimir Lukin, introduced a draft resolution to declare the 1954 transfer of Crimea invalid and illegal. Weeks later, a parliamentary study of the constitutionality of the 1954 transfer was approved. Lukin also advised the Kremlin to use the status of Crimea as a bargaining chip in negotiations with Ukraine, to gain total control over the Black Sea Fleet.[66] In May 1992, a Russian newspaper quoted Sergei Baburin, then Vice Speaker of the Russian Duma, telling the Ukrainian ambassador to Moscow that "[e]ither Ukraine reunites with Russia again, or [there would be] war."[67] In 1994, Konstantin Zatulin, director of Russia's Institute for CIS countries, expressed opposition against recognizing the "historically nonexistent borders of a historically nonexistent state, that is Ukraine."[68] In 1996, Moscow's mayor, Yurii Luzhkov, went as far as to state on Russian television that Sevastopol "could be taken by force" because Russia had "adequate forces to defend its sovereignty."[69] This rhetoric did not sit well with authorities in Kyiv, who stayed the course of negotiations on a bilateral treaty.

Not all Russian politicians took the position that Crimea should be "returned" to the Russian fold. For instance, in 1995 when pro-Russia Crimean politicians called on Moscow not to ratify a draft of the bilateral treaty of friendship with Ukraine, the Russian Foreign Ministry, the State Duma speaker, and other high-level politicians declined to interfere and called the Crimea issue a Ukraine internal matter. They all called on Ukrainian authorities to be sensitive to the status of the Russian population in Crimea.[70]

This rhetoric delayed and complicated negotiations for a bilateral Russia-Ukraine Treaty of Friendship that would have settled the Crimea and the Black Sea Fleet issue. In May 1997, the treaty was eventually agreed upon and signed by then presidents Yeltsin and Kuchma. The treaty guaranteed the inviolability of the Russian-Ukraine border, and Crimea was recognized as integral part of Ukraine. Provisions were made for the division of the Soviet Black Sea Fleet between Russia and Ukraine. The agreement stated that the Russian navy was to remain in the Crimean port of Sevastopol until 2017, in exchange for an annual rent.

The treaty was vigorously opposed by Russian politicians for the following two years. Senator Georgii Tikhonov argued that ratification would give recognition to the "false idea" that Russians and Ukrainians are separate peoples, and recognize *de jure* the territorial integrity of Ukraine.[71] Zatulin wrote a highly publicized article in a Russian newspaper arguing that the 1954 transfer of Crimea from the Russian SSR to the Ukrainian SSR was unconstitutional. He further argued that the transfer

of Crimea did not affect the status of the city of Sevastopol which had been designated as an independent administrative and economic center under the direct
authority of the government in Moscow. He concluded that Ukraine had no right
to "the city of Russia's military glory," as Sevastopol was sometimes called, nor to
its Fleet. Mayor Luzhkov spoke before the Russian Federation Council in January
1999, managing to persuade some senators to postpone the ratification of the treaty.
He argued that ratification would *de facto* separate Sevastopol from Russia for ever.[72]
Krasnoyarsk Krai Governor Aleksandr Lebed further underscored that Sevastopol
"must belong to Russia."[73]

The treaty was ratified by the State Duma in December 1998, and by the Federation Council in February 1999. Crimea was recognized as an integral part of Ukraine
and the Black Sea Fleet was divided between Ukraine and Russia. The Russian portion of the fleet was to be stationed in Sevastopol until 2017, in exchange for rent.

Various aspects of the agreement were challenged, particularly by the Orange leaders of Ukraine, and a renegotiated agreement was sought. Many Ukrainians view the
presence of Russian troops on their territory as undesirable. Popular demonstrations
demanded that Russian troops go home. Under the government of Viktor Yushchenko, demands for the departure of the Russian fleet took various forms. Officially,
a renegotiated agreement was suggested, demanded but never agreed to by the Russian
administration. The confrontation over the Russian-Ukrainian border through the
Azov and Black Seas and the Kerch Strait erupted in summer 2003 when Russia
attempted to construct a dam on the Tuzla Island in the Kerch Strait. Ukraine accused
Russia of encroaching onto its territory, and deployed border guards on the small
island. Ukraine accused Moscow of deliberately procrastinating the definition of the
maritime border, insisting that the Sea of Azov and the Kerch Strait should be assigned
the status of territorial waters for both countries, and that the demarcation line should
pass along the seabed. Kyiv insisted on an arrangement that would help Ukraine keep
the bigger part of the Sea of Azov with its gas-bearing shelf. In this arrangement, the
Kremlin would lose one of the potential levers of energy pressure on the Ukrainian
authorities, and is therefore delaying the formal demarcation of the seabed.

Ukraine also took Russia to court over ownership of a hundred lighthouses in
Crimea, which the Russians kept under control as part of the 1997 agreement.
Ukraine argued that the agreement did not cover the lighthouses and won in court.
Russia vowed to disregard the court order and retain the lighthouses until 2017. In
early 2007, Ukraine won an appeal ordering Russia to turn over seventy-seven lighthouses to the Ukrainian Transport Ministry and demanded prompt return of its
property. Russia continued to ignore the court ruling and the Ukrainian demands.[74]

Continued popular demands for a renegotiated treaty and an earlier departure of
the Russian Fleet from Sevastopol made the Kremlin nervous. Asked about Crimea
in a telephone question and answer session with the Russian people on October
25, 2006, President Putin stated that "Crimea...[is] a special territory. Crimea is a
part of the Ukrainian state and we cannot interfere with another country's internal
affairs. This is the answer we have to give ourselves. Of course we are not indifferent
to what happens there...Russia does not aspire to remove its fleet from the Crimea

ahead of term and, as you know, the agreement is set to last until 2017."[75] In 2007, the Ukrainian foreign minister articulated that the Russian fleet would not be forced out of Crimea before the agreed 2017 date. "We do not claim early withdrawal of the fleet because...the agreements are signed, and whether anyone likes it or not, we must fulfill them."[76] Ukrainian authorities tried to raise the rent on the Russian fleet, arguing that the value of real estate had gone up since the agreement was signed, and an adjustment in light of market prices was in order. In typical double standard fashion Russia refused. Although Russia justified higher gas prices for its former republics due to rising market prices, it did not recognize the right of the Ukrainian government to adjust the land rent based on the same principle.

Holodomor

Between 1932 and 1933, Josef Stalin's forced campaign of collectivization of independent farms contributed to the death of millions of Ukrainians, an event known as the Great Famine, or Holodomor. During the Cold War, Holodomor was not a topic for public discussion in Ukraine. Post-Soviet Ukrainian politicians demanded that the historical record be set straight and the Holodomor recognized as an intentional act of genocide against the Ukrainian nation by the Soviet authorities. Russia refused to admit intent and political tensions escalated.

Among historians and politicians, there is no denial that the Great Famine occurred. The issue of contention is whether the death of millions of people was an intentional Soviet policy.

Soviet authorities started the collectivization of agriculture throughout the Soviet Union in the twenties. Collectivization involved confiscating privately-owned farm lands and pooling them into collective lots, to be cultivated by groups of farmers based on a five-year plan set by the communist authorities. Proceeds from the harvest were divided between the government and the farmers. Under Stalin, each village was ordered to provide the state with a quota of grain, determined not by scientific (or realistic) calculations of crop yield but by the communist party's estimates of demand for food. The remainder of the harvest was divided among farmers. Collectivization destroyed private farms and, over years, impoverished farmers throughout the communist world.

During the first years of collectivization, state quotas were often times higher than the harvests themselves. In Ukraine and a few other Soviet republics, by the end of the summer, village after village failed to meet the quota requirements. Overzealous Soviet bureaucrats blamed the smaller amounts of harvest on the (fierce) opposition of the Ukrainian farmers to collectivization. Farmers were assumed to either hide, not disclose the true yields, or keep the crops for themselves, and were put on a government blacklist. The government then proceeded to seize all food from the blacklisted villages and prohibited villagers from leaving in search for fresh sources of food. Left without any means of subsistence, one village after another died of starvation. Some records place the death toll at 25,000 villagers per day. Cases of cannibalism were reported. The villagers who resisted the Soviet requisition of food supplies were either labeled "enemies of the state" and executed, or sent to Siberia.

Depending on which sources one believes, the death toll during the Great Famine ranged from 1.54 million to 10 million people. Recently declassified Soviet archives place the toll from the famine in Ukraine at a million and a half. It is worth noting that Kazakhstan and Russia also witnessed mass starvation due to low crop yields and government requisition of the harvest.[77]

The famine lasted several years. Memoirs and testimonies by former Soviet party leaders and bureaucrats indicate that the authorities in the Kremlin were aware of the situation in Ukraine.[78]

Defenders of the Holodomor as a phenomenon caused by poor party planning and unrealistic harvest expectations quote declassified communist party documents that support the view that the famine was unintentional. For instance, documents indicate that party officials were informed that the harvest of 1932 was going to be poor. The reasons for that ranged from blaming local authorities of deliberately wanting "to underestimate the harvest,"[79] to poor management of the harvesting process. "The harvest campaign is obviously proceeding unsatisfactorily," read a party document in September 1932. "...[A] number of regions are still far from completing the reaping and are stacking the grain inadequately."[80] Stalin was made aware of the poor harvest but attributed it to organizational deficiencies and ordered the Politbureau to deal with those who were "undermining the Soviet system."

Defenders of the thesis that the Holodomor was an unintentional result of Soviet policies argue that four conditions combined to produce lower harvests than expected, which in turn contributed to the famine. Overextension of the sown area led to pressure to overuse agricultural technology and disrupted the traditional arrangements for the cultivation of the soil. Trying to sow a larger area to meet party directives for bigger agricultural production next led to a decline in the "draught power," where more grain was necessary for sowing, and less was available for human consumption and for feeding farm animals. Third, the quality of cultivation went down due to demoralized farmers and overused tractors. Finally, the weather played a factor in the diminished harvest yields. The year 1931 was a drought year, and 1932 had poor weather as well. The combination of all four factors, coupled with the unwillingness of Soviet leaders to attribute the poor harvest to their own policies of overplanning, led to the famine.[81]

Other sources argue that Stalin deliberately provoked the Holodomor in Ukraine, in order to bring Ukrainian nationalism to its knees and impoverish peasants. Defenders of the Holodomor as intentional genocide against the Ukrainian nation generally agree that there is no document signed by Stalin ordering the famine, and understand that intentional Soviet action may arguably never be proven. They liken this argument to that of Hitler's responsibility for the Holocaust and argue that there was not a document signed by Hitler calling for the Jewish Holocaust either. They point to the fact that Stalin was informed about the famine, an aspect that defenders of the "unintentional" thesis do not dispute. Evidence shows that Stalin's wife informed him directly about the deaths caused by the famine, and he chose to silence and scold her for "collecting Trotskyite gossip."[82]

The defenders of the genocide thesis conclude that first, the Soviet party leaders knew about the famine; second, they chose to systematically suppress any information about it; and third, they closed the border between Ukraine and Russia to keep hungry Ukrainians from going to Russia. As such, even if the Soviets may not have designed the famine, they deliberately let it continue without doing anything about it.[83] In the view of the Ukrainian government, this silent passivity constitutes an act of genocide.

In post-Soviet years, Ukrainian authorities sought recognition from the Kremlin that Soviet leaders deliberately subjected their country to starvation amounting to genocide. Russia remained opposed to this terminology and argued that the famine did not specifically target Ukrainians; it also argued that the famine affected other nations, including Russia and Kazakhstan. In October 2006, a Russian Foreign Ministry statement condemned the "unilateral [Ukrainian] interpretation" of the famine as genocide. "It was wrong to apply the notion exclusively to Ukraine, because it deals with a sad page in our common history." The famine, the statement said, was part of Communist repressions that affected other ethnic groups in the former Soviet Union as well, and was not to be considered as a targeted attempt only on the population of Ukraine.[84]

Ukrainian authorities did not give up their claim and raised the political stakes further. During the official address to the 61st Session of the General Assembly of the United Nations Organization, Ukrainian Minister of Foreign Affairs Borys Tarasiuk called on member-nations of the organization to recognize the 1932–33 famine in Ukraine as an act of genocide against the Ukrainian people.

> Having committed this inhuman crime, the communist regime tried to conceal its scale and tragic consequences from the world community. And they succeeded for a long time ...Ukraine calls upon the United Nations as the collective voice of the international community to contribute to the commemoration of the 60th anniversary of the Convention [on the Prevention and Punishment of the Crime of Genocide] by recognizing Holodomor as an act of genocide against the Ukrainian people.[85]

President Yushchenko proposed that the Verkhovna Rada recognize the Holodomor of 1932–33 as genocide against the Ukrainian people. He also proposed supplementing the Code on Administrative Violations with an article on public denial of the famine of 1932–33 in Ukraine. The article proposes fines and punishment against any public materials that deny the famine.[86] "I do not ask, I demand that the Ukrainian parliament recognize Holodomor as genocide," President Viktor Yushchenko told the crowd gathered on Kiev's Mykhaylivska Square on November 26, to commemorate the tragic event.[87] The Ukrainian parliament passed the resolution and Holodomor is defined by law as genocide. Despite strong Russian opposition against an interpretation of Holodomor that points the finger in the Kremlin's direction for atrocities committed by the Soviet Union, Ukraine stood its ground and adopted a resolution regarding this unfortunate event that matches national perceptions. Knowing that such resolution would further strain relations with the Kremlin, Ukraine acted on its interests and defined history the way its citizens see it.

Deportations

Between 1944 and 1956, Poland and Ukraine experienced a difficult page of common history. As Poland lost eastern territories to the Soviet Union and gained western territories from Germany, Soviet Ukraine lost western territories to Poland as well. In the process, the local population found itself in a "new" country and resisted the seemingly arbitrary way in which its fate had been decided.

The symbol of Ukrainian aspirations for independence, and of resistance against the territorial rearrangements following WWII, was the UPA (Ukrainian Insurgent Army). UPA fought the Nazi German occupation in the forties, the Soviet occupation in the forties and the fifties, and the shifting of Ukrainian land to Poland through and through. In the process, crimes against the civilian population were committed by all sides, and the role and place of UPA in the history of Ukraine remains controversial. In Soviet textbooks, UPA is designated as a "terrorist" organization, whereas in Ukrainian memory, it is considered the symbol of the nation's spirit of independence. In recent years, various organizations asked the Ukrainian government that UPA be rehabilitated and its members recognized the same social benefits as Soviet army veterans. Naturally, Moscow reacted angrily and asked the Ukrainian government not to rehabilitate UPA. Ukraine's minister of foreign affairs retorted that UPA was "Ukraine's internal matter" and advised the Kremlin to back off.[88]

By far the most contentious issue involves the relocation of Ukrainian population from western Ukraine to Polish lands, sometimes in the far western lands gained from eastern Germany. In 1947, the so-called Operation Visla involved the relocation of some 140,000 Ukrainians to territories in northern and western Poland, gained from Germany. The deportations were justified as a Polish reaction against the atrocities of the UPA toward the Polish population residing in what used to be Ukrainian land. Operation Visla was for many years after the end of the Cold War still a matter of deep disagreement between Poland and Ukraine. It was only in 2002 that a formal apology was articulated by then Polish President Kwasniewski. In a letter to the Polish National Remembrance Institute and the conference it organized on the subject of Operation Visla, he characterized the matter as follows:

> It was believed for years that Operation Visla was the revenge for the slaughter of Poles by the Ukrainian Insurgent Army (UPA) in the east in 1943–1944. Such reasoning is fallacious and ethically inadmissible. It [invokes] a principle of group accountability, with which we cannot agree. The slaughter of Poles cannot serve as an excuse for the brutal pacification of Ukrainian villages and the expulsion of populace. Operation Visla should be condemned...
>
> On behalf of the Polish Republic, I would like to express regret to all those who were wronged by [this operation]...The infamous Operation Visla is a symbol of the abominable deeds perpetrated by the Communist authorities against Polish citizens of Ukrainian origin.[89]

This public acknowledgment of crimes committed by both sides paved the way for the beginning of bilateral reconciliation on the matter. In 2007, both Polish and Ukrainian presidents attended a memorial concert held in one of the towns affected by the 1947 deportations. It was the Ukrainian president's turn to reach out.

> Only great nations can forgive. Deep and brotherly reconciliation is the sole way to a new life both nations are creating...Today, I am thankful to the Polish side, the President of Poland, the citizens of Poland for the opportunity to remember those sad events of the 1940s. It is pleasant for me to be in Poland today and demonstrate deep respect for our history and our present day together with the Polish president, together with the Ukrainian community. Unfortunately, history has left many issues for us, and today's event, today's visit confirm the fact President Kaczynski and I deeply share the formula for historical mutual understanding and historical reconciliation, which is extremely important to the Ukrainian and Polish peoples.[90]

Since 2002, both governments have taken measures to set the historical record straight by collecting eyewitness accounts and compiling lists of deportees, to be published in remembrance of the collective history of the two countries. New discoveries of remains of what were believed to be victims of the Soviet occupation were reburied in Ukraine, with the proper ceremony and publicity.[91] In contrast, no such joint venture was initiated between Ukraine and Russia.

It is therefore worth underscoring that when there is a will, reconciliation of views and relationships is possible, even with respect to difficult pages in the common history of this geographic space. Ukraine and Poland were able to find common ground on the issue of deportations, even if differences remain. This common ground allowed the two countries to start the process of healing together. Russia refuses to seek common ground and dismisses the criminal premises of the Holodomor in Ukraine, and of deportations throughout its former Soviet space altogether. The different approaches in dealing with difficult episodes in the common history of these countries highlight that Russia is not willing to look critically at its own history, and make amends where necessary. This tendency does not bode well for the future of relations between the Kremlin and its former republics, particularly as the latter become more assertive and sovereign-minded. As these three cases of settling the historical record indicate, Russia remains uncomfortable with the breakup of the Soviet Union and with the legacy of the communist regime. It has difficulty treating its former republics as equals and admitting past wrongdoing. As such, Russia leaves the door open to further contentious exchanges and less than friendly relations with Eurasian countries.

Developing Democratic Institutions and a More Open Market

Throughout Central Asia, democratic reform was not an initial domestic priority, as was the case in Central Europe and the Baltic countries. Building sovereignty and gaining a level of independence from the Kremlin were more acute priorities for all former republics. During the nineties, late-blooming republics witnessed slow and uneven transitions to a form of governance that combined democratic elements, such as elections, with Soviet-style leadership.

The beginning of the twenty-first century found these countries slowly opening up to democratic practices by allowing more freedom for the media and cracking down less often on NGOs. The populations of three countries rose up in popular revolts against the governments of the nineties, in Georgia, Kyrgyzstan, and Ukraine. The "color revolutions," that Russia thinks were orchestrated by Western powers, were prompted by wide popular dissatisfaction with the course of the countries' politics and economic developments. Corruption at the highest levels of government, widespread poverty, and poor human rights records were major factors in the color revolutions of Central Asia. The revolutions were an expression of the people's will for change, not orchestrated by the Kremlin, nor by other centers of power.

Much like Central Europe in the beginning of the transition, Central Asian countries suffered from a chronic lack of democratic culture and traditions. Throughout the years of Soviet identity, the model of politics was that of a strong, authoritarian center and an equally authoritarian local leader. Populations were expected to listen to and execute whatever their leaders decided. Any opposition was considered state treason, or the work of "forces from abroad" trying to undermine the communist system, and suppressed.

Post-Soviet developments witnessed some of these characteristics as well. Elections took place, but they were hardly free and fair. Political opposition to incumbent authorities was repressed, and the media was rarely allowed to question or criticize the powers that be. In some countries, when civil society tried to perform its checks and balances function by highlighting government abuses and calling for accountability and transparency, civic leaders, the media, or NGOs were harassed, imprisoned, shut out of the public eye, or labeled "organizations funded by the West" to push a foreign agenda on the country. Belarus, for instance, remains one of the former republics with the least amount of freedom of speech and association, and crackdowns on domestic and international NGOs are part of the political landscape. Turkmenistan had virtually no freedom of expression until Turkmenbashi died. Uzbekistan is run with an iron fist by an authoritarian leader who makes no secret of the fact that he would order the repression of any popular upheaval against his rule.

These countries have laws according to which it is a crime to criticize the head of state or the government. Legislation gives authorities a free hand to harass political opponents or imprison them if need be. Investigative journalism remains a challenge, and those journalists who try it sometimes pay with their lives for the audacity of exposing government corruption and scandals. In Ukraine, the case of the beheaded journalist Heorhiy Gongadze remains unresolved as of this writing, and existing evidence about his murder points to the highest levels of government.

In other late-blooming republics, laws were passed to enshrine lifetime privileges for people in top positions, as is the case in Kazakhstan. President Nursultan Nazarbayev tightened the grip on power by pushing through the parliament lifetime privileges for himself and his family, including access to future presidents and immunity from criminal prosecution. A direct result of the poor record of democracy and human rights in the country was the response of the Council of Europe Parliamentary Assembly to Kazakhstan's inquiry about observer status in 1999. The official position of the Council was that Kazakhstan was in its right to apply for full membership, but that would not be granted until progress in the area of human rights and democratic process was visible in the country.

Freedom of expression and of the media remains a major obstacle to the development of democratic institutions in late-blooming republics. Appendix III offers a summary of these countries' rankings in freedom of the press. Of all the countries discussed in this book, the late-bloomer republics rank the poorest. Of 139 countries in the 2002 RwB study, Tajikistan ranked 86, Kyrgyzstan 98, Azerbaijan 101, Ukraine 112, Kazakhstan 116, Uzbekistan 120, Belarus 124, and Turkmenistan 136. In 2003, Armenia ranked 90, Moldova 94, Kyrgyzstan 104, Azerbaijan 113, Tajikistan 114, Ukraine 133, Kazakhstan 138, Belarus 151, Uzbekistan 154, and Turkmenistan 158 of 166 countries under study. For comparison, the United States ranked 32 and Russia 148. In 2004, Moldova ranked 78, Armenia 83, Georgia 94, Tajikistan 95, Kyrgyzstan 107, Kazakhstan 131, Azerbaijan 136, Ukraine 139, Uzbekistan 142, Belarus 144, and Turkmenistan 164 among 167 countries. The pattern was maintained in 2005 and 2006, with Belarus, Turkmenistan, and Uzbekistan having the poorest records, and the rest of the late-blooming republics scoring poorly by comparison to the vanguard Central European and the Baltic states.

In the economic transition from a centralized, Soviet-style economy to a more open market, the distinctive element in former republics was their heavy dependence on Russian or domestic "barons," businessmen who reportedly owned much of the countries' most profitable enterprises. Some of the domestic barons had strong ties with Russian barons, and privatizations of state assets seemed to favor sales to such individuals. In Ukraine, the public concern that privatization would favor Russian businessmen or Ukrainian barons with strong ties to Moscow was significant. Such privatization would *de facto* lead to Moscow buying the most lucrative enterprises and making Ukraine further dependent on Russia. In 1998, rumors and public anxiety about this possibility were so high that then President Kuchma felt compelled to offer a public disclaimer. "I have not sold Ukraine to Russia," he was quoted in the media. "The course of integration with the West and Ukraine's cooperation with NATO remain unchanged...We are only interested in military and technical cooperation [with Russia]."[92] This concern was equally mirrored in the Ukrainian parliament's move to pass legislation that would close all legal loopholes in the possible sale of the gas transmission network to a foreign company. When pro-Russia Prime Minister Victor Yanukovych proposed the sale of shares in the distribution network to Russia, the Rada moved decisively to prevent such sale.

The index of economic freedom of the Fraser Institute did not include all the late-blooming republics in its analysis. As Appendix II highlights, the data are fairly sketchy, although by 2004, the Caucasus had a fair degree of freedom comparable to the vanguard Central European countries. Armenia and Georgia were found to have the same level of economic freedom as Poland, with a ranking of 6.7, where 10 is the highest ranking. Ironically, the richest Caucasus country, with the highest foreign investment in the only non-Russian oil pipeline in the region, Azerbaijan, trailed Armenia and Georgia in economic freedom, with a ranking of 6.0. Ukraine's level of economic freedom in 2003 and 2004 was comparable to that of Slovakia in 1995. The fact that Ukraine's level of economic freedom was not only relatively low, at a 5.3–5.4 midpoint, but that it stagnated for three years in a row (2002–4) is also an indication of the relative absence of reforms in the last years of Kuchma's second administration. Those were the years when it was believed that Russia was making inroads in the economy of Ukraine and barons were allowed to capture state assets for a fraction of what they were worth.

Between insufficient and incomplete political reforms, as the freedom of the press index highlights, and partial economic reforms, as the index of economic freedom summarizes, populations in late-bloomer republics eventually reacted against their governments. The color revolutions in Georgia, Ukraine, and Kyrgyzstan were a manifestation of the populations' will for change for the better. Government under-performance in countries rich in natural resources, widespread corruption, and the sense that populations had not benefited from post–Cold War changes contributed to the popular despair that prompted the color revolutions. In the words of political analysts, the revolutions "were the response of [the] people to bad governance and worsening conditions, and [to] the new leaders that came in [and] have shown themselves unable to offer improvements."[93]

The overthrow of authorities in Georgia and the crowds gathered in Kyiv in freezing temperatures in December 2004 to demand new elections were a testimony of the people's will for change. The Tulip Revolution in Kyrgyzstan was believed to be a function of both popular despair with living conditions and a spillover effect from Georgia and Ukraine. In the words of another analyst, "recent events in Ukraine have made people everywhere understand that taking to the streets gets the authorities' attention."[94]

The extent to which the color revolutions were the product of domestic conditions arising from poor government management or instigated by NGOs "financed from abroad" remains a topic of intense debate in the region. If the argument forwarded throughout this book is correct, the color revolutions were the result of the people's will for change, without interference from the Kremlin or other centers of power. However, the argument may be challenged on the basis of counterclaims widely distributed in the Russian media.

History has seen numerous cases of popular uprisings against the political establishment. In most cases, abuse of power, corruption, and despair were the main contributors to such dramatic events. It is in this particular geographic space that popular uprisings tend to be interpreted as the result of illegal and disingenuous work by foreign forces who seek to undermine legitimate, pro-Russian governments. Russian politicians and analysts charge that the revolutions were financed by American and Western centers of power, in an effort to export Western-style democracy and undermine the Kremlin's vision of democracy. In Vladimir Putin's words, "democracy cannot be exported. It should be a product of internal development of a society."[95]

When the color revolutions started to develop, the Kremlin administration feared a spillover effect in Russia. Putin's administration moved to significantly curtail the freedom of Russia's own NGOs, which were perceived to be instrumental in the conduct of color revolutions in Central Asia. When the Kremlin was criticized for cracking down on civil society, analysts countered back, "the new [legislation] aim[s] only at blocking the operation of those who use the cover of public activities to import color revolutions technology to Russia." The coauthor of the new legislation restricting the activities of NGOs claimed that "Duma deputies have concluded that at least 20–25% of the 450,000 [Russian] NGOs live on the money of the Western community...These are primarily human rights groups, whose registration forms proclaim their activity as the protection of the rights of Russian citizens. In fact, they are engaged in shady operations on the money of foreign sponsors."[96]

When the post–Tulip Revolution governants proved no better than the previous ones, domestic unrest was recorded again. The Russian rhetoric continued to blame the United States and the West for domestic developments in Kyrgyzstan. "...in the name of democratic reform, a U.S.-backed coalition of political activists and NGOs was making yet another effort—the third this year alone—to bring down the elected leadership of Bakiyev and Prime Minister Feliks Kulov," argued a Russian political analyst.[97] Russian political circles paid no attention to eyewitness accounts of the beginnings of the Tulip Revolution, who described the following grassroots developments:

> ...the poor, as well as the wealthy, who had grown tired of Akayev's regime, joined the protests...Women with their children came straight from the bazaars; teenagers and the elderly also turned out...Many in Kyrgyzstan believe that Askar Akayev usurped his power because the Constitution dictates that the country's leader may only serve two terms, and Akayev swore on the Constitution at least three times. Another contributing factor is the enormous gulf that exists between rich and poor and the attendant absence of a large middle class.[98]

The official Russian explanation that color revolutions were a product of Western interference in these countries' affairs does not give credit to the will of populations in this vast area to demand a better course for their countries. It belittles the people's intellectual capabilities and makes them look like easily maneuverable puppets. As patterns of sovereign behavior in this chapter show, that is not the case. Late-blooming republics stood up to the Kremlin on energy issues, asserted their sovereign interests in reducing their dependence on Gazprom, stood up to the core regarding history-related disputes, and even attempted modest domestic changes. To view all these developments as the result of forces other than the countries' sovereign will does not take into consideration the evidence to the contrary and makes a mockery of millions of people. As the final part of this chapter shows, late-blooming republics were able to assert a degree of sovereign-mindedness in foreign policy as well.

FOREIGN POLICY ASSERTIVENESS

Resisting the core-periphery format of relations with Russia was high on many late-bloomer republics' foreign policy agenda, particularly in the twenty-first century. The notion that newly independent countries were expected to either consult with the Kremlin or favor courses of action that the Kremlin approved was not fully spelled out, but ran like an undercurrent through bilateral relations. As the institutional (and psychological) transition from Soviet republics to fully independent states set in, late bloomers realized their economic potentials and geostrategic importance. They started to take independent-minded positions, taking courses of action that did not necessarily originate in the Kremlin's hallways. They also assumed a more assertive tone in their relationship with Russia. In the process, countries started establishing regional cooperative agreements with or without Russia's blessing, and some conducted (successful) rapprochement with NATO, the EU, and the United States. None of them assumed an inimical position toward Russia in this process. On the contrary, to the best of their abilities, most countries tried to maintain good relations with Russia.

Resisting the Core-Periphery Format

The Commonwealth of Independent States

Relations between Russia and its former republics in the format of the CIS best illustrate the Kremlin core-periphery approach. Initially established between the High Contracting Parties of the Republic of Belarus, the Russian Federation, and Ukraine in December 1991, the Commonwealth grew to twelve member states by 1994, representing all the former Soviet republics except the Baltic countries.[99] In theory, relations among CIS members were guided "on the basis of mutual recognition and respect of state sovereignty, the inherent right to self-determination, the principles of equality and noninterference in internal affairs, a rejection of the use of force, economic or other methods of pressure, regulation of disputed issues through negotiations, and other generally recognized principles and norms of international law."[100] In reality, the perception that Russia used CIS to influence the course of politics in former republics persisted.

CIS members used the organization to conduct economic and trade consultations, cultural exchanges, and other negotiations. Throughout the nineties, CIS countries met somewhat regularly, rotated the presidency of the CIS, and discussed trade and the formation of a single economic zone. On occasion, member states were able to make modest progress on economic and trade issues.

During Vladimir Putin's second term, characterized by a more pronounced comeback of Russia's influence in global affairs, some CIS countries started to question the continued usefulness of the commonwealth, and suggested that the organization might need significant reform. Other countries went as far as to suggest that a "dignified divorce" might be needed.

A September 2003 CIS meeting in which Russia, Belarus, Ukraine, and Kazakhstan formed a SES triggered fears that Russia was moving in the direction of recreating the Soviet Union. The Moldovan president voiced disappointment with the decision and commented on "the lack of perspective" and the "depreciation of the CIS stock" brought about by SES. He concluded that since there were few ways to secure Moldova's national interests through organizations in Central Asia, Moldova would "likely step up its efforts to join the EU."[101]

With Turkmenistan's withdrawal from CIS in 2005, remaining members agreed on the necessity of institutional reform. Even Alexander Lukashenko, Russia's staunch ally, admitted that the "CIS [was] undergoing the most critical phase in its history...there [was] more and more talk about its uselessness...it had transformed but no one [knew] into what anymore."[102]

Once the "color revolutions" started to make their way into Central Asia, Russia's allies in Georgia, Ukraine, and Kyrgyzstan were replaced by more assertive leaders, some of whom favored a Euro-Atlantic option for their countries. These leaders started to question the *raison d'etre* of the organization.

Ukrainian authorities underscored the lack of progress in reforming the organization into a body that could be useful to all its members, and said the government was considering halting its financial support for the CIS.[103]

On May 2, 2006 at a cabinet meeting, President Saakashvili instructed the government to consider the possible consequences of Georgia's withdrawal from CIS. He made his position clear in a speech at the School of Public Administration in Kutaisi.

> In 1991 Georgia's independence was recognized by many countries and Georgia refused to become a member of the Commonwealth of Independent States, like the Baltic States. Then, in 1993, during the Abkhaz tragedy, a kneeling and humiliated Georgia was forced to join the CIS. I think that, despite the fact that it was a humiliating act, we found many benefits from CIS membership. We were able to maintain ties with many former Soviet states...we were able to establish trade links, we were able to maintain free movement between [former Soviet states]...And we had partnership with the Russian Federation for a long time; our products were sold in Russia and demand [for Georgian products] has recently increased in Russia...Today I instructed the Georgian government to thoroughly study...the exact economic estimations over whether it is worth it or not for Georgia to remain in the CIS. If there is still the possibility to gain certain benefits, we will consider remaining in this organization. And if Georgia can no longer benefit from this organization—which I suspect is the case—and if we can not receive anything but humiliation, then the Georgian people, with its Parliament and government, should make a decision which honorable nations should take.[104]

Coming after a number of serious disagreements with the Kremlin over the closing of Russian military bases on Georgian territory, the exorbitant raises in gas prices, and a Russian ban on Georgian wines and fruit, Georgia's decision to reassess the usefulness of the CIS was perceived as a veiled attempt to undermine the organization, and the influence that Russia was able to exert through it. "We had placed great hopes in the CIS for peaceful conflict resolution, freedom of movement of our citizens, and improvements in economic relations, but everything turned out exactly to the contrary. For Georgia in any case. Our hopes in the CIS were not justified, so there is no longer any sense in staying in the CIS," Deputy Prime Minister Georgy Baramidze also underscored.[105]

The Kremlin and the remaining CIS countries attempted to revamp the organization among fears of its dissolution. In October 2006, a CIS anniversary meeting was cancelled by Russia and Kazakhstan without consulting the other members. The decision came unexpectedly and caused consternation in CIS capitals. Andrei Ryabov from the Carnegie Moscow Center argued that the cancellation had to do with the Kremlin's and Astana's inability to garner support from the other members for a plan to revamp the organization. "Russia and Kazakhstan, which have decided they cannot offer solutions to existing problems that are acceptable to all sides, suggest taking a break and drafting new proposals," Ryabov was quoted by *Ria Novosti.*[106]

These developments indicate that while, during the nineties, former republics may have felt comfortable interacting in a framework resembling the Soviet Union, that level of comfort dissipated as member states transitioned to more sovereign and single-minded governments. The mere act of questioning the effectiveness of an organization championed by the Kremlin indicates that countries that used to be on the periphery of power need to be approached differently, as stand-alone, independent-minded countries. Ironically, the charter of the CIS makes provisions for relations based on "mutual recognition and respect of state sovereignty." The likely dissolution of the CIS indicates that the theory did not square with the practice of multilateral relations, and that the rising sovereign-minded Eurasian states no longer see themselves obligated to indulge the Kremlin. As of this writing, CIS has not dissolved but its status remains uncertain.

Assertive Rhetoric in Relations with Russia

Some late-blooming republics adopted political positions that did not conform to the Kremlin's choices, and were not afraid to advocate for their own national interest. From asking the Kremlin to pull Russian troops out of Georgia and Moldova, and stay out of domestic conflicts in the breakaway republics, to demanding a level of respect in bilateral relations, countries such as Georgia, Moldova, and Ukraine set a new tone in their bilateral relations with Russia. The tone was sometimes difficult, sometimes contentious, and often times fueled anti-Russia conspiracy theories.

Georgia proved by far the boldest of the late-bloomer countries with respect to resisting the core-periphery relationship with Moscow. From starting talks about the withdrawal from the CIS, to demanding the pullout of Russian troops from Georgian military bases, post–Rose Revolution politicians caused much trouble for the Kremlin.

Under the terms of a 1999 agreement negotiated under the auspices of the Organization for Security and Cooperation in Europe, Russia was to close the Vaziani and Gudauta bases by July 2001, and negotiate with Georgia toward the closure of the Batumi and Akhalkalaki bases. Despite the relatively small number of Russian troops in Georgia, approximately 7,000, Moscow later argued that it needed fourteen years to complete the withdrawal, and requested financial compensation from Georgia for the relocation of its military personnel. The Georgian government insisted on Russia respecting the terms of the 1999 agreement. The pullout eventually started in 2006.

The diplomatic rhetoric leading to the pullout was inflammatory and sometimes escalated into a war of words. In 2005, President Saakashvili refused to go to Moscow for the sixtieth anniversary of Victory Day, in a symbolic gesture of dissatisfaction with Russia's stonewalling the negotiations on troop withdrawal. In the words of Georgian foreign and defense ministers,

> We have not reached progress [on withdrawal of troops] and...the president of Georgia will not be able to come to the festivities in Moscow because, as we emphasized, something mutually beneficial was expected to happen...We see that nothing like that is taking place. Therefore, the Georgian president should stay in his country for the 60th anniversary of the Great Patriotic War...We have not agreed upon a timeframe of the withdrawal of the Russian bases because, as the Georgian side sees it, a date not later than January 1, 2008 would be preferable...Nor has a withdrawal of the Akhalkalaki military base prior to 2006 been coordinated...[107]

Closely related to the issue of Russian troop withdrawal is the perceived interference by Russian authorities in Georgia's conflict with the breakaway republics. Georgian authorities accused Russia of interfering in its internal affairs by supporting the separatist movements in Abkhazia, and North and South Ossetia. On numerous occasions, Georgian leaders showed their determination to send a strong message to the Kremlin that support for separatist movements was not going to be tolerated. Foreign Minister Gela Bezhuashvili presented a letter to the UN Secretary General's Group of Friends calling on Russia to stop its military exercises in Abkhazia's Kodori Gorge region. "...[t]he exercises are held on the background of unusually frequent violations of the Georgian air space and missile strikes in the Georgian territory by Russian war planes, as well as military exercises held by the Russian Armed Forces in North Caucasus," the minister charged.[108]

At the 2006 UN General Assembly gathering, President Mikheil Saakashvili accused Russia of inciting and supporting territorial conflicts in his country, with the covert intent of annexation of Georgian territory. The Federation distributed Russian passports among the people of North and South Ossetia, in direct violation of Georgian law and contrary to international law.

> ...the painful but factual truth is that these regions are being annexed by our neighbor to the north, the Russian Federation which has actively supported their incorporation through a concerted policy of mass distribution of Russian passports...Few examples [in history] are more poignant—when one State seeks to annex another, when one State seeks to undermine another—on its internationally recognized sovereign territory... I would like to ask all of you in this hall if you would tolerate such interference on [your] own soil. I doubt it.[109]

Moldova had similar issues with Russia due to the Kremlin's interference in the country's internal conflict with the Trans-Dniester breakaway republic. Russia initially intervened in the conflict at the Moldovan president's request in 1992. A Russian-brokered cease-fire agreement was signed by the Russian and Moldovan presidents in the presence of the leader of Trans-Dniester in July 1992. Despite a 2001 Russian-Moldovan Treaty of Friendship and Cooperation, the persistence of the breakaway republic to demand independence hardened positions between the Kremlin and Chisinau, the capital of Moldova.

In early March 2006, the Moldovan government imposed new customs regulations on Trans-Dniester, requiring all goods bound for Ukraine to bear an official Moldovan stamp. The regulations came after years of Moldovan government's claims that illicit trade was occurring across the border into Ukraine, with drugs, weapons, and other unauthorized merchandise crossing into Moldova without proper customs checks. The new regulations were outlined in a joint communiqué adopted by the Moldovan and Ukrainian prime ministers on December 30, 2005 and endorsed by the Ukrainian Cabinet in a March 1 decree. As Trans-Dniester is landlocked between Moldova and Ukraine, the decree gave Chisinau full authority over the trade flow in and out of the breakaway republic.

Russian Ambassador to Moldova accused Chisinau of breaking international norms by imposing the new customs regulations. While stressing that Russia "respects Moldova's sovereignty and territorial integrity," Ryabov added that "Russia is seriously concerned about the heightened tensions around Trans-Dniester," which the Kremlin blamed on Ukraine's direct involvement into "attempts by Moldova to further lock the region into its economic space. . ."[110] His remarks drew protests from Moldovan Foreign Minister Andrei Stratan, who retorted that the Russian Ambassador's behavior was "unacceptable," and that his comments were "clearly provocative and do not fit the diplomatic dialogue between two sovereign countries."[111]

By late March, Trans-Dniester local leaders were requesting humanitarian aid from Russia, as trade came to a full halt due to the new customs regulations. A convoy of twenty-four trucks of medicine and other goods was sent across Ukraine toward the breakaway republic. This gave Ukraine an opportunity to complain about Russian abuse of its territory on the eve of parliamentary elections in the country. Ukrainian foreign minister called the convoy a "provocation" intended to intimidate and influence elections in his country, and demanded that Russian trucks travel only at night, on a route of Kyiv's choice.[112] This type of assertive tone rarely occurred before in relations between the two countries, and Russia complained that Ukraine was making the situation even more difficult.

As Yulia Tymoshenko first underscored a year before these events occurred, Ukraine was also determined to stand up more to its former core of political influence. Tymoshenko cancelled her first scheduled visit to Moscow as prime minister in 2005, when Russia's state prosecutor warned that she remained on a wanted list of persons linked to claims of fraud in the nineties. Tymoshenko cited a busy schedule, cancelled the visit, and warned Russia that Ukraine needed to be treated with the respect deserved between equal partners. "I know the Russian elite has gotten used to Ukraine suffering from an inferiority complex, but I want this to disappear from our relationship," she was quoted by the *BBC*.[113] As these examples indicate, late-blooming republics' tone and approach to relations with Russia has become increasingly assertive in recent years, in their attempts to decouple from the Kremlin's influence and advocate for their national interests.

Establishing Regional Cooperative Agreements with or without Russia

Late-blooming republics opted to belong to a variety of cooperative arrangements, some of which do not have Russia as a member. Some of them use their membership to balance Russian influence in Central Asia. A foreign minister of a Central Asian country speaking off the record acknowledged that SCO membership offered his country the opportunity to strengthen its position vis-à-vis Russia when his country disagreed with the position of its former core.[114]

One of the first regional cooperative arrangements not to include Russia was GUAM. Named after the initial letters of each cofounding country—Georgia, Ukraine, Azerbaijan, and Moldova—GUAM was established in 1997. The overall goal of the organization was to foster political and economic cooperation among its members. In 1999, Uzbekistan joined and the group was renamed GUUAM.

The group is perceived by Moscow as anti-Russian, an attempt to counter Russian influence among former republics, although that charge was naturally rejected by member countries. The organization's relevance has been questionable, having few tangible results to show. While member countries met to foster relations among themselves, by 2004, only two countries attended a Yalta meeting. In 2005, Uzbekistan gave up its membership and the group reverted to its initial membership and name. In 2006, members announced expansion of member relations and renamed the group GUAM Organization for Democracy and Economic Development. Proposals were made to establish a multinational peacekeeping force to replace the Russian peace-keeping forces deployed in breakaway republics, but those proposals have not yet materialized. Other areas of regional cooperation included energy and trade.[115]

The CDC is another regional cooperation arrangement in which Russia does not participate. Initially agreed upon between the presidents of Ukraine and Georgia at a bilateral meeting in August 2004, the CDC was conceived as an organization to support member states in the pursuit of democracy, market economy, and rapprochement with Western European countries and institutions. Member states include the Baltic countries and one vanguard Central European country, Romania, as well as two South European countries, the Republic of Macedonia and Slovenia.

In official statements celebrating the new organization, Viktor Yushchenko was careful to state that the new organization was "not directed against any third countries or institutions" and indicated that it was an "open dialogue between friends, adherents of ideas for promoting democracy and the supremacy of law."[116] Russia was invited to participate but declined.

Like GUAM, CDC has few tangible results to show but both represent modest attempts to recreate neighborly relations based on a philosophy of full equality and respect for member countries. Organizations in which Russia is involved usually tend to be dominated by Russia. Whether intentional or not, Russia behaves like the "leader" of the member states in organizations such as the CIS, and such format of relations resembles too closely the core-periphery format of the Soviet times. As such, the Russia-dominated format is becoming increasingly unpopular among late-bloomer republics who favor a more fair treatment of their sovereign identities.

A number of other regional arrangements involved cooperation on energy and water issues. Water resources have long been a point of contention among countries in the region. Kyrgyzstan and Tajikistan, located in the upper course of the Syr Darya River basin, use the river for power generation. This affects Kazakhstan and Uzbekistan down the river, which have traditionally used it for irrigation. Both Kyrgyzstan and Tajikistan used water resources for political leverage in their relations with Kazakhstan and Uzbekistan.

While full-scale conflict has not erupted over the shared use of water resources, many observers warn of the potential for such conflict if countries do not find a formula for water usage that they can all agree upon and respect. From swapping energy for water, to building reservoirs and rationing water use, these countries have been trying to work out an arrangement since 1992, many times without involving Russia as a broker. The World Bank and several international lending institutions helped with loans for building adequate facilities for water retention, with limited results. Yet, it is worth noting that Central Asian countries refrained from full-scale war and made decisions, good or bad, based on their perceived national interests. The relatively limited role that Russia played in water and energy arrangements speaks to these countries' abilities to think and act for themselves.[117]

Other cooperative arrangements were attempted, many times involving the search for increasing energy independence from Russia. Armenia established an intergovernmental commission to open up a political dialogue with energy resource-rich Iran. The bilateral relationship grew despite U.S. disapproval, which considers Iran a sponsor of terrorist groups. Ukraine struck up an energy alliance with Kazakhstan in early 2007. Azerbaijan is working to help Georgia with its energy needs.

On security issues, vanguard Poland and the Baltic countries have been particularly supportive of Ukraine, Moldova, and the Caucasus in their search for Euro-Atlantic integration. In doing so, they aggravated political circles in Russia who regarded them as pawns of the United States in the latter's attempts to interfere in Central Asia, as the next and final chapter will discuss.

Good Relations with Russia and the Euro-Atlantic Community

Since the breakup of the Soviet Union, late-blooming republics tried to maintain good political, trade, and security relations with Russia, even as they were increasingly interested in relations with the Euro-Atlantic community.

Some countries never showed substantial interest in rapprochement with Euro-Atlantic centers of power and remained committed not only to a pro-Russia foreign policy but also to a political and economic union. Belarus is a case in point.

Other countries pursued a multi-vector approach to foreign policy, remaining on good terms with Russia as they invited Euro-Atlantic investment in their countries and flirted with deepened relations either with the EU, the United States, or NATO. Kazakhstan conducted the most prominent example of multi-vector policy.

Other countries only warmed up to a relationship with the Euro-Atlantic community in the aftermath of the September 11, 2001 attacks, inviting the United States and antiterrorism coalition forces to use their domestic military bases for operations in Afghanistan. U.S.-led coalition forces are based in Kyrgyzstan and Uzbekistan. Tajikistan provides support in the form of over flight rights, emergency landing and refueling, and other operations connected to the antiterrorism campaign. An additional layer of security is provided by Russia's 201st Division located in Tajikistan.

Finally, a small number of late-blooming republics chose integration with NATO and the EU, and pursued domestic policies conducive to membership. Most prominent in this category are Georgia, Moldova, and Ukraine.

The Euro-Atlantic community extended a helping hand to Central Asian countries that reached out for assistance. NATO opened its doors for late-bloomer membership in PfP and all the countries took advantage of this opportunity, some faster than others. Russia itself participates in PfP. In 2006, the EU adopted the Neighborhood Strategy, to bolster financial aid to countries aspiring to membership. Various other bilateral arrangements were adopted, depending on the level of late-bloomer interest in deeper levels of cooperation.

The relation of Central Asia with the United States strengthened particularly after the September 11, 2001 attacks in New York and Washington. The antiterrorism campaign was particularly important to late-blooming republics with ethnic tensions of their own. It also gave some of the more authoritarian Central Asian governments an opportunity to crack down on domestic separatist movements waged in the name of human and religious rights, as was the case in Uzbekistan.

Kazakhstan floated the possibility that it would open up access for American military, if the United States requested it. "We are going to provide [the U.S.] with use of the Zhetigin air base for free, if they need it. This is one way of assisting them and, in return, the U.S. side promised to give us $10 million, which will mainly be used for increasing the armed forces in western Kazakhstan," Defense Minister Altynbaev offered in 2003.[118]

The use of Kazakh bases never materialized, but Kyrgyzstan opened its base at Manas for the use of American military, starting in the fall of 2001. Negotiations leading to this unprecedented event were held with Moscow's full knowledge and approval. Russia was also offered the use of the Kant base in connection with the antiterrorism campaign, just a few miles away from the Manas base. Kyrgyz officials clarified on several occasions that the use of the country's bases was not permanent. The government "supports the presence of coalition forces until the mission of fighting terrorism has been completed," read a public statement.[119]

Uzbekistan similarly opened the country's air base Karshi-Khanabad (also known as K-2) to American military forces, as a hub for military activities in Afghanistan. The first U.S. military personnel and airplanes arrived in Uzbekistan's Khanabad airport in November 2001. Bilateral relations were close until the Uzbek government ordered violent repressions of popular uprisings in Andijan, in 2005. The United States called for an investigation into the crackdown, and Karimov responded by telling the American forces to vacate the air base.

In the heydays of Uzbekistan's good relations with the United States, President Karimov was careful to stress that his country was pursuing good bilateral relations both with Washington and with Moscow. He said that good relations with Russia did not come at the expense of good bilateral relations with the United States and vice versa. In a 2003 opening of the fall parliamentary session, Karimov underscored the importance of good bilateral relations with both centers of power and warned against interpretations of his foreign policy as "drifting towards Russia." Even as Karimov underscored the intention of his country to consolidate good bilateral relations with Russia, he was equally assertive about Russia's initiatives through CIS, such as the Customs Union Agreement of 1996, which he called "stillborn." He was dismissive of initiatives such as the Eurasian Economic Community and the economic space between Russia, Ukraine, Kazakhstan, and Belarus, and called them "populist."[120] Once again, as the former near-abroad became less near, and more abroad, former republics showed that they had grown a spine in relations with their former core of influence. They were also not shy to show the door to American soldiers when they perceived that the United States was trying to interfere in their affairs.

Several years into the antiterrorism campaign, Kyrgyzstan also took a sovereign-minded stance in its relations with the United States and demanded a higher rent for the use of the Manas base. In doing so, it elected not to ask Russia for a similar rent increase for its use of the Kant base. Parliament speaker Marat Sultanov said that since Kant was not a Russian base, but a Kyrgyz base "the question of asking for rent does not exist...our friends in Moscow say we should decide about the U.S. air base by ourselves."[121] Clearly, the Kyrgyz authorities "decided by themselves" that the Americans should pay more for the use of one of their bases and that Russia should not. Whether this was a decision they thought up themselves or was suggested to them by "their friends in Moscow" is less important than the fact that the authorities made a decision and stood up to a center of power such as Washington. As chapters two and three showed, assertiveness can go in all directions.

In 2005, whether due to increased perceptions about the inappropriateness of the Iraq war or to fears of too much American influence in Central Asia, the SCO demanded that the United States set a date for the withdrawal of its troops from bases in Kyrgyzstan and Uzbekistan. Underscoring their continued support for the antiterrorism campaign, member countries also decided that "the active [combat] phase of the anti-terrorist operation in Afghanistan has been completed, the[refore] SCO member countries deem necessary that the coalition countries involved should set the final dates for their temporary use of those infrastructure installations and stationing of their troops on SCO member countries' territories."[122] As of this writing, U.S. military remain at Manas base, although support for their continued presence is waning.[123]

A final word should be said about Turkmenistan. Under Niyazov, the country's foreign policy of neutrality and the president's dictatorial tendencies pushed the country into complete isolation. With the administration of Berdymukhammedov, the country started cultivating relations with countries east and west. It reached new economic agreements with China, Kazakhstan, and Russia, and has reached out to the United States, particularly for energy investments.

During his first visit to the United Nations in 2007, Berdymukhammedov indicated that his country supported plans to open a preventive diplomacy center in Central Asia, to be located in his country's capital, Ashgabat. The center was expected to be a "strong positive force in resolving the problems our region faces," and Turkmenistan was ready to "do everything necessary to make the center's work effective and fruitful," vowed the new Turkmen leader.[124] As Turkmenistan becomes more open in relations with its regional neighbors and beyond, the country's energy resources may attract more than Russian investment. It, too, should be expected to diversify its investments and energy clients.

Three late-blooming republics moved toward full-fledged integration either in the EU or NATO or both, although none of them dashed to apply for membership as soon as they became independent. Neither Georgia, Moldova, nor Ukraine started out their post-Soviet transformation from the premise of Euro-Atlantic membership; consolidating statehood was their main priority. NATO and the EU were reluctant to consider any former Soviet republic as a serious candidate but that reluctance seems to be softening, particularly in the aftermath of September 11.

Moldova is only interested in EU membership. In 1998, it signed a PCA with the EU, which set the legal foundation for further cooperation. In 2004, it developed the Moldova-EU Action Plan, and adopted the plan in 2005. The Action Plan constitutes the first step in the process of integration. In 2006, the European Commission launched its Communication on Strengthening the European Neighborhood Policy, and started publishing progress reports regarding the fulfillment of the Action Plans. As of 2007, Moldova is working toward goals set in the Action Plan and continuing its course of integration with the EU.[125] While Russia is not happy to see Moldova drifting away from the CIS, it seems to accept the possibility of Moldova in the EU.

Before the Rose Revolution in Georgia, talks about the possibility of membership in either NATO or the EU were scant and mostly tentative. After the revolution, the dialogue to join NATO and the EU intensified between Georgia and Brussels. In October 2004, the North Atlantic Council approved Georgia's IPAP, and the country moved to a second stage of integration. In 2005, a Georgian state commission was appointed by the president to implement the IPAP. In 2006, NATO positively assessed Georgia's progress and the country was invited to join the Intensified Dialogue process for NATO membership. It also signed an Action Plan as part of the EU's European Neighborhood Policy. The Georgian parliament voted unanimously for a bill calling for integration in NATO. In the words of the country's then deputy defense minister, Levan Nikoleishvili, "We look to NATO...as an organization, which will not only be a guarantee for security but will also be a guarantee for development for us...After that we are looking to other steps to join other European institutions."[126] In June 2007, Georgia was given the right to subscribe to EU political statements as part of the Georgia-EU Action Plan agreed in November 2006.[127]

As of this writing, Georgia is set on a course for NATO membership. Russia is disturbed by this possibility and expressed its opposition on numerous occasions. Relations with Russia have been particularly tense after the Rose Revolution, and the diplomatic dialogue continued to escalate as Georgia accused Russia of interference in its affairs. Of all the late-blooming republics, Georgia is probably the most assertive country in setting the limits on Russia's persistence to interfere in Georgia's breakaway republics, and in other affairs. Russia sees Georgia's foreign policy as a direct threat to its geopolitical position in the Caucasus.

Ukraine's rapprochement with NATO and the EU was a mutually slow process, unraveling throughout the nineties. At times, it appeared that Ukraine was interested in rapprochement but unwilling to compromise its relationship with Russia in the process. At other times, it seemed that Kyiv was more interested in a solid Russia-first relationship than in rapprochement with Western institutions. This uneven direction came to an end with the Orange Revolution and the election of Viktor Yushchenko to the country's presidency in December 2004.

The EU-Ukraine Action Plan was adopted in early 2005. The European Commission approved the directives for holding talks on signing an expanded agreement on partnership and cooperation with Ukraine in September 2006. In October, the EU offered Ukraine stronger economic and trade relations and a commitment to start official negotiations in early 2007 on a new Enhanced Agreement. While maintaining the position that "Ukraine is not ready and we are not ready" for further enlargement, EU President Jose Manuel Barroso recognized the need to form a free trade zone. The EU's intention was not to give a "negative signal" by delaying membership talks, but rather to spur political and economic reforms necessary for accession.[128]

In October 2006, after months of domestic political instability, the general strategy of Euro-Atlantic rapprochement and eventual membership was strongly reiterated. Defense Minister Anatoliy Hrytsenko told a Kyiv conference that "NATO is not only a military-political bloc, but a community of democratic states, which creates a high standard of living for their citizens, for their society...If we resolve both those questions, [NATO membership and energy independence] Ukraine will be a stable, independent state."[129]

The political instability that continued in Ukraine after the Orange Revolution and Yanukovych's return to power cast a cloud on Ukraine's possible Euro-Atlantic membership. Yanukovych took the position that NATO membership should be decided through a national referendum. The prime minister called for a go-slow approach, in a resolution approved by the Rada (242 in favor, 208 against). "Ukraine's further moves toward NATO membership should be made only by taking the will of the Ukrainian people into account," the resolution read.[130] But even as the Rada put the brakes on Yushchenko's membership drive, it also directed the country's government to "promote the distribution of objective information on NATO's role in the modern world, and on the direction of reforms, as a key to raising public awareness."

Even as he pursued a pro-Russia domestic and foreign policy, Yanukovych announced numerous times that he would "defend Ukraine's European choice consistently and decisively."[131] He pressed the parliament to pass the necessary legislation to enable the country to join WTO (World Trade Organization) by February 2007. In early November 2006, the Rada passed five laws required for Ukraine's accession to WTO in the first reading and adopted two more in full. In December, the Rada voted to pass the last bill required to bring Ukraine's legislation in line with WTO requirements for membership.[132]

Throughout the process of strengthening relations with NATO and the EU, Ukraine leaders never equated membership in either organization with a rejection of Russia as a strategic and regional partner. "While getting closer to the European Union, we should not be coming with two suitcases of problems in our relations with Russia," Yushchenko told a media conference in November 2006.[133] Throughout the postindependence period, Ukraine maintained a strategically close relationship with Russia even as it argued with the Kremlin over Crimea, the Black Sea Fleet, and other Soviet-era unresolved issues. For instance, in 1998, then President Leonid Kuchma signed a ten-year economic cooperation agreement with then Russian President Boris Yeltsin in Moscow. The agreement included a wide range of mutual economic relations, from the media to the space industry. Then Russian Prime Minister Viktor Chernomyrdin called the agreement "unprecedented...Russia ha[s] not achieved anything similar with any of the other countries in the Commonwealth of Independent States."[134] Even with Ukrainian reassurances and gestures of cooperation, Russia regards "the loss of Ukraine to NATO" as a significant threat to its security and a clear sign that "the West" is trying to encircle it.

Controversial and still under investigation remains the attempt on the life of Ukraine's current president, Viktor Yushchenko, at the time he was running for election against Moscow-backed candidate Viktor Yanukovych. If the investigation will ever be completed, and if it will be proven that a Russian state-controlled laboratory produced the type of poisoning agent that claimed Yushchenko's health, this act would qualify as a clear interference in the domestic affairs of a sovereign country by Russian authorities. Just as the Soviet Union interfered in Eastern Europe after the war, and influenced election results, modern Russia may be tempted to revert to old Kremlin schemes of keeping countries under its control.

The story is straightforward. Viktor Yushchenko running for president in 2004 against Viktor Yanukovych was poisoned during the election campaign, just when polls showed that he was widely popular and likely to win. These elections were held under the shady practices of an election commission appointed by then President Leonid Kuchma, who also feared a Yushchenko win. There was ample speculation that a Yushchenko victory would lead to a significant investigation of the abuses of two Kuchma administrations. Power abuse allegations ranging from selling the country out to special interests in Moscow to pocketing millions of dollars from the national budget abounded. None of those allegations were proven in a court of law as of this writing. The fear that such law suits could be filed was, however, significant. As a result, when Yushchenko was poisoned, speculations abounded that powerful interests tried to get him out of the race for fear of uncovering substantial fraud.

Yushchenko fell ill and was rushed to the hospital, where it was proven that he had been poisoned with a type of dioxin that only three laboratories in the world produce. The investigation proceeded. Two laboratories provided samples of the type of dioxin they produced, the Russian laboratory refused to offer samples. Russia invoked national security secrecy in withholding samples, and the investigation could not proceed further.

As of September 2007, the investigation is inconclusive in the absence of the relevant evidence. Yushchenko cannot claim to have been poisoned by the Russian side, but when asked about his suspicions, Yushchenko only said, "[t]his was not a private act."[135] It may never be known who ordered the poisoning of Yushchenko. Speculations, however, abounded that Russia had the most to gain from his disappearance from the political scene of Ukraine. The rationale is that without Yushchenko, Ukraine would not have changed course toward Euro-Atlantic integration, and Russia would still retain a significant amount of influence over the country.

CONCLUSION

Late-blooming republics had a difficult transition to full statehood, as they developed independent and sovereign governments, economies, and societies. Their Soviet identity left psychological and institutional scars on their mode of operation, and subtly influenced the way they governed themselves in the beginning of the transition.

As countries became more stable and moved away from authoritarian tendencies and toward (incomplete) democratic practices, they started to assert their national interests in ways that did not consistently conform with the Kremlin's preferences. From trying to gain energy independence from Russia to adopting domestic and foreign policies of their own choosing, late-blooming republics seem set on decoupling from their former core of influence. Even as late-blooming republics showed interest to cooperate with Russia and maintain good relations, they moved away from a display of submissiveness into a display of assertiveness of their opinions, preferences, choices, and ultimately policy and strategy decisions. The final chapter shows that Russia not only does not take these countries' sovereignty fully seriously, it also translates these independent choices in ways that have little to do with reality. Russia's persistence in concocting conspiracy theories to explain away these countries' sovereign choices can be a very dangerous practice and could become a self-fulfilling prophesy.

Russia and Eurasia—Where To?

So why is Russia so convinced that there is a broad Western conspiracy to isolate and encircle it? What concrete acts of aggression from either NATO or its newest members lead Russian politicians to believe that the world is entering a second Cold War? If Russia is the target of Western encirclement, what explains rising Eurasia's assertiveness toward its allies in the Euro-Atlantic community? Does it all matter or should we stop worrying and let the chips fall where they may?

At first glance, these questions seem to have foregone conclusions. It has been argued that Russian politicians tend to be distrustful and suspicious, and project their own fears and values on others. It has also been argued that in the final analysis, Russian persistence in conspiracy theories is not that important, that with diligent diplomatic activity, all these misunderstandings and misperceptions about a presumed hidden agenda of the West will eventually subside.

One needs to remember, however, that these arguments have been voiced throughout the nineties and the rhetoric of Russian elites only intensified with time. Misperceptions allowed to grow into alternative realities can damage all sides involved, unless they are unpackaged from the layers of suspicion, fear, distrust, and past patterns of thinking and behavior.

The historical and statistical evidence presented in this book is not new. It has been and remains in the public domain. However, the cumulative effect of this information should supersede rhetorical sound bites according to which rising Eurasia is still in an uncertain transition, Russia is recreating its sphere of influence in this region, and the standoff between Russia and the West is inevitably leading to a second Cold War. This book does not present a revisionist approach to post–Cold War events, it simply presents them from the vantage point of rising Eurasian countries, to highlight the dynamics of *intentional,* sovereign change. It does so in hopes that Russian and Euro-Atlantic policy communities pay attention and give the credit that is appropriately due to millions of people who sometimes chaotically, tentatively, or mistakenly selected domestic and foreign policy courses that seemed to fit their national interests.

These countries' pursuit of a political and economic system that served their domestic interests, not those of the Kremlin, Brussels, or Washington should be recognized and given appropriate credit as a phenomenon in its own right. The dynamics of intentional, sovereign change are by no means easy, perfect, tidy, or successful; but they are formulated in the countries' capitals, as a function of priorities determined by born and bred, elected leaders. This dynamic is misinterpreted as a Western conspiracy mostly by Kremlin policy circles. The final thoughts on how this dynamic may unfold reflect directly on Russian policy circles.

In Russia, the Eurasian dynamic of intentional, sovereign change is widely viewed as a function of first, Western influence in "turning" Eurasia toward the Euro-Atlantic community, and second, a deliberate encirclement of Russia. There is little credit given to the sovereign choices of these countries to adopt domestic and foreign policy directions of their own persuasion. A "Western hand" is seen in any event that the Kremlin does not approve of, from NATO and EU enlargement, to demanding a level of recognition for the Soviet Union's past wrongs toward these countries. Most recently, Russia claimed responsibility for events it does not even approve of, such as the democratization of the former communist world. If crisis scenarios can and should be feared in the region, the evidence presented in this book also offers legitimate grounds for hope that developments in these countries are not a (negative) foregone conclusion and are not biased toward a sole source of power.

As far as Russia is concerned, the sooner the country's elites change the tone and direction of their fears to allow for the possibility that Central Europe, the Baltic countries, and the late-bloomer republics have a right to choose their own system of government, the allies they want, and the geostrategic positioning that makes sense for them, the better for all parties involved. The unfortunate and persisting reality is that Russia translates any political move that is not favored by the Kremlin as a direct affront and infringement on Russia's national interests. Imbedded deeply in the national psyche is a fear of being left out, of becoming isolated and irrelevant. In the words of a Russian analyst, "the fear of being isolated, marginalized...in Europe...[is a fear that] goes deep into Russian history. There is a perception in Russia that we are not [considered] Europeans, and we are literally pushed out of Europe. We are getting isolated on the continent."[1] If and when Russian politicians stop fearing isolation and start building neighborly relations on the basis of mutual respect, Russia may be able to change the international perception about its neo-imperialist tendencies and start a new page in its relations with the Euro-Atlantic community. Until then, Russian elites' persistence in conspiracy theories will continue to generate alternative realities that, just as in Soviet times, will captivate the imagination of millions of people.

A start in the direction of unpackaging layers of misperceptions may have occurred in the immediate aftermath of the end of the Cold War. At that time, conditions were ripe for a recasting of international relations away from the superpower standoff toward a world of cooperation and collective security. Seventeen years later, the Soviet Union let go of its near abroad and fifteen independent countries replaced it; NATO and the EU enlarged to six former East European communist countries and three former Soviet republics; NATO and EU both have bilateral arrangements of cooperation with Russia; and the United States used Central Asian bases in former

Soviet republics, with Russian consent, in order to fight terrorism. At no point during these dramatic changes occurring in a relatively short period of time, did the West and Russia come close to confrontation—that is, if one does not count the stepped up Russian rhetoric to oppose many of these developments. Post–Cold War cooperative arrangements helped all sides air differences, argue, agree to disagree, and eventually have dinner together. The future of relations can be respectful, if all sides agree that Eurasian countries have as much right to assert their national interests as Russia, the United States, or the EU do.

Between now and whenever that auspicious day comes, Russia needs to accept responsibility for known facts of life. Russia needs to acknowledge the Soviet Union's role in past wrongdoing, such as denying these countries a sovereign identity after 1920. It needs to drop creating alternative realities of its choosing, such as claiming that these countries favored communism over capitalism at the end of WWII, and that Russia democratized the entire communist world after the end of the Cold War. These claims are troubling aspects of modern Russian rhetoric. They indicate that Russian leaders and politicians persist in propagating alternative realities and refuse to give the credit that is due to the countries themselves for their efforts and sovereign choices. Alternative realities are as dangerous as conspiracy theories. They take on a life of their own and, with effective marketing, they become self-fulfilling prophecies. If this rhetoric continues, the world may be faced with a second Cold War sooner, rather than never. As such, leaders on all sides of the Atlantic have a special responsibility to pay enhanced attention to developments in Eurasia and Russia, and address misperceptions as soon as they are articulated, not after they become mainstream pop culture.

CONSPIRACY THEORIES AND ALTERNATIVE REALITIES

NATO and EU enlargement to former communist countries; the planned positioning of military bases in Romania and Bulgaria, and a missile defense site in Poland and the Czech Republic; Western criticism of Russia's state of democracy; and Eurasian countries' criticism of Russia's refusal to take full responsibility for Soviet abuses, add up to the fundamental reasons why Russian political elites believe that the West is "out to get them." Russian authorities often times connect the dots between Western criticism of any kind and a desire to "humiliate" Russia. There is a strong trend among Russian citizens to believe their leaders when they claim that the West concocted "color revolutions" in their backyard, in order to destabilize the Russian democracy. The rhetorical record speaks for itself.

NATO and EU "Expansion" in Russia's "Traditional Sphere of Interest"

Russia views NATO enlargement to former communist countries as an expansion of "the West" into its "traditional sphere of interest." It views EU enlargement as an acceptable trend, as long as Russia's interests are protected. It also views proposed positioning of Western weapons and military bases on the territories of NATO's newest members as a concrete expression of the West's intention to encircle Russia.

Russia does not accept the explanation of Central European, Baltic, and late-bloomer republics that their Euro-Atlantic choice is not aimed against Russia. In the words of a Moscow-based military analyst, "For the Baltic countries, for Poland and for those who want to join NATO, like Georgia, their main reason. . . is to have a guarantee against the Russians. . . That makes NATO and Russia basically enemies. In a sense they are on a collision course. . . any expansion of NATO is seen in Russia, in Moscow, as a threat to our interests."[2]

In the early nineties, Boris Yeltsin initially seemed to agree to NATO enlargement, only to radically change his position later in his presidency. Gennady Gerasimov, Yeltsin's former spokesperson, quoted his boss on the possibility of reaching an agreement between Russia and NATO as the equivalent of "mat[ing] a hedge hog and a grass snake."[3] Clearly, Yeltsin did not think such agreement could be reached, yet a Russia-NATO Council is in operation, and is used by both sides to address political and military issues of mutual interest.

A period of Russian bemoaning of the lack of trust displayed by the Central Europeans seeking NATO membership followed. By the mid-nineties, when enlargement to Poland, Hungary, and the Czech Republic seemed inevitable, Russia turned to semi-threats and warnings of a "Cold Peace" potentially following NATO's enlargement. By 1997, Russian leaders turned to persuasion. After the 1997 NATO Madrid Summit, Yeltsin sought the help of Finnish President Martti Ahtisaari to convince the Baltic countries not to seek NATO membership, following the example of Finland which did not seek membership once the Cold War was over. Russia "will be strongly against the admission of countries of the Commonwealth of Independent States and of the Baltic states to NATO," he told Ahtisaari.[4] Instead of NATO membership, Russia offered a two-way security system for the Baltic states, where both NATO and Russia would offer guarantees to the three countries.

What Yeltsin and Russian elites after him refused to acknowledge was the right of each country to choose the allies they wanted. Russia used political pressure to influence developments in these countries for such a long time in history that Russian politicians forget these countries have identities of their own. Not only does Russia sometimes forget that countries have sovereign rights, it takes their decisions very personally, particularly when their choices do not conform to the Kremlin's views. The position of being "strongly against" a country's sovereign choice, whether that choice is to join NATO or the EU, or have an American military base on one's territory, is the equivalent of trying to influence the country's politics and interfering in its affairs. Ironically, this is not how post–Cold War Russia wants to be perceived in the world, and yet this is the image it has created for itself since 1991.

After pouting, warning, and threatening against NATO enlargement, Russia eventually had to concede that there was nothing it could do to stop the former communist countries of Europe from joining whatever institutions they chose. Yet when some of its former republics started to make the same overtures to NATO and the EU, Russian elites adopted a more bullish approach. The evidence provided in chapters three and four highlights that, with Putin's presidency, Russia applied increased political and economic pressure on Eurasian countries that moved toward Euro-Atlantic membership. Even when Eurasian countries were already members of the Euro-Atlantic community, Russian pressure was applied. From raising gas prices unexpectedly and breaking existing contracts, to insisting on political and military outcomes of Russia's choice (seen in episodes such as the Pristina airport in Kosovo, the war of monuments in the Baltics, or the strong reaction against the color revolutions in Central Asia), Russia reverted to a bullish, disrespectful treatment of Eurasian countries.

Policy makers in the Kremlin never seemed to understand that the more vocal their opposition to NATO enlargement, the more determined the applicant countries were to move forward with membership. They may have counted on the stereotypical Cold War response, when strong words from the core intimidated the periphery into submission to whatever the Russian leaders demanded. As their anti-NATO rhetoric intensified, so did the pressure from Central European and Baltic countries on centers of power in Brussels and Washington to move ahead with enlargement. It can be argued that Russian opposition to NATO enlargement strengthened the perception that Russia had a hidden agenda in this postcommunist space. At any rate, Russian opposition did not help the anti-NATO enlargement case.

As the United States opened negotiations with Poland and the Czech Republic regarding a new missile defense shield, Putin warned that the new weapons could threaten Russia. In that case, he threatened that Russia could aim new weapons at Europe. "If part of the U.S.'s strategic nuclear arsenal is located in Europe and our military experts find that it poses a threat to Russia, we will have to take appropriate retaliatory steps...We will have new targets in Europe."[5]

When the United States offered Russia bilateral cooperation on the proposed missile site in Europe, Putin mocked the proposal and called into question the legality of the decision to deploy the system. "We have heard talk of European solidarity...Two countries, the Czech Republic and Poland, made a decision to deploy the missile defense elements on their territories. They say it is needed for Europe's protection. Has anyone asked Europe? Has there been any pan-European decision?" Putin asked at a press conference before the G-8 summit in 2007.[6] "Our American partners want us to provide them with our missiles as targets, so that they can conduct exercises using our missiles. This is just brilliant. What a great idea they've thought up," he complained mockingly. In fact, the United States offered that Russia join the new defense system. U.S. proposals included a testing system to find out how and if the system worked on missiles of the kind Russia had; that proposal prompted Putin's sarcastic reaction. Observers noted that if Russia wanted to improve its own missiles, they would have welcomed the American proposal, and used the tests to design even better weapons. As in the case of NATO enlargement, the more opposed Russia seems to be to a military- or security-related development in Europe, the more likely it is to provoke the exact opposite reaction to what it is hoping to achieve from the Euro-Atlantic community. Fears and suspicions go, after all, both ways.

In the case of EU enlargement to Eurasian countries, Russia initially saw enlargement as an opportunity for itself, and hinted at membership.[7] Europeans, however, discouraged the Kremlin from seeking membership and offered an alternative framework of bilateral cooperation. The EU and Russia designed mechanisms of cooperation in all fields of activity, and Russia gets a fair hearing on all the issues it raises.[8] What it does not get is blind acceptance of all its proposals.

In particular, the field of energy has become contentious, especially after Russia's interruption of gas supplies to Ukraine and Moldova in 2006, when the two countries refused to pay more than doubled new gas prices. Russia justified the new prices it imposed on its former republics in no uncertain terms: it was in Russia's best interest and it was consistent with world market prices. As early as 2005, Russia informed its CIS partners that the relationship between Russia and its former republics needed to "move away from gray, unclear barter payments and switch to civilized payments, to world prices."[9]

However, the imposition of sharply higher prices and new fees was accompanied by Russia's leveraging energy resources to acquire the distribution networks of former republics, thus making them fully dependent on the Kremlin. For instance, as chapter 4 showed, the new duty on crude oil exported to Belarus imposed in January 2007 was levied as Belarus continued to refuse to sell its gas pipeline operator Beltransgaz that carries Russian gas to Europe. The move was justified by the Russian Cabinet in the name of protecting "Russia's economic interests," in connection with Belarus failing to observe an intergovernmental agreement on sharing exports earnings from oil products exports.[10]

Political pressure on Ukraine to sell the main natural gas company Naftogaz was sustained over a period of years, starting in the nineties. When pro-Russia Prime Minister Viktor Yanukovych seemed to lean toward selling the company to Gazprom in 2006, in exchange for lower gas prices, the Ukraine parliament went as far as to pass specific legislation to insure that the national distribution network would not be sold off to a foreign entity. Extended talks preceding the 2007 gas price increase led to speculations that Russia leveraged lower than market value gas prices in exchange for Ukraine's commitment to slow down on NATO accession and permission for the Russian fleet to remain stationed in Crimea until 2017 or later. Officials on both sides denied that gas negotiations were linked to political demands but talks on gas and political concessions did take place in parallel. Since Ukraine ended up with the lowest price for gas in 2007 relative to the other former Soviet republics, speculations abounded that the Ukrainian authorities must have agreed to some Kremlin demands. The conditions of the deal were not made public.[11]

The doubling of gas prices for Georgia in 2006 came after months of increasing tensions between Russia and Georgia regarding Russian military involvement in the separatist republics of Abkhazia and South Ossetia, and Georgia's arrest of four Russian diplomats on charges of spying.

Moldova caved, as did Armenia. Both sold off pieces of the national operators to Russia, in order to escape the doubling of gas prices.

Yet Russian authorities reject any criticism of their market practices and blame it on an anti-Russian conspiracy. Putin repeatedly rejected the charge that Russia was using its energy resources to pressure its former republics.

> We have no obligation to provide huge subsidies to other countries' economies, subsidies as big as their own national budgets. No one else does this, and so why are we expected to do it?...the experts understand this situation very well; thanking us would be more appropriate, but instead, we see a dishonest attitude to the interpretation of events taking place. This is, of course, the work of Russia's ill-wishers...*there are people out there who do not wish Russia well* [emphasis added].[12]

Other Russian officials took a similar position. In early 2007, then first Deputy Prime Minister Dmitry Medvedev told the World Economic Forum in Davos, Switzerland that Russia was starting to conform to European market rules, therefore it would stop selling oil and gas at lower, subsidized prices. "Being a part of the European economy and therefore of the world economy, we should accept the rules that have evolved in Europe, as well as in the world. This means that there will be no more free natural gas for anyone."[13]

The EU, on the other hand, stood by its newest members. It expressed concerns over Russia's market practices and delayed negotiations on extending the EU-Russia agreement of cooperation. At a 2007 EU-Russia summit, both the EU's foreign policy chief and the president of the European Commission traced the lack of a new agreement back to Russia's seeming politically-motivated embargo of products from new EU member countries. Javier Solana had this to say before the summit started:

> We had hoped to be able to launch negotiations on a new EU-Russia Agreement at the Summit, but regrettably this will not be possible, as we still need to overcome the problem of the Russian ban on imports of meat and plant products from Poland. The recent events surrounding Estonia have not gone unnoticed [internet attacks after the relocation of Soviet monuments], nor have the continuing problems surrounding the interruption of oil supplies to Lithuania via the Druzhba pipeline.[14]

Jose Manuel Barroso underscored Solana's message at the end of the summit. He said that Russia's embargo on Polish meat imports was unjustified. "If there were grounds [for an embargo], we would not allow Poland to circulate meat in the European Union."[15]

As the European Commission further decided to "place tough conditions on ownership of assets by non EU companies to make sure that we all play by the same rules,"[16] Russia took issue. The new EU conditions effectively prevented further Russian acquisition of national operators. Russia charged that the EU was not motivated by "fair competition rules," and concluded that the decision was specifically aimed at "ban[ning] Russia's giant Gazprom...from conducting future investment activities in Europe."[17]

The European decision came in the aftermath of two observed patterns of Russian business practices. On the one hand, Russia acquired majority stakes in national distribution networks in several former republics. On the other hand, Russia protected its own natural resource exploration and distribution networks from foreign investment. In other words, while Russia found the principle of acquisition of national distribution networks to be a legitimate business practice, it did not agree that the principle applied to its own resources and networks.

These patterns were displayed most prominently in the aftermath of the Kremlin terminating, then taking over the operations of Russia's largest privately owned oil company, Yukos. Yukos was auctioned off to companies that proved to be extensions of Gazprom or with strong ties to the Kremlin. Further, in 2006, the Kremlin moved to limit foreign company participation in oil and gas production in the long awaited Sakhalin exploration project by awarding a majority stake to Gazprom, after years of promising open tenders. Western companies thus understood that Russia's philosophy of world market practices was not related to transparent competition, but to the principle of protectionism. While Russia is in its right to do whatever it wants with its energy resources and exploration, presenting protectionism as a world market practice shows a misunderstanding of free market principles. This is a fundamental issue on which Russia and the Euro-Atlantic community differ.

These developments showed that Russia would not allow foreign majority stakes in its major operators, nor open its resource exploration and production to the rest of the world, irrespective of what it promised publicly. Such developments further diminish the level of trust and cooperation between the Euro-Atlantic community and Russia, and reinforce the perception that Russia is not motivated by market practices.

The EU has been trying to convince Russia to agree to a new Charter on Energy that would stipulate the rules of supply, demand, and distribution, and introduce a predictable schedule even for raising prices, if Russia so chooses. To date, Russia refused to sign on, stating that the proposed charter infringes on its interests and accusing the new EU members of boycotting its interests from within.

It is true that the EU's newest members pick fights with Russia more often than the other EU members. It is also true that Russia takes more trade liberties with the EU's newest members. The cases of banned meat imports from Poland and of canned fish from Latvia are just two examples. Russia complained that the quality of the products no longer complied with its domestic health standards and refused to import the products despite contracts in force. Yet the quality of the same products was good enough for the EU markets, which raised the question of whether Russia had a genuine health concern or was using quality standards as an excuse to punish Poland and Latvia for their non-Kremlin-mindedness.

When the EU sides with its newest members, or potential members such as Ukraine, Russian elites and analysts are prompted to elaborate on one of their favorite alternative reality theories: The EU is no longer in control of its own affairs. Rather, it is the newer members, and the United States working through them, that are the root of the problem in EU-Russia relations. Here is an excerpt written by a Russian analyst after Poland blocked negotiations on a new partnership agreement with the EU.

Russia's relations with EU countries have been often marred by disputable issues but not once has any major EU nation raised them at a summit...The attitude of East European countries is totally different—Poland and the Baltic nations do not have Western Europe's diplomatic potential and do not want a compromise with Russia. Moreover, they have been deliberately trying to hurt it by exploiting its only doubtless element of national identity—the victory over Nazism...united Europe does not want to assume responsibility for creating a new model of relations with Russia. As a result, the European agenda for Russia is regrettably bleak...This situation could change if the Europeans opened their energy market to Russian companies, but they have made it clear more than once that they are not going to let the "uncivilized Russians" take part in the retail...The Europeans are not masters in their own house if they allow the United States to turn Eastern Europe into an instrument of threatening Russia...East European states are settling old accounts and blocking dialogue between key regional players.[18]

Some Russian analysts were facetious about the increasing assertiveness of the Central Europeans and the Baltics and called it "an international contest in deteriorating relations with Russia," with Estonia winning over Poland and Latvia.[19]

President Putin downplayed the influence of EU's new members on bilateral relations. "The European Union has changed, the number of members has increased, and it is more difficult to resolve the issues that were easy to settle in the past," Putin said. "However, we must defend our own interests as professionally as my [European] colleagues do." He also added that the inability to reach a solution on the import on Polish meat was solely due to the Polish lack of willingness to resolve the issue. "We have not yet solved the Polish meat problem, since our Polish colleagues have not been on speaking terms with us for over a year," Putin argued.[20]

In a much publicized 2007 Munich speech, Putin vigorously defended Russia's actions. The claim that Russia was leveraging energy resources in Eurasia for political ends was countered as a misinterpretation of Russia's intention to "create uniform market principles [where]...energy prices must be determined by the market."[21] As the Gazprom takeover of national distribution networks in several Eurasian countries and the protection of Russia's own distribution networks and exploration project showed, Russia's understanding of world market practices is monopolistic and protectionist. This pattern of doing business is something that Western allies will have to learn to deal with.

Russia's Democracy and Alternative Realities

Western criticism of the direction and state of Russian democracy also causes irritation in Moscow, and further fuels conspiracy theories about the West's agenda to humiliate Russia. The Kremlin is convinced that Russia is a democracy. Western criticism of the Kremlin's restrictions on the activities of the media and NGOs infuriates Russia's elites. According to President Putin and the Russians who believe in him, Russia is a "major European power" in pursuit of "the ideals of freedom, human rights, justice and democracy...sometimes behind and sometimes ahead of European standards."[22] It is a country

...that has freed itself from...80 years when one political force dominated the scene and had a monopoly on power in the country...[where] development of democratic institutions [are] at an early stage...but...are growing stronger and asserting themselves ...[where] There is no doubt that the main democratic institutions are already in place. Even the mentality of our society has become democratic...We have a multi-party system. It is still weak and requires consolidation but this is an absolute fact. We conduct very important democratic law-based elections to a representative body of government, the parliament. The head of state, who is entitled to be in power for no more than two four-year terms in succession, is democratically elected as well...Our judicial system is making headway, even though there have been some problems...the legal system is independent...We haven't just created conditions but achieved a real division of power between the executive, legislative (representative) and judicial bodies of government. [Freedom of the] mass media, and the development of democratic institutions and a civil society, are the main indications of the Russian Federation's democratic development... Therefore, it is beyond any doubt that Russia is a democratic state.[23]

Russia feels strongly that the West is applying double standards in the evaluation of its democracy in order to deny Russia the status it deserves among the community of great powers of Europe. One issue of significant contention has been the West and particularly the United States denying Russia membership in the WTO on account of Russia not meeting WTO standards of economic openness. Putin and other analysts complained that the demands for Russia's compliance with a host of conditions in exchange for membership are unfair and unacceptable.

We have carried out quite a few absolutely revolutionary reforms in the economy. We have drastically reduced taxes. The income tax for individuals in Russia is 13 per cent, the lowest in Europe. We are reducing VAT, profit tax, a single social tax. We are trying to cut taxes for individual economic entities, introducing new systems of accounting, shifting the tax burden in the economy from [commodities] production to processing industries...We are against [Western demands for specific economic reforms] being used as instruments in bilateral relations for achieving certain goals, as an element of pressure. OK, you do this, and in return we'll make sure you are accepted into the WTO. This is absolutely unacceptable.[24]

Russians seem to agree with their president. The chair of the political science department at the Higher School of Economics in Moscow had this to say during a meeting of the national conference of humanities and social science teachers:

...[W]e find ourselves in a situation where someone comes to take a look at how we are doing. It is as if we are in school, or rather, not even in school but in kindergarten. Just take the example of democracy. We were told: you have renounced communism and will now build democracy, but we will judge when and how you build it...the principles of democracy are universal, but each country has its own political culture, and Russia too has its own political culture, and without the appropriate adjustments we will not achieve anything...How long can we continue to be school pupils? This is a vast country with immense achievements and we [are] still sitting at our school desk and anyone

from Freedom House, say, can come mark our results and say "you are in 161st place!"
...This is just one of the facts that creates a hopeless and hurtful situation for our entire
people, and all the more so for our young people.[25]

The Freedom House ranking of Russia among the countries with the lowest level
of freedom and democracy quoted above is, unfortunately, reflected in rankings compiled by other institutions as well. Appendix III highlights how Russia ranks systematically among the countries with the least amount of media freedom among the
countries evaluated by RwB. Russia was ranked better relative only to Turkmenistan
and Belarus in 2002, in 121st place of 139 countries in the study. In 2003 and 2004,
Russia placed higher than only Azerbaijan, Belarus, Turkmenistan, and Uzbekistan.

It does not help that journalists who criticize the Kremlin seem to get murdered
more often in Russia than anywhere else in the former Soviet empire—although
Ukraine and a few Central Asian republics have seen their share of politically motivated murders of journalists.

Instead of taking the rankings at face value and trying to correct what needs
correcting, the Russian leadership defends positive aspects of media freedom and
downplays the negatives. Putin takes pride in the fact that Russia has a substantial
number of television and radio stations, and claims that his government does not influence most of them. There are "...3,200 television and radio companies. And only
10 per cent of them are state-owned...Russia has 46,000 registered and operating
print media. Even if the authorities wanted—at the federal or regional level—to control this vast number of media...it is practically impossible to do...So rumors of
the Kremlin's total control over the media in Russia, as Mark Twain put it regarding
his death, are greatly exaggerated."[26]

Putin agrees that the government should retain a certain amount of power over the
political message. "...[T]he state, in my opinion, has the right to possess a mechanism for presenting its official position through official and state mass media. The
second channel, which is called Channel One in [Russia], is a joint-stock company
...It is true that one is state-owned...[It] is a joint stock company with a sufficiently
noticeable proportion of state capital. Honestly, I do not remember how much, but
the state does not hold the controlling stake." He also believes that while the
government could control even more media activity, it does not actually do that precisely because of democratic, institutional levers set in place by Russian legislators.

> The state in effect is in a position to control whatever it likes. The question is the extent
> to which internal legislation allows the state to do so. As for the relations between society
> and the media, they are always somewhat strained. It is because mass media are designed
> to identify problems and issues and show them to society, while the bureaucratic struc-
> tures are trying to soft-pedal and play them down. Incidentally, in my view, this is typical
> not only of Russia, but also of many other countries.[27]

In cases where an obvious breach of the media's right to speak up occurred, such as
the murder of a prominent critic of the Putin administration, Anna Politkovskaya,

the authorities blamed the breach on "...a conspiracy beyond Russia's borders," intended to make Russia look bad and destabilize the country. In the words of the prosecutor general who ordered arrests of individuals suspected of murdering the journalist in 2006,

> The individuals interested in eliminating Politkovskaya *can only be ones living beyond Russia's borders* [emphasis added]...Above all, people and structures interested in destabilizing the country, changing its constitutional order, stoking a crisis in Russia...could gain from the crime...The group was headed by a leader of a Moscow criminal group of Chechen origin...Unfortunately, this group included retired and acting interior ministry and FSB [Federal Security Service] officers.[28]

While laying the blame for the murder on unspecified forces from abroad, the prosecutor general made an unexpected acknowledgment that government officers had also been involved. It is not clear what prompted such acknowledgment, and the case is still unsolved as of this writing. Politkovskaya had been a long-time critic of the Putin administration, his handling of the war in Chechnya, his authoritarian style of leadership, and warned of the return of autocracy in Russia. To claim that "individuals living beyond Russia's borders" would benefit from her death was an astounding charge, especially since individuals living within Russia's borders would clearly benefit from her being silenced. How her death would destabilize the constitutional order was not clarified either. Why a person of Chechen origin would organize her murder was also left unaddressed, a charge all the more puzzling as it was widely believed that Chechens appreciated Politkovskaya's reporting of atrocities committed by Russian troops against the Chechen population. It is fair to say that Chechnya lost in Politkovskaya one of its few allies. It thus makes no sense why someone of Chechen origin would eliminate her.

Defenders of freedom of speech and democracy in Russia have accused the government of orchestrating the murder, to silence one of Putin's most verbal critics. Politkovskaya herself predicted that she would be murdered due to her anti-Putin views and outspoken manner of asking for government accountability.[29]

The belief of Russian authorities that a crime of this nature could "only" be orchestrated by someone outside of Russia's borders highlights, once again, the conspiracy theories that the Kremlin is so fond of. Taking events at face value would possibly involve the Kremlin starting a process of self-evaluation to see if there are things that it could do to prevent criminal events of this nature from happening again. Besides, the notion that Politkovskaya's murder would "change the constitutional order and provoke a crisis in Russia" is not only far-fetched, it reiterates the long-held belief of Russian elites that foreign forces conspire against Russia.

Another element of Russia's democracy that has come under Western criticism is the freedom of NGOs. Legislation to restrict, limit, or otherwise monitor the activity of NGOs in Russia was implemented in 2006. The argument of the government in favor of such legislation was that NGOs were a conduit for spy activities, were ruining the county's image abroad, and that regulations of NGO activity existed in other countries as well. An alternative reason was that the Kremlin suspected that NGOs helped bring down Kremlin-friendly regimes and helped install Russia-unfriendly regimes in Georgia, Ukraine, and Kyrgyzstan.

Restrictions on registration of foreign nongovernmental groups were implemented in late 2006. Of an estimated 500 NGOs operating in Russia in late 2006, only 108 were able to reregister, in conformity with the new legislation. Organizations that were affected by the new law and had to reapply for license included adoption agencies, social welfare groups, and human rights organizations. Human Rights Watch was one of the organizations that tried to reapply and failed. It charged that Russian officials kept changing the list of documents needed to regain the license. As of August 2007, over 600 NGOs were known to have been crossed out of the Unified State Register of Legal Entities according to the Voronezh Interregional Group of Rights Defenders.[30] The apparent discrepancy between known numbers of NGOs operating inside Russia (500) and known numbers of NGOs crossed off registration lists (600) underscores the lack of reporting transparency and the unreliability of existing statistics. This may be a deliberate government policy—or not.

The director of the Federal Registration Service, Sergei Movchan, restated the government's interest to "look at the aims and purposes announced by the organization [applying for license] and what funds are being spent. . .and whether these funds are being spent on [stated] aims and purposes."[31] The Kremlin's position remained that it had no interest in banning NGOs or repressing their freedom of expression, but that activities should be held in a responsible fashion. President Putin described NGOs as an "important component of the social system," a component that society needed "to monitor the state itself." Yet he and other Kremlin officials stressed their belief that Russia's poor image abroad was being "financed" through NGOs. "It is no surprise when Russia's foreign policy is perceived inappropriately and falsely abroad," said Russian Deputy Foreign Minister Alexander Yakovenko. "This happens because the Russian and Western media quote the opinions and views of NGOs well funded by foreign capital. This situation should be urgently corrected."[32]

Instead of trying to fix the malpractices of the Russian democracy identified by a watchdog agent such as the media or the NGOs, the Kremlin prefers to find fault with the reporting process or blame the West for sponsoring anti-Russia criticism.

A psychiatrist would look at these patterns of thinking and probably assess that Russian elites are in denial about the state of affairs in their country; again, even if a professional could suggest such a diagnosis, the Kremlin would probably label it a "Western conspiracy to further humiliate Russia" and pay no attention to it. The rhetoric of the Russian elites indicate that this mode of thinking will persist. In the Munich speech, Putin claimed that the government had not "refused registration to almost any organization" but that authorities object "when these NGOs are financed by foreign governments; we see them as an instrument that foreign states use to carry out their Russian policies."[33] When Russian leaders at the highest government level articulate such beliefs, they feed long held anti-West biases. The Euro-Atlantic community should be mindful of these tendencies, interpret them from the vantage point of the Russian elites, and adjust their strategies accordingly.

Instead of taking a critical look at itself, the Russian government prefers to turn the tables on the Euro-Atlantic community and highlight the latter's democracy deficits. Putin charged that undemocratic practices such as "secret prisons and torture exist in Europe," problems with the media and firing of journalists occur even in hundred-year old democracies, and "immigration laws...in some European countries are not in line with the general principles of international law or democratic order" either. As such, he called on Euro-Atlantic allies to stop talking about "having immaculate, white fluffy partners on one side, and on the other a monster who has just come out of a forest with claws and corns growing instead of legs."[34] As these excerpts highlight, the combination of denial and retaliatory rhetoric remains a constant of the Russian government.

History and Alternative Realities

Finally, the Russian tendency to invoke a Western plot to isolate it closely relates to another tendency: that of dodging responsibility for past decisions that negatively impacted neighboring countries and its own domestic population.

When Russia is criticized about the past, politicians and analysts tend to hide behind alternative explanations that either exonerate the Soviet past or attenuate it by laying most of the blame in the West's backyard. For instance, Gorbachev explained the Soviet decision to sign a nonaggression pact with Nazi Germany in 1939 as a result of Western refusal to ally itself with Red Russia. The pact "...could have been avoided...if the ruling circles of Britain and France had agreed to cooperate with the Soviet Union against the [Nazi] aggressor at that time."[35]

While Gorbachev's statement is correct, it is incomplete. It leaves out the well-known fact that the ruling circles in Britain and France had a valid reason to refuse to cooperate with Soviet Russia: the Stalinist leadership promised to spread communism throughout the Western world, by force if necessary. Such promise was a threat to the identities and way of life of millions of people before the rise of Nazism. Naturally, the West refused to cooperate with Red Russia as a way to protect its identity from the spread of communism.

Similarly, Gorbachev blamed the division of Germany on the West's failure to work with Soviet leaders at the end of WWII toward a solution that Moscow could accept. "...[A]fter Yalta and Potsdam...we [the Soviet Union] were for the establishment of an integral, sovereign and above all, peaceful German state on the basis of denazification, democratization and demilitarization...But in the West, there were forces which acted in a way that led to the present set-up [i.e. two German states]."[36]

If Truman and Churchill were alive, they could offer a counterargument by changing one of Gorbachev's words: at the end of the war, the allies were also for Germany's denazification, democratization, and demilitarization, but "in the East" there were forces that led to the partition of the country. Like his successors, Gorbachev did not recognize shared responsibility for postwar events. He did not clarify what the Soviet Union authorities meant by the "democratization" of Germany and glossed over the fact that at the time, the "democratization" of Eastern Europe had nothing to do with free elections, and more to do with the Kremlin's agenda to turn these countries into buffer, communist states. He hid behind the alternative explanation that the West refused to follow Soviet proposals for the status of Germany, without mentioning that the West also had good reason to distrust the ultimate Soviet intentions. The pattern of Soviet behavior dictating the political order in postwar Eastern Europe was testimony of things to come. Naturally, the allies refused to go along.

An even more alarming conspiracy theory-related phenomenon is the tendency to rewrite the Soviet history itself. Gorbachev's position on the post-1945 division of Europe into communist and capitalist states is that it reflected the countries' own choices. "...[I]n postwar history of Europe...European states, in accordance with the concrete conditions and opportunities, made their choice: some of them remained capitalist while others moved towards socialism."[37]

From the Eastern European and Baltic perspective, to claim that Poland, Lithuania, and Romania moved toward socialism of their own volition is to add insult to injury. From the ordinary Russian citizen's perspective, if Kremlin leaders say Eastern Europe went socialist of their own choice, then it must have been so. From the West's perspective, such statements only reinforce the notion that Russian leaders continue to be in denial about the past. Such positions solidify the impression that Russian leaders continue the process of recreating alternative realities of their own liking, in which their version of history is always right, and Russia never did wrong to anybody.

Vladimir Putin also thinks that his country's role in WWII has been misrepresented and recently called for a rewriting of history textbooks. He called for modern textbooks to offer a "factual" presentation of events, a balancing of the information written about the war elsewhere in the world with the Russian view. Putin quoted views expressed by Russian educators such as Vladislav Golovanov to defend this new initiative. A middle school teacher, Golovanov argued that Russia should not find itself feeling guilty for the events of the war. "...[J]ust imagine that one of your pupils says, 'Vladislav Alexeyevich, I read this book, and it turns out that we [Soviet Union] attacked first' [a reference to the Stalin-Hitler secret protocol and invasion of the Baltic states]. Who only knows what junk heap this book came from?...our history should not be cause for self-flagellation."[38]

The proposed new history textbook is also intertwined with Putin's attempt to create a sense of national pride in the history of the country.

We do have bleak chapters in our history [but]...we must not allow others to impose a feeling of guilt on us...we must not forget our own past and we will not forget it. We have fewer such pages than do some countries, and they are less terrible than in some countries...we have never used nuclear weapons against civilians [a reference to America's use of nuclear bombs at the end of WWII], and we have never dumped chemicals on thousands of kilometers of land or dropped more bombs on a tiny country than were dropped during the entire Second World War, as was the case in Vietnam...All states and peoples have had their ups and downs through history.[39]

This type of rationale led Putin and his administration to commission the rewriting of history from a Russian perspective. It appears that the new history book essentially glorifies Stalin. He is apparently described as "the most successful [Russian] leader ever." The Stalinist mass purges were a necessary part of the leader's plan to make Russia "great." Putin did acknowledge that the Great Purge of 1937 was a terrible thing but he reverted to the familiar pattern of justification of past wrongs as not being as bad as what happened in other countries. "We had no other black pages, such as Nazism, for instance."[40]

A final note on the Russian leadership's view of history has to include the much debated Putin remark according to which the disintegration of the Soviet Union was "a major geopolitical catastrophe of the century...a genuine drama" of the Russian nation. Speaking before the federal assembly in his April 25, 2005 address, Putin's remark sent shock waves in the Western world and was the subject of much controversy.[41] Putin later clarified what he meant with his remark.

> ...[A]fter the Soviet Union's disintegration, 25 million Russian people found themselves outside Russian territory. Twenty-five million! They had lived by tradition in other Soviet republics, had moved there some time in the past, or left Russia to work there after receiving a higher education. And all of a sudden, 25 million people become foreigners for Russia. Isn't this a tragedy?...Take the Baltic Republics, for instance. Do you know that they have documents there, where the column on citizenship reads: "Non-citizen." I'd like to tell you that this is something very new both in modern international law and in modern law in general. Modern law on citizenship has the following categories: citizen, foreigner, a person with dual citizenship and apatrid, a person who has lost his or her citizenship. And who are they? This approach does not tally at all with modern humanitarian law...And what about contacts with relatives, kin, and friends?...Living in a foreign country is still very different from living in the framework of a whole country. In this sense, this is of course a tragedy for millions of people. I believe that the definition that I used to describe the disintegration of the Soviet Union is correct. It is also linked with the loss of savings. After the collapse of the Soviet Union all the savings that people had collected during their entire lives were eliminated, and the social sphere was destroyed. It goes without saying that all this was an enormous tragedy for millions of people.[42]

Other times, Putin admits that the recreation of the Soviet Union is not possible and was not something the Russian Federation aspired to do. The Soviet Union had been a "heroic, creative and tragic" chapter in Russia's history that was closed for good.[43]

To be fair, there are also occasional signs that Russia can come to terms with its own past. Reestablishing the historical facts has been a long-standing sore point for all the countries in whose affairs Russia interfered. Russia has been oftentimes very stubborn in refusing to admit historical blunders such as the occupation of the Baltic countries. On occasion, it displayed an unexpected willingness to embrace its history. For instance, in October 2006, the upper house of the Russian parliament, the Federation Council, commemorated fifty years since the 1956 Hungarian Revolution.

Over 2,500 Hungarians were killed by Soviet troops sent to Budapest to squash the revolution, thousands were wounded, and approximately 200,000 fled the country. Russia officially apologized for the events in 1991. On the fiftieth anniversary of the revolution, Russian Senators paid respect to the memory of those who died in 1956 and said Russia could not be blamed for the actions of the Soviet leadership. "However, moved by the feelings of honor and dignity, we feel a moral responsibility for certain pages of our history, and hope that present-day Hungarian society will appreciate the sincerity of our regret for the events in Hungary in October-November 1956," read an official statement of the Federation Council.[44]

In another instance, Polish President Kaczyński visited Russia and a cemetery in Katyn, where the remnants of thousands of Polish officers massacred under Stalin's orders were buried. This unique visit was organized on the sixty-eighth anniversary of the Soviet invasion of Poland. The chairman of the foreign affairs committee in Duma, Konstantin Kosachov, remarked that "[t]he more openly we speak of that tragedy, without turning it into a political affair, the less it disturbs our [Russia-Poland] relations."[45]

Such sincere statements of regret and compassion for past wrongs are a healthy, occasional sign of Russian acceptance of the country's involvement in difficult pages of history. The Baltic countries are still in the waiting room, hoping for a sign that Russia can similarly embrace and denounce the occupation they were subjected to. Occasional signs indicate that some Russian politicians understand the importance of controversies over historic events and accept the notion that Russia should be more flexible in addressing its own responsibilities.

Russia's difficulty in coping with history does not apply solely to its relations with countries it used to occupy, such as the Baltics or its other former republics. The duality of personalities such as Joseph Stalin and their significance to Russian history is debated in inner and outer circles of Russian intellectuals. For instance, on the occasion of the sixtieth anniversary of the victory over Nazi Germany in 2005, a Russian professor teaching in the United States called for a renunciation of the public glorification of Stalin's role in defeating fascism. "Our people defeated Nazism not thanks to Stalin but despite his crimes committed before the war, his lack of preparation and resolve in the beginning of the war," wrote Russian poet Yevgeni Yevtushenko. "The attempt once again to ascribe to Stalin, who not once was on the front, the main role in that victory is actually not extolling but denigrating the popular feat. Our great victory belongs to the people." Yevtushenko further condemned those who, under the guise of "patriotism," gave Stalin the credit for the achievements of the Russian people and thus misrepresented historical facts. "It is the triumph of historical illiteracy when, despite the mighty books of Solzhenitsyn and a huge number of irrefutable documents of Stalin's war on his own people, our self-proclaimed 'patriots' behave as if they are innocent of history."[46]

Other Russians see things differently. For them, the victory over Nazi Germany remains a victory of the Russian people led by a Soviet leader whose name was Stalin. Army General Makhmut Gareyev, who led the offensive of the Red Army to the final victory in the Far East, remembered Stalin's "flawed" policies, "especially his domestic policies," but argued that "our leader was very consistent in his international relations and he observed the Allied agreements." The general was referring to those aspects of Stalin's commitments which he indeed kept, such as the promise to enter the war against Japan and help end WWII. "[A]t the Yalta Conference Stalin gave a firm commitment that the Soviet Union would go to war against Japan two to three months after the defeat of Germany. And he kept his word: the war in Europe ended on May 9, 1945, and exactly three months later, on August 9, 1945, we attacked Japan."[47] He did not comment on other agreements reached at Yalta that Stalin did not respect, such as the Poland question and holding free elections in Eastern Europe.

Apart from taking pride in the way they fought WWII, Russians also feel that the West does not give them sufficient credit for their wartime sacrifices. In General Gareyev's words, "There are some 'analysts' who claim that we fought without skill. This is a lie. Our military leaders had a lot of very inspired ideas." He complained that the Soviet Union had to make hard choices that are no longer remembered or appreciated. For instance, General Gareyev remembered a Japanese offer to the Soviet Union to act as mediator between Japan and the United States, and promised South Sakhalin and the Kuril Islands in return. "This would have provided us with a political solution to our territorial problems, and the only lives lost would have been American ones. But Stalin was so consistent in his international relations that he chose to act honorably and keep his promise to the Allies. He rejected Japan's attractive proposal and the Soviet Union went to war."[48]

Gareyev also pointed to agreements the American side did not respect at the end of the war, such as the sharing of the occupation of Japan. ". . . [t]here were a lot of agreements that Washington did not honor. For example, it had been agreed that we would take part in the occupation of Japan, and that we would send one or two Soviet brigades to Tokyo. . . MacArthur did everything he could to prevent the Red Army from landing in Japan." If one remembers that at the time, the Soviet Union was maneuvering elections in Eastern Europe to secure communist victories in defiance of Yalta agreements, it might not come as a surprise that the Allies did not feel bound by wartime commitments regarding the shared occupation of Japan.

Gareyev did clarify, however, that Russians have long memories. That might serve as a good reminder to current policy makers on both sides of the Atlantic in their dealings with Russia. "You will remember Russia's shameful defeat by Japan in 1905," continued the General. "This had left the peoples of the Soviet Union deeply embittered and the older generation had waited for decades for the chance to erase that humiliating memory. When Russians feel their desire for revenge is just, they cannot let it go."[49] We can safely extrapolate that when Russians feel that they are unfairly treated, they will reciprocate. If that is indeed the case, correcting misperceptions is all the more important to the state of future relations between the Euro-Atlantic community and Russia.

It should be noted that historical revisionism stirs intense emotions in other parts of the world as well; this is not a phenomenon unique to Russia and the countries in its former sphere of influence. Such emotions are understandable. On the one hand,

Russians believe they shed their blood to liberate countries occupied by the Nazis. On the other hand, liberated countries believe they were freed from one form of totalitarianism, the Nazi regime, only to be forced into another form of totalitarianism, the communist regime and the occupation of the Soviet Union. Irrespective of what each side currently believes, an honest untangling of historical data is urgently needed. In the absence of a shared version of history, there cannot be new ground for respectful bilateral relations between the Euro-Atlantic community and Russia.

A SECOND COLD WAR?

All these developments lead Russia to harbor a sense of being misunderstood and mistreated by the Euro-Atlantic community. The country's politicians and political pundits seem to believe that the West cheated Russia in the post–Cold War era. Gorbachev and Yeltsin made agreements with Western leaders regarding the end of the Cold War, the unification of Germany, and the status of Eastern Europe. Russia delivered on its promises, Western leaders defaulted on theirs. Russia made numerous concessions in the nineties, but received little in return. This sense of betrayal intensified in the aftermath of the U.S. decision to move forward with the installation of a missile defense site in Poland and the Czech Republic. In the words of a Russian editor,

> In Putin's eyes, Russia has done a great deal for the West and America. Putin removed the military base from Vietnam, he shut down the radar station in Cuba, he did not stand in the way of the U.S. opening bases in Central Asia. The U.S. believes that Russia had no choice and that it was in Russian interests anyway [to take all these actions] but Russia believes that all it got for its efforts was the Orange Revolution in Ukraine, the dispute with Georgia, NATO expansion and now these anti-missiles sites.[50]

Furthermore, the West did not only cheat Russia about Eastern Europe, it did the same about Central Asia. Russia believes that the "color revolutions" in Georgia, Ukraine, and Kyrgyzstan were sponsored and orchestrated by Western countries. In a press conference with then French President Chirac and German Chancellor Schroeder in Paris, Putin asked, "The West actively supported President [Eduard] Shevardnadze [in Georgia] over a period of many years. Why was it necessary to topple him through revolution? And if it was necessary to topple him through revolution, then we can't help but ask [whom] the West was supporting and why."[51] Other Russian leaders consider the color revolutions unconstitutional. In a 2005 interview, then Security Council Secretary Igor Ivanov referred to the color revolutions as "changes of power by undemocratic methods."[52]

As a result of these beliefs, Russian analysts argue that the Euro-Atlantic community is the one persisting in Cold War stereotypes, not Russia. "Cold War thinking has prevailed, especially on the western side," Yevgeny Myasnikov, a senior research scientist at Moscow's Centre for Arms Control, told the *Guardian*. "Russia has been deeply disappointed by what has happened after 1991. NATO started to expand, and the U.S. started to think it had won the Cold War. We had hoped for a partnership. But it didn't happen."[53]

This type of reaction feeds into another Russian open wound: the issue of who won the Cold War. Vladislav Surkov, a deputy head in the administration of the Kremlin and rising political figure, advocates a very interesting interpretation of the end of the Cold War. First, Russia won the Cold War, it was not defeated by the West. Second, Russia defeated totalitarianism on its own. In Surkov's words, "we do not believe that we were defeated...We think that we defeated our own totalitarian regime...We defeated ourselves...We do not consider ourselves a defeated nation...We simply believe that we have chosen our own destiny."[54]

In addition, Russians are also becoming convinced that the West "likes it when Russia is down and weak," as it used to be in the nineties, and feels threatened by Russia's new found economic power. The West's criticism of Russian democracy is not motivated by facts, but by jealousy and economic rivalry. The conviction that the West was happy with "Russia's humiliation" in the nineties seems to originate with those Moscow political circles who disagreed with the breakup of the Soviet Union. In the words of Gennady Gerasimov, Gorbachev's former spokesperson, the circles who use this type of rhetoric are former communists and nationalists who prefer to have an enemy in the West and incite public spirits against it.[55] A search of Russian opinions on the BBC "Have Your Say" section highlights that these beliefs are held not only by high-level politicians but also by Russian citizens.

Further, Russian leaders claim credit for post–Cold War changes in Eastern Europe and argue that it was the Kremlin who contributed to the transformation of the region. In Putin's words, "I'd like to draw your attention to the fact that the fall of the Berlin Wall, the liberation of Eastern Europe, the granting of independence to the former republics of the Soviet Union were possible owing to domestic changes in Russia itself and in our foreign policy that is based on these changes. These countries can and should themselves choose their foreign policy priorities, their partners, and develop relations with all countries."[56] In a disturbing, revisionist vein, Surkov similarly claimed that Russia should be given credit for the changes in Eastern Europe and Central Asia. "*It was Moscow that democratized this gigantic space* [emphasis added], which is now being revitalized," he said, adding that recognition for Russia's contributions to democracy would lead to increased respect for the country abroad.[57]

Apart from the fact that Russia had little to no say in how the countries in this space selected their domestic and foreign policies, as the evidence in chapters two, three, and four shows, taking credit for "democratizing" the region seems to be the most recent stretch in the Kremlin's creation of alternative realities. Russian leaders may be trying to say that their country contributed to the changes in the region by not forcefully interfering to stop the unfolding events, per Kremlin's past mode of operation. Russian politicians forget to acknowledge that noninterference is an international right of every sovereign country. To acknowledge such right would invite the question of why the Soviet Union did not stay out of the countries' affairs in 1920, 1945, 1956, and 1968. To present the lack of interference in other countries' domestic affairs first, as evidence of Russia's greatness and second, as something for which Russia should be given special credit indicates that Russia's politicians still do not understand basic rules of international relations, such as respect for other countries' affairs and territorial integrity. In the twenty-first century, such basic lapses can lead to dangerous outcomes and, indeed, to a second Cold War.

WHERE THE CHIPS ARE AND WHERE THEY COULD FALL

Does the hyper-rhetoric about conspiracy theories, encirclement, intentional isola-tion of Russia, and a second Cold War matter or should politicians on all sides of this debate let the chips fall where they may? A summary of the current *status quo* from the three vantage points considered in this book offers a sense of the precarious balance between Russia's version of history, current facts on the ground, and the Euro-Atlantic community's view of events.

From the rising Eurasian vantage point, countries chose to transition from a totali-tarian political system to a system of their own choosing in the post–Cold War period. It is less important whether the resulting political system conforms neatly with Western notions of democracy or not, the ownership over the choice is what counts. All of them opened their economies to the outside world, even if not all are considered market economies. They liberated themselves from communism, transi-tioned to democracy—or something resembling it—built freer economies with more opportunities for all, and freed themselves from "big brother" Russia's influence. Some of them chose to ally themselves with the Euro-Atlantic community, others remained neutral, yet others prefer to continue a close relationship with Russia. In some countries, Russia is trying to recreate its political influence and leverage, and occasionally interferes in domestic affairs through direct political pressure or indi-rectly by withholding energy resources. The choice of democracy, market economy, and Euro-Atlantic integration is a sovereign, *intentional* choice, not imposed from the outside as used to be the case during half a century of communism.

From the Euro-Atlantic vantage point, Russia is an integral part of global security. Russia has not completed its democratic reforms, is backsliding on democracy, and is becoming increasingly autocratic. It is displaying patterns of neo-imperial tendencies toward the former communist countries and tries to bully them into agreements that favor the Kremlin's economic and political interests. Russia's economy is protectionist, and there is too much state interference in the economy. Relations with Russia are nevertheless important, and the security of the Euro-Atlantic space depends on good relations with the Kremlin. That is not always easy to achieve but it should be some-thing to strive for and is worth trying to bring Russian leaders to the negotiating table.

From the Russian vantage point, Russia is an (unrecognized) great European power. As first Deputy Prime Minister Dmitry Medvedev told audiences in Davos, "Russia has every chance of becoming the Number One oil producer, leaving Saudi Arabia behind," and will be a leading producer and supplier of oil and gas in world markets.[58]

Russia regards itself as a democracy, greatly responsible for the transformation of the Eurasian space, and directly responsible for the democratization of Central

Europe. It has special national interests in all the territories that used to be the Soviet Union, hence it is entitled to oversee developments in these territories and make its preferences known, with the expectation that its preferences prevail. When the situation dictates, it is entitled to defend its interests against adverse courses of events, even if that means interfering in other countries' affairs or choices. Russia also believes that some Eurasian states are trying to demonize it in European circles, and that the EU and the United States should use their influence to convince these countries to treat Russia with the respect due to a great power.

The Euro-Atlantic community does not give Russia sufficient credit for its greatness, its potential, and its historical contributions to peace on the continent. A Western conspiracy is at work to corrupt Russia's image in the world, embarrass it, and isolate it. Another conspiracy tries to encircle Russia, by sponsoring color revolutions in its traditional area of national interest, and by hoping to infiltrate the homeland with color revolutionaries. The West prefers to see Russia weak, as the country was in the nineties, because it feels threatened by a strong Russia. Therefore, Russia should continue on its course of doing everything possible to secure its interests, by whatever means necessary.

As this summary suggests, the sides are thinking and talking past each other. Alternative realities are being created based on wishful thinking, incomplete history storytelling, and a misplaced sense of national pride. That bears the question: is there a way out of this dialogue of the deaf?

To continue in the same vein of analyzing the situation from three vantage points, here are possible scenarios of relations between Russia, Eurasia, and the Euro-Atlantic community based on observed patterns of behavior in the post–Cold War period.

Assuming that Russia will continue to refrain from the use of military force to intervene in countries' affairs, Eurasia will continue to assert national sovereign interests based on domestic and foreign policy priorities identified in home capitals. If countries feel it is in their interest to democratize, they will introduce mechanisms conducive to more transparency in civil society and political governance. If countries feel they can and should strive to retain control over their national resources, become leading producers or exporters of energy resources, they will do so, and grow their economic potential. If they evaluate that a close relationship with Russia should be maintained, they will maintain it. If they think a close relationship with the Euro-Atlantic community is necessary, they will retain or invent it. If neutrality is preferable, they will adopt and enforce it. Any one of these possibilities may lead to more color revolutions or to voting out inefficient regimes or to the continuation of the *status quo*. Change is not inevitable, and sometimes it is not useful. It will remain the prerogative of each country to recreate its own domestic and foreign policies however good or bad, based on the identified needs of the country.

Assuming that the Euro-Atlantic community continues to require Russia and Eurasia to respect economic and democratic processes based on shared values and transparency, a continuation of the current assertive dynamic should be expected. Some Eurasian countries will grow closer to Brussels, while others will keep to their own. Some will adhere to more, others to less Euro-Atlantic political or economic norms. The Euro-Atlantic community will respond to either alternative based on its long-term interests defined in terms of peaceful cohabitation and cooperation. If the situation in Kosovo or other areas of potential civil conflict turns violent, the Euro-Atlantic community will rely on its newest allies as it relies on its oldest allies, with an expectation of jointly sharing the burden of resolving the conflict. If an out of area conflict emerges, the community will decide jointly how to respond, and hopefully will respect the position of its newest allies as it respects the position of its oldest allies.

Assuming Russia continues to create alternative realities and believe in conspiracy theories, a hardening of positions can be expected between Russia on one hand and Eurasia and the Euro-Atlantic community on the other hand. If Russia persists in propagating the alternative reality that the Soviet Union did not occupy the Baltic states, did not impose communism on Central Europe after 1945, respected the republics' right to self-determination, and helped them democratize at the end of the Cold War, Russia can expect to see a hardening of positions particularly among Eurasian countries. If Russia continues to blame Western criticism of its economic protectionism and backsliding on democracy on anti-Russian conspiracies, it will continue not to address its own domestic problems. As such, a time will come when Russians will blame their own leaders for the ills of their society. A color revolution or an overthrow of the Kremlin administration may become a real possibility, depending on the amount of popular dissatisfaction with the domestic situation.

These possible outcomes assume little to no change from the dynamic of sovereign, intentional change described by previous chapters. It is entirely possible that elections in Ukraine may bring to power leaders who give up the Euro-Atlantic direction for a pro-Russia foreign policy. The Russian fleet could then be stationed indefinitely in the Black Sea, and even an increase of Russian soldiers on Ukrainian territory may be possible. Kazakhstan may decide that trying to compete with Russia for the title of reliable energy supplier is not worth the effort, and sell most of its assets to Gazprom. Belarus may overthrow its regime and organize competitive elections. It may still want a union with Russia and move forward toward reunification—or not.

Any number of configurations are possible as long as countries act based on their national interest, not because the Kremlin tells them what to do. It is therefore incumbent on all parties to select courses of action that respect the other party's position, with the expectation that respect is reciprocated.

For instance, all the countries discussed in this book should understand that Russia has legitimate security concerns. During the first stage of postcommunist NATO enlargement, Central Europeans were careful to address Russia's security concerns and not irritate it with an aggressive rhetoric. As any big change, this endeavor took a lot of multilateral effort, numerous commissions, and discussion forums to alleviate Russian apprehensions. It took the setting of an additional mechanism of bilateral coordination, the NATO-Russia Council, and systematic consultations with the Euro-Atlantic community. Seven years after the enlargement to Central Europe, and three years after the enlargement to the Baltic countries, there have been no confrontations between Russia and NATO. With the exception of the cooling of relations provoked by the NATO air strikes over Kosovo and Belgrade in 1999, there is no reason to believe that bilateral relations would have been different between NATO and Russia whether enlargement occurred or not.

Russia should equally show understanding for the other countries' security concerns and work toward a compromise. Only by trying to formulate choices that accommodate all the parties involved can a compromise be reached. Invoking the national interest to adopt mutually exclusive security solutions has never yielded peaceful cohabitation in history, and will continue not to do so.

Most importantly, all the participants have to find a way to agree on a shared version of history. The Baltic countries have to accept and respect the proposition that the Soviet Union freed them from Nazi Germany, as much as Russia has to accept that in so doing, the Soviet Union occupied these countries and denied them sovereign rights for over half a century. Western allies must explain their denying a Japan zone of occupation to the Soviet Union, as much as Russia must explain the orchestration of elections in Eastern Europe in 1945.

Russia must also stop defending itself for the Soviet Union's role in history-related controversies by pointing fingers at other countries for worse historic tragedies. There is nothing untrue about the fact that the United States dropped atomic bombs on Japan. The problem with countering one historic wrong, say the occupation of the Baltic countries, with another historic wrong, say the United States dropping nuclear bombs on Japan, is that this is not a contest of who made the worst decision in history. The United States is not the main actor in this particular controversy, Estonia, Latvia, and Lithuania are. Russia cannot point fingers at these countries to claim that they were also participants in historic tragedies of their own doing, therefore it points fingers at the Baltics' biggest ally, the United States. In doing so, Russia hopes to impress on the world community that the United States is no better as far as history-related controversies go. This is a backward rationale and one that will never serve as excuse for the wrongs that Russia did inflict on the Baltic countries and other former republics, for which it still has to show genuine regret and acknowledgment.

In the same vein, Russia's image would be better served if its politicians dropped the complaint that their country was also "robbed" in 1988. Russian officials occasionally bemoan the agreement between Gorbachev and Reagan to "let go of" Eastern Europe in exchange for a seat in WTO and G-7. To assert that Russia agreed to the trade-off is to implicitly admit that for half a century, Russia denied these countries their sovereign identity. This is inconsistent with other Russian pronouncements that at the end of WWII, Eastern Europe chose communism over capitalism. What Russia did in 1988 was a restoration of the countries' rightful place in the community of sovereign nations, a place they were deprived of by Soviet encirclement and pressure. When analysts point to Russia's good intentions in restoring the sovereignty of these countries and ask for brownie points, they do not seem to understand that they admit past wrongdoing for which the Kremlin has yet to atone.

Before any untangling of history can proceed, all sides have to make an effort to stop mutual incriminations. Russia must stop interpreting constructive criticism as a conspiracy theory, and Eurasian countries must stop talking as if the Kremlin is attempting to reconstruct its former sphere of influence. As the evidence demonstrates, misperceptions go both ways. A concerted and intentional effort by all involved can put an end to a spiral of incriminations and misunderstanding that may otherwise turn rhetoric into the very reality it is warning against.

Historic wounds could be addressed by intergovernmental commissions that would pledge to analyze facts, work cooperatively and in good faith, and try to come to terms with ambiguities on both sides of a controversial issue. A Baltic-Russia Commission to Analyze Shared History could be set up to move beyond disagreement in the direction of common ground. Putin is correct in pointing out that if humanity were to begin to go back in reclaiming history and territory, there would be no end in sight to historic rectifications. For starters, Americans would have to give back their land to the native Indian tribes, or worse, return to the places they emigrated from. Only by finding common ground can the relationship between Russia and Eurasia be reenergized.

As far as security goes, all sides need to open a fresh can of creative thinking. The global village is increasingly interdependent and the Euro-Atlantic community cannot secure itself behind a tall wall any more than Russia is able to do the same by surrounding itself with Russia-friendly states. If Russians continue to think about former communist countries and republics as "theirs," as some of the evidence suggests, then the relationship between both Russia and these countries, and between Russia and the West, will continue to be a dialogue of the deaf. This will affect the manner in which all sides can engage in collective security to meet the challenges that will undoubtedly be greater in a century of terrorist threats and proliferation of nuclear weapons.

The fact that Russian politicians refer to "losing Eastern Europe" to the West, "losing the Baltics to the West," and "cannot lose Ukraine and Georgia too" is symptomatic of an imperial nostalgia. Such pronouncements should be avoided. Russia should accept that these countries are not, and have not been, theirs—ever. They were merely occupied and held under an artificial border by fear, not by loyalty to a Soviet identity. Such talk frightens sovereign countries that have barely started their new journey as free and independent states, and makes them worry about their security. Such talk produces the kind of anti-Russian security measures that the Kremlin fears the most.

If Russia's security cannot be secured other than by surrounding itself with countries that have pro-Russian governments, then Russia must feel very insecure. As the largest country in the world, with abundant natural and human resources, with nuclear weapons and advanced military technology, this insecurity is problematic and indicative of old mentalities. This mentality says that irrespective of military arsenal, human talent, gas and oil riches, Russia will continue to desire an influence in the affairs of its neighbors, for the sake of its own security. More importantly, Russia will not see that neighboring countries are entitled to the same right. This one-sided view of national security will remain problematic not only for Eurasian countries but for the Euro-Atlantic community as a whole. For the sake of all the parties involved, there is still time to avoid zero-sum security games and the second Cold War that such games are bound to bring. The question is, will the parties be willing to talk a new talk?

Appendix I ────────────────────────────────────

Postcommunist Parliamentary Election Turnout Results in Central Europe and the Baltic Countries

Country	Population (in million)	First post-communist election	Second post-communist election	Third post-communist election	Fourth post-communist election	Fifth post-communist election
Bulgaria	8.5	87% (91)	62% (96)	59% (97)	54% (03)	55% (05)
Czech R.	10.4	90% (90)	76% (96)	73% (98)	58% (02)	65% (06)
Hungary	10.2	65% (90)	68% (94)	56% (98)	65% (02)	67% (06)
Poland	38	43% (91)	52% (93)	47% (97)	46% (01)	40.6% (05)
Romania	22	86% (90)	76% (92)	70% (96)	65% (00)	56% (04)
Slovak R.	5.4	84% (92)	75% (94)	84% (98)	70% (02)	54% (06)
Estonia	1.48	67% (92)	69% (95)	57% (99)	58% (03)	61% (07)
Latvia	2.4	91% (93)	72% (95)	68% (98)	72% (02)	61% (06)
Lithuania	3.7	75% (92)	48% (96)	53% (00)	37% (04)	

Note 1: Turnout percentages are rounded up. Election turnouts are for legislative rounds; presidential, municipal, and local elections were not included. Where elections involved two rounds, the turnout for the first round was used; second rounds have lower turnouts. Country populations fluctuated slightly, as EU membership caused waves of Central European workers to move into Western European countries in search for work.

Note 2: Election results provided from the following official sources:
For Bulgaria, Central Election Commission Web site, http://www.2005izbori.org/results/index.html.
For the Czech Republic, the Czech Statistical Office elections Web site, http://www.volby.cz/index_en.htm.
For Hungary, Ministry of the Interior Central Registration and Election Web site, http://www.election.hu/index_en.html.
For Romania, Central Electoral Bureau Web site, http://www.kappa.ro/guv/bec/prz-e.html.
For Estonia, Estonian National Electoral Committee, www.vvk.ee/engindex.html.

For Latvia, Central Election Commission, http://web.cvk.lv/pub/public/28334.html.
For Lithuania, Central Electoral Committee, http://www3.lrs.lt/rinkimai/pgl_data_e.htm.

Note 3: Some of the official government Web sites are not regularly updated with election information. Where information was not available on official Web sites, the following resource was used:
"The Project on Political Transformation and the Electoral Process in Post-Communist Europe" based in the Department of Government at the University of Essex, UK (http://www.essex.ac.uk/elections/) provided statistical information for the following countries and election years: Czech Republic (1998), Poland (1991, 1993, 1997, 2001), Romania (1990, 1992), Latvia (1993), and Lithuania (1992).

Appendix II ─────────────────────────

Economic Freedom of the World Index (EFW), Fraser Institute Ratings

	1990	1995	2000	2001	2002	2003	2004
Bulgaria	4.3	4.6	5.1	5.7	6.0	6.3	6.3
Czech R.	NA	5.8	6.7	6.8	6.7	6.9	6.9
Hungary	5.1	6.3	6.7	6.8	6.7	6.9	6.9
Poland	3.9	5.2	6.3	6.1	6.3	6.2	6.7
Romania	4.8	3.8	4.9	5.1	5.5	5.7	5.7
Slovak R.	NA	5.4	6.3	6.3	6.3	6.4	6.9
Estonia	NR	5.6	7.1	7.6	7.7	7.8	7.7
Latvia	NR	5.1	6.6	6.8	7.1	6.9	7.1
Lithuania	NR	4.9	6.3	6.4	6.8	6.8	7.0
Armenia	NR	NR	NR	NR	NR	NR	6.7
Azerbaijan	NR	NR	NR	NR	NR	NR	6.0
Georgia	NR	NR	NR	NR	NR	NR	6.7
Ukraine	NA	3.4	4.7	4.8	5.3	5.4	5.4
Russia	NA	4.0	4.9	4.9	5.1	5.2	5.6

Source: Economic Freedom of the World: 2006 Annual Report, www.freetheworld.com.

Note: EFW ratings are on a continuum from 0 to 10, 10 the highest level of economic freedom. NR, not recorded; NA, not applicable.

Appendix III

Reporters without Borders Index of Press Freedom

	2002 (139)	2003 (166)	2004 (167)	2005 (167)	2006 (168)
Bulgaria	38	35	36	48	36
Czech R.	41	12	19	9	5
Hungary	25	21	29	12	10
Poland	30	33	32	55	60
Romania	45	60	70	70	61
Slovak R.	NA	14	7	8	8
Estonia	NA	13	11	11	6
Latvia	NA	11	10	17	11
Lithuania	NA	18	16	22	27
Armenia	NA	90	83	102	101
Azerbaijan	101	113	136	141	135
Georgia	NA		94	99	89
Belarus	124	151	144	152	151
Moldova	NA	94	78	74	85
Ukraine	112	133	139	112	106
Kazakhstan	116	138	131	119	128
Kyrgyzstan	98	104	107	111	123

Tajikistan	86	114	95	114	117
Turkmenistan	136	158	164	165	167
Uzbekistan	120	154	142	156	158
Russia	121	148	140	138	147

Note: The number in parenthesis next to each year represents the number of countries included in the study for the particular year. Each country number represents the ranking of the country relative to the total number of countries in the study. A smaller number represents better ranking in freedom of the media than a larger number.

Rankings for 2002 from RwB, Regular Reports, Worldwide Press Freedom Index 2002, http://www.rsf.org/article.php3?id_article=4116.

Rankings for 2003 from RwB, Regular Reports, Worldwide Press Freedom Index 2003, http://www.rsf.org/article.php3?id_article=8247.

Rankings for 2004 from RwB, Regular Reports, Worldwide Press Freedom Index 2004, http://www.rsf.org/article.php3?id_article=11715.

Rankings for 2005 from RwB, Regular Reports, Worldwide Press Freedom Index 2005, http://www.rsf.org/article.php3?id_article=15331.

Rankings for 2006 from RwB, Regular Reports, Worldwide Press Freedom Index 2006, www.rsf.org/rubrique.php3?id_rubrique=639.

Appendix IV

Gazprom Fees for Gas to Europe and Central Asia

	−2000	2005	2006	2007
Austria		221	221	
Germany		217	217	
Turkey		243		
Estonia			110	
Latvia			110	
Lithuania			110	
Armenia	50	50	110	110
Azerbaijan			110	235*
Belarus			47	100
Georgia		60	110	235
Moldova	62	80	110/160	170
Turkmenistan**	36	36	65	100
Ukraine	50	50	95	130

Sources: "Turkey Pays $243 to Russia, $236 to Iran for Gas," *Turks US Daily News,* February 1, 2006; Maria Danilova, "No More Cheap Gas, Russia Tells Neighbors," *The Associated Press,* Moscow, November 28, 2005; "Moldova turns to Ukraine for gas after Russia cut off supply," *XINHUANET* January 3, 2006; "Russia Reaches Turkmen Gas Deal," *BBC World News* (September 5, 2006).

Note: Gas prices per thousand cubic meters.

*Price asked by Gazprom, refused by country.

**Gas prices charged to Russia.

Notes

CHAPTER 1

1. Understandably, such arguments tend to come from Russian leaders and policy analysts. Boris Yeltsin warned of a Cold Peace as early as 1995, and of a new world war in 1996, should Central Europe be "permitted entry into NATO." See Bill Delaney, "On Invasion's Anniversary, Yeltsin Preaches Against NATO Expansion," *CNN World News,* June 22, 1996. Vladimir Putin made no secret that he opposed NATO expansion even before he became president. He did not change his mind afterward and accused the United States of imposing its economic, political, educational, and cultural policies on other countries, in an attempt to create a unipolar world of its choosing. See Vladimir Putin, "Speech and the Following Discussion at the Munich Conference on Security Policy," February 10, 2007, President of Russia Web site, www.kremlin.ru/eng/. Mikhail Gorbachev joined his voice to complain about the increasing imperialist tendencies of the United States and its Western allies. See Alex Nicholson, "Gorbachev Blames U.S. for 'Growing Global Disarray,'" *Associated Press,* July 28, 2007. Policy analysts picked up on their leaders' position and some suggested that the Iron Curtain that separated "the East" from "the West" during the Cold War was being replaced by a "velvet curtain" in the nineties, in an allusion to the creeping Western influence into Central Europe and beyond. See Viatcheslav Morozov, "The Forced Choice Between Russia and the West: The Geopolitics of Alienation," *Program on New Approaches to Russian Security,* Policy Memo 327, 11 (Washington DC: Center for Strategic and International Studies, January 2005).

2. There is an increasing literature dealing with the reemergence (or continuation) of "Russian imperialism," or "Russian nationalism" as some critics would call it. Russia is accused by some of trying to establish itself as the center of power in Central Asia, by leveraging energy resources and political influence on countries that do not seem to make decisions favorable to the Kremlin's point of view. See Mete Skak, *From Empire to Anarchy: Postcommunist Foreign Policy and International Relations* (New York: St. Martin's Press, 1996); William Zimmerman, *The Russian People and Foreign Policy: Russian Elite and Mass Perspectives, 1993–2000* (Princeton: Princeton University Press, 2002); and Janusz Bugajski, *Cold Peace: Russia's New Imperialism* (Connecticut: Praeger, 2004).

3. Eurasia is used throughout this book to signify the geographic space that came under the influence of the Soviet Union after WWII. Eurasia includes countries of CEE that retained sovereignty without full political power to choose their domestic political system, and the former Soviet republics that lost their identity by being incorporated into the Soviet Union.

4. This argument was first formulated in Georgeta Pourchot, "Towards a New Dynamic in the Post-Soviet Space," *Eurasia Heritage Foundation,* Eurasian Home Analytical Resource online (October 14, 2005), www.eurasianhome.org.

5. Lithuania, Estonia, and Latvia form what is commonly known as "the Baltic countries." All were independent between the two world wars, and were annexed by the Soviet Union in 1940. The annexation was never recognized by the United States and other Western countries, and still forms the battlefield of political discord between Russia and the Baltics. Historical details follow in chapter 3.

6. This book deals with developments in CEE and the former Soviet Union. Yugoslavia was technically never part of the Soviet sphere of influence and the secessionist wars of the mid-nineties set the region apart in terms of political and economic transitions. Developments in the countries of the former Yugoslavia are therefore not discussed in this book. The post-Balkan wars were about secession from the Yugoslav "center," i.e., Serbia, and asserting independent-mindedness from Belgrade rather than from Moscow. For the same reason, Albania is not discussed either. While originally a party to the Warsaw Pact, Albania withdrew from the Pact in 1961, never returned to the Soviet sphere of influence, and joined the Group of Non-Aligned states.

7. Various definitions of Central Asia exist. For the purpose of this book, Central Asia refers to the following former constituent republics of the Soviet Union: Kazakhstan, Kyrgyzstan, Tajikistan, Turkmenistan, and Uzbekistan. The Caucasus countries are Armenia, Azerbaijan, and Georgia.

8. See Mikhail Gorbachev, *Perestroika. New Thinking for Our Country and the World* (New York: Harper & Row, 1987).

9. By some estimates, the total amount of German loans to the Soviet Union and its successor states is 70 billion Deutche Marks (DM). See Manfred R. Hamm, "Soviet Withdrawal from Germany," *Perspective* 2, no. 5 (May–June 1992).

10. During my brief tenure as a member of the Romanian Chamber of Deputies after the first free election in May 1990, the "debates" were shouting games. Parliamentarians had many good ideas but little practical experience. Reforms were adopted in the absence of institutional structures to implement them, and many of the early reform packages had to be completely revised and voted on.

11. Jane L. Curry, "Pluralism in Eastern Europe: Not Will It Last but What Is It?" *Communist and Post-Communist Studies* 26, no. 4 (December 1993): 446–61.

12. Raymond M. Duch, "Economic Chaos and the Fragility of Democratic Transition in Former Communist Regimes," *Journal of Politics* 57, no. 1 (February 1995): 121–58.

13. Fareed Zakaria, "The Rise of Illiberal Democracy," *Foreign Affairs* (November–December 1997): 22–43.

14. Ilya Prizel, "The First Decade after the Collapse of Communism: Why Did Some Nations Succeed in Their Political and Economic Transformations While Others Failed?" *SAIS Review* (Summer–Fall 1999): 1–15.

15. Gorbachev, *Perestroika,* 151.

16. Interview given to Austrian journal *Neue Kronen-Zeitung* (July 23, 1988), in Foreign Broadcast Information Service (July 26, 1988).

17. "'Sinatra Doctrine' at Work in Warsaw Pact, Soviet Says," *Los Angeles Times,* October 25, 1989.

18. Fredo Arias-King, "From Brezhnev Doctrine to Sinatra Doctrine, Interview with Gennadi Gerasimov," *Demokratizatsiya,* Spring 2005, www.findarticles.com/p/articles/mi_qa3996/is_200504/ai_n15328179.

19. Robert L. Hutchings, *American Diplomacy and the End of the Cold War. An Insider's Account of U.S. Policy in Europe, 1989–1992* (Washington DC: The Woodrow Wilson Center Press, 1997), 6–7.

CHAPTER 2

1. City on the Crimean peninsula, used to be part of the Soviet Union, now part of Ukraine.

2. *The Yalta Conference,* Protocol of Proceedings of Crimea Conference, chapter II Declaration of Liberated Europe (February 1945), The Avalon Project at Yale Law School, http://www.yale.edu/lawweb/avalon/wwii/yalta.htm.

3. The Fulton Address (also known as the Sinews Address) was offered by Winston Churchill at Westminster College in Fulton, Missouri on March 5, 1946. The "Iron Curtain" phrase had been used before but Churchill made it famous. For a text of the address, see Winston S. Churchill, *Memoirs of the Second World War,* abridged edition (Boston: Houghton Mifflin Comp., 1990), 996–98.

4. In 1990, this author took an American professor from Virginia Tech on a visit of small, Romanian towns. Almost everywhere we went, the professor received the same warm welcome from the local population, usually accompanied by hands thrown up in the air and a comment "My prayers have been heard, the Americans have finally arrived."

5. Initially an anticommunist workers' movement in the northern port of Gdansk, Solidarity grew to become the symbol of anticommunist resistance in Poland and elsewhere in Eastern Europe. Established in 1980, it was the first noncommunist trade union in a communist country. Led by Lech Walesa, who was to become the country's first elected postcommunist president, Solidarity opposed the communist government through petitions and nonviolent protests.

6. Kieran Williams, *The Prague Spring and Its Aftermath: Czechoslovak Politics 1968–1970* (Cambridge: Cambridge University Press, 1997).

7. *Declaration of Charter 77,* http://libpro.cts.cuni.cz/charta/docs/declaration_of _charter_77.pdf.

8. Dennis Deletant, *Communist Terror in Romania: Gheorghe Gheorghiu-Dej and the Police State, 1945–1965* (New York: Palgrave Macmillan, February 2000).

9. Vessel Dimitrov, *Bulgaria: The Uneven Transition* (London: Routledge, 2002).

10. Brussels is the symbol of European power because the main headquarters of the EU, European Commission, European Parliament, and NATO are located in this city.

11. A rich Western literature debates aspects of democratic governance and the "necessary and sufficient" conditions needed for a country to be considered a democracy. There is much agreement on the necessity of free elections, and much disagreement on their sufficiency for democracy to take root. Numerous theorists argue that free elections cannot solely turn a country into a democracy. Other criteria make a country more or less democratic ranging from the existence of a civil society, individual freedoms, and the presence of free enterprise. For a review of democratic theory, see Arend Lijphart, *Democracy in Plural Societies: A Comparative Exploration* (New Haven: Yale University Press, 1980); Robert A. Dahl, *On Democracy* (New Haven: Yale University Press, 2000); and Samuel P. Huntington, *The Third Wave: Democratization in the Late Twentieth Century* (Oklahoma: University of Oklahoma Press, 1993).

12. Constitutional references for Bulgaria, the Czech Republic, Hungary, Poland, Romania, and the Slovak Republic are from a collection of Constitutions published by the Council of Europe, *The Rebirth of Democracy. 12 Constitutions of Central and Eastern Europe,* 2nd ed. (Council of Europe Publishing, 1996).

13. For Bulgaria, preamble to the Constitution. For the Czech Republic, preamble, Art. 1, 9.2 and 9.3 and 10. For Hungary, Art. 2.1 and 8.1. For Poland, part 2. Constitutional Provisions, Ch. 1, Art. 1. For Romania, Art. 1.3. For the Slovak Republic, Art. 1.

14. For Bulgaria, Art. 10 of the Constitution. For the Czech Republic, Art. 6 and 18.1, 18.2, 18.3. For Hungary, Art. 71.1. For Poland, Art. 3.1 and 3.2. For Romania, Title III, Art. 59. For the Slovak Republic, Art. 30.3 and 74.1.

15. For Bulgaria, Art. 11.1 and 11.2. For the Czech Republic, Art. 5. For Hungary, Art. 3.1. For Poland, part 2. Constitutional Provisions, Ch. 1, Art. 4.1. For Romania, Art. 8.1 and 8.2. For the Slovak Republic, Art. 29.2.

16. For Bulgaria, Art. 13.1 stipulates that the practicing of any religion is free even as Art. 13.3 states that Eastern Orthodox Christianity is the traditional religion. For the Czech Republic, Art. 10 is more general and refers to the constitutionality of all international treaties on human rights and fundamental freedoms that the country adhered to. That includes freedom of movement, association, speech and the right to petition and protest. For Hungary, chapter 5 includes several articles involving the rights of minorities and introduces a government job for Commissioner for Civil Rights. Chapter 12 is entirely dedicated to fundamental rights and duties. For Poland, part 2, chapter 8 includes twenty-seven articles dedicated to the specifications of the fundamental rights and duties of citizens. For Romania, Title II on fundamental rights, freedoms, and duties has four chapters with a total of forty-three articles on the subject. For the Slovak Republic, part 2 includes eight chapters on fundamental rights and freedoms.

17. For Bulgaria, Art. 35.1. For the Czech Republic, Art. 10. For Hungary, Art. 58.1. For Poland, this right is indirectly addressed in Art. 89. For Romania, Title II, Chapter II, Art. 25. For the Slovak Republic, Art. 23.

18. For Bulgaria, Art. 39.1 and 40.1. For the Czech Republic, Art. 10. For Hungary, Art. 61.1 and 61.2. For Poland, part 2. Constitutional Provisions, Ch. 8, Art. 83.1. For Romania, Title II, Chapter II, Art. 30 and 31. For the Slovak Republic, Art. 24.2 and 26.

19. For Bulgaria, Art. 43.1, 44.1, and 45.1. For the Czech Republic, Art. 10. For Hungary, Art. 62.1, 63.1, and 64. For Poland, part 2. Constitutional Provisions, Ch. 8, Art. 84.1, 84.2, and 86.2. For Romania, Title II, Chapter II, Art. 36, 37, and 47. For the Slovak Republic, Art. 27, 28, and 29.

20. For Bulgaria, Art. 19.1. For the Czech Republic, the principle of a market economy is not enshrined in the Constitution, but in legislative acts. For Hungary, Art. 9.1. For Poland, part 2. Constitutional Provisions, Ch. 1, Art. 6. For Romania, Title IV, Art. 134. For the Slovak Republic, Art. 55.

21. Samuel Huntington argues that one criterion to measure democratic consolidation is the two-turnover test. According to this test, if a country's incumbent politicians lost elections and turned over power peacefully in two consecutive elections, the country could be considered a consolidated democracy. See Samuel P. Huntington, *The Third Wave*, 266–67.

22. Adrian Karatnycky, Alexander Motyl, and Charles Graybow, eds., *Nations in Transit 1998. Civil Society, Democracy and Markets in East Central Europe and the Newly Independent States* (Piscataway, NJ: Freedom House, Transaction Publishers, 1999), 155.

23. National Assembly of the Republic of Bulgaria, Archives, thirty-ninth and fortieth National Assemblies, www.parliament.bg.

24. Czech Elections Office, http://www.volby.cz/index_en.htm.

25. Karatnycky, Motyl, and Graybow, *Nations in Transit 1998,* 279.

26. Hungarian Ministry of the Interior Web site, Central Registration and Election Office, www.election.hu/index_en.

27. Karatnycky, Motyl, and Graybow, *Nations in Transit 1998,* 442.

28. National Electoral Commission, Elections for Sejm, http://www.wybory2005 .pkw.gov.pl/SJM/EN/WYN/M/index.htm.

29. Karatnycky, Motyl, and Graybow, *Nations in Transit 1998,* 465.

30. Camera Deputatilor, Repertoriul Legislativ, Legea 27 (April 26, 1996), http:// www.cdep.ro/pls/legis/legis_pck.frame.

31. Central Electoral Bureau, http://www.kappa.ro/guv/bec/ceb96.html.

32. Karatnycky, Motyl, and Graybow, *Nations in Transit 1998,* 517.

33. Statistical Office of the Slovak Republic, www.statistics.sk/struk/volby.htm.

34. Andrey Vyshinsky, Soviet statesman, lawyer and diplomat was sent to Romania in 1945 to orchestrate the success of the communist party in postwar elections. Ana Pauker, Romanian activist with strong Stalinist political views, was instrumental in the implementation of a strictly Moscovite political approach in postwar Romania. See Robert Levy, *Ana Pauker: Dilemmas of a Reluctant Stalinist,* presentation at the Woodrow Wilson International Center for Scholars, report #273, http://www.wilsoncenter.org/index.cfm?topic_id=1422&fuseaction =topics.publications&doc_id=35705&group_id=7427.

35. The Visegrad Group was created at the initiative of the leaders of three countries, Czechoslovakia, Hungary, and Poland, in the Hungarian town of Visegrad. When Czechoslovakia split, the Czech and Slovak Republics joined the group. More on the group in the foreign policy assertiveness part of this chapter.

36. David Lipton and Jeffrey Sachs, "Creating a Market Economy in Eastern Europe: The Case of Poland," *Brookings Papers on Economic Activity* 1 (1990): 75–145; Ben Slay, "Poland: The Rise and Fall of the Balcerowitz Plan," *Radio Free Europe Radio Liberty Research Report* 1, no. 5 (January 31, 1992): 40–47.

37. Ben Slay, "Poland: An Overview," *Radio Free Europe Radio Liberty Research Report* 1, no. 17 (April 24, 1992): 15–21.

38. Ivan Svitek, "An Assessment: Czechoslovak Economic Reform in 1991," *Radio Free Europe Radio Liberty Research Report* 1, no. 21 (May 22, 1992): 45–49.

39. Ira A. Liberman, "Mass Privatization in Central and Eastern Europe and the Former Soviet Union: A Comparative Analysis," in Organization for Economic Cooperation and Development (OECD), *Mass Privatization: An Initial Assessment* (Paris: OECD Publications, 1993), 13–38.

40. The EBRD (European Bank for Reconstruction and Development) started researching the process of transition to a market economy and democratic institutions as soon as communism collapsed. The statistical information provided by annual Transition Reports permits a comparative analysis across categories of transition and countries in the region. For an evaluation of the economic slump witnessed in 1997 and 1998, see *Transition Report 1997. Enterprise Performance and Growth* (London: EBRD, 1997), chap. 1, and *Transition Report 1998. Financial Sector in Transition* (London: EBRD, 1998), chap. 1.

41. Interview with Mihaly Kupa, *Le Figaro,* Paris (June 4, 1991).

42. Ibid.

43. "Berlin Businesses to Boost Presence in Hungary," *Interfax Hungary Daily Business Report,* Headline News 1, no. 155 (October 5, 1999).

44. "Parliament Passes Bills Increasing State Control," *FBIS-EEU-95-137* (July 18, 1995). The law provided for the state to retain a golden share in companies that were considered "strategic." The golden share gave the state the right to veto decisions regarding the management and development of the strategic companies. The direct result of the law was that

strategic companies were sold off to a few people, at low prices. This practice prompted the first popular demonstrations against the government's economic policy, see "First Mass Rally by Trade Unionists since 1989," *FBIS-EEU-95-190* (October 2, 1995).

45. *Transition Report 1997. Enterprise Performance and Growth, European Bank for Reconstruction and Development,* 198–99; *Transition Report 1998,* 188–89.

46. *Transition Report 2005. Business in Transition, European Bank for Reconstruction and Development* (London: EBRD, 2005), 178–81.

47. Vladimir Philipov, former policy advisor to President Petar Stoyanov, quoted in Elisabeth Pond, "Reinventing Bulgaria," *Washington Quarterly* 22, no. 3 (Summer 1999): 41.

48. *Romania Libera* (Bucharest, April–May 1990).

49. For economic progress data, see *Transition Report 2003. Integration and Regional Cooperation* (London: EBRD, 2003), 128–31, 180–83; *Transition Report 2004. Infrastructure* (London: EBRD, 2004), 110–13, 162–65; and *Transition Report 2005,* 114–17, 166–69.

50. The Fraser Institute ratings were chosen as example because of their complex methodology, their credibility with over seventy research institutes around the world, and the longevity of the study. Studies with similar goals, such as the index of economic freedom of the Heritage Foundation and the Wall Street Journal, found similar patterns of economic progress in the region. See www.heritage.org/index/.

51. For more information about methodology, datasets, and annual reports, see www.freetheworld.com.

52. Karatnycky, Motyl, and Graybow, *Nations in Transit 1998,* 156, 210, 280, 443, 465, 518.

53. The Czech Republic and Poland ranked "free" after 1990. Bulgaria ranked "partly free" after 1990. Hungary ranked "free" from 1990 to 1992, "partly free" in 1993, "free" in 1994, "partly free" from 1995 to 1997, and "free" after 1998. Romania ranked "not free" in 1990, "partly free" in 1991, "free" in 1992, then "partly free" after 1993. The Slovak Republic ranked "free" from 1990 to 1992, "partly free" from 1993 to 1998, and "free" after 1999. See specific country reports in Karatnycky, Motyl, and Graybow, *Nations in Transit 1998,* and Freedom House, *Nations in Transit 2006. Democratization from Central Europe to Eurasia* (Lanham, MD: Rowman & Littlefield Inc., 2006).

54. Library of Congress, Federal Resource Division, *Country studies: The Soviet Union,* Appendix C, the Warsaw Pact; http://memory.loc.gov/frd/cs/soviet_union/su_appnc.html.

55. There is a vast literature regarding the topic of Warsaw Pact dissolution. A good Web site to access historical documents of the Pact's meetings and decisions is the Parallel History Project which focuses on security dimensions of the Cold War, at www.php.isn.ethz.ch. Another good source of information for the development of events is Jacques Levesque, *The Enigma of 1989. The USSR and the Liberation of Eastern Europe* (Berkeley and LA, CA: University of California Press, 1997), chap. 14.

56. "Declaration on Cooperation between the Czech and Slovak Federal Republic, the Republic of Poland and the Republic of Hungary in Striving for European Integration," Visegrad Declaration (1991), Visegrad official Web site www.visegradgroup.eu.

57. Check official Visegrad site for specific projects and events. Another listing of cooperative arrangements in the region can be found in George W. Handy, Georgeta Pourchot, and Eric Hatch, *Learning from Successful Cooperation in the Expanding Euro-Atlantic Region* (Washington DC: Center for Strategic and International Studies, May 2003).

58. "London Declaration on a Transformed North Atlantic Alliance," NATO online library, nato.int/docu/update/1990/9007e.htm (July 1990).

59. Prezydent Rzeczpospolitej Polskiej, *Tenets of the Polish Security Policy* (Warsaw, November 2, 1992), 2.

60. Foreign minister Krzysztof Skubiszewski on Poland's long-term policies, interview with Polska Zbrojna (June 19–21, 1992); Deputy Defense Minister Jerzy Milewski speaking at NATO headquarters, *Open Media Research Institute Daily Digest* 49, part II (March 9, 1995).

61. Jan Obrman, "The Czechoslovak Armed Forces: The Reform Continues," *RFL/RL Research Report* (February 7, 1992): 50–51.

62. "Czech President Says NATO Should Re-Define Itself Before Expanding," *Open Media Research Institute Daily Digest* 84, part II (April 28, 1995).

63. Juraj Schenk, Slovak Minister of Foreign Affairs, in "Schenk Disassociates Himself from Slota on NATO," *FBIS-EEU-95-204* (October 23, 1995): 14; and "Ministry Denies Country Moving Away from NATO," *FBIS-EEU-95-195* (October 10, 1995): 19.

64. "Deputy Foreign Minister Meets NATO's Balanzino," *FBIS-EEU-95-202* (October 19, 1995): 16.

65. "Horn Urges More NATO Involvement in Europe," *FBIS-EEU-95-193* (October 5, 1995): 16–17.

66. "Iliescu: Military Ties with U.S. Positive," *FBIS-EEU-95-190-A* (October 2, 1995): 27; and "Roman on Joining NATO 'With Hungary,'" *FBIS-EEU-95-136-A* (July 17, 1995): 17.

67. Stephen Foye and Douglas L. Clarke, eds., "Military and Security Notes," *RFL/RL Research Report* (March 13, 1992): 48.

68. "Security Strategy Geared to European Integration," *FBIS-EEU-95-135-A* (July 14, 1995): 3–4; and "Reactions to NATO Expansion Document Reported," *FBIS-EEU-85-191* (October 3, 1995): 3–4.

69. Stephen Foye and Douglas L. Clarke, "Military and Security Notes," *RFL/RL Research Report* 1, no. 19 (May 8, 1992): 53.

70. *NATO Study on Enlargement,* NATO official Web site, www.nato.int/issues/study _on_enlargement.

71. Defense Minister Stanisław Dobrzański in interview with News Editor Juliusz Urbanowicz, "Polish Forces Are Fully Capable of Joining Allies," *Warsaw Voice,* April 28, 1996.

72. "NATO Expansion Is Russia-Friendly," *Warsaw Voice,* April 28, 1996.

73. A vast literature discusses the arguments for and against enlargement. The NATO Review is a very good online resource.

74. Gen. Wesley K. Clark (ret.), *Waging Modern War. Bosnia, Kosovo and the Future of Combat* (New York: Public Affairs, 2001), 401.

75. Robert Anderson et al., "Mixed Views from the New Members," *Financial Times* (April 23, 1999): 2.

76. John Tagliabue, "Crisis in the Balkans: The Neighborhood; Front-Line Hungary Feels Anxiety," *New York Times* (May 2, 1999): 16.

77. Adam Szostkiewicz, "By Invitation: Where Do You Stand?" *Warsaw Voice,* April 4, 1999.

78. Tomasz Oljasz, Dorota Warakomska, and Jarosław J. Szczepański, "Poland and Kosovo Just War or Just a War?" *Warsaw Voice,* April 4, 1999.

79. "Poland Threatens Veto in EU Row," *BBC News,* December 11, 2003.

80. For a text of the draft Constitution, see European Convention Secretariat, *Draft Treaty Establishing a Constitution for Europe,* CONV 850/03 (Brussels: July 18, 2003),

http://european-convention.eu.int/docs/Treaty/cv00850.en03.pdf. For the "Alternative Report: The Europe of Democracies," see European Convention Secretariat, *Report from the Presidency of the Convention to the President of the European Council,* CONV 851/03, Annex III (Brussels: July 18, 2003), http://register.consilium.eu.int/pdf/en/03/cv00/cv00851en03.pdf.

81. "Poland Takes Uncompromising Stance on EU Constitution," *Warsaw Voice,* May 31, 2007.

82. "EU Chiefs 'Satisfied' with Treaty," *BBC News,* June 23, 2007.

83. George Jones, "Polish PM Adopts WW2 Rhetoric at EU Summit," *Telegraph,* June 22, 2007.

84. "Poland to Opt Out of EU Treaty," *Warsaw Voice,* September 14, 2007.

85. Oana Lungescu, "Chirac Blasts EU Candidates," *BBC World News,* February 18, 2003.

86. "Europe's Hard-Won Unity on Iraq—quotes," *BBC World News,* February 18, 2003; "'New Europe' Backs EU on Iraq," *BBC World News,* February 19, 2003.

87. Harry Truman, *Memoirs: Year of Decisions* (Garden City, New York: Doubleday & Comp., Inc., 1955), 368.

88. W. Z., "Claims, Complaints & Controversy," *Warsaw Voice,* January 3, 2007.

89. Ibid.

90. "Poland Threatens Germany with Treaty Review over Property Row," *Deutsche Welle,* December 20, 2006, www.DW-World.de; Jan Puhl and Andreas Wassermann, "Suit Evokes Ghosts of War," *Spiegel Online International,* January 2, 2007, www.Spiegel.de/international/.

91. "Plans for Missile Shield in Europe Not Understandable—Lavrov," *Ria Novosti,* February 25, 2007; "Russia Sole Target for U.S. Missile Shield in Europe—Ivanov," *Ria Novosti,* April 19, 2007; "Putin Accuses U.S. of Starting a New Arms Race," *Moscow News,* May 31, 2007; "Putin Warns of Measures Against U.S. Missile Shield in Europe," *Ria Novosti,* June 4, 2007.

92. "U.S. Asks to Build Radar in the Czech Republic," *Prague Post,* January 24, 2007.

93. "Poland Needs U.S. Base to Cede from Russian Influence—PM," *Ria Novosti,* February 20, 2007.

94. "Missile Shield in Europe Could Lead to Cold War—Slovak Ex-Premier," *Ria Novosti,* February 20, 2007.

95. Radek Sikorski, "Don't Take Poland for Granted," *Washington Post* (March 21, 2007): A15.

96. Andrzej Ratajczyk, "Difficult Trade with Russia," *Warsaw Voice,* February 14, 2007.

97. Quoted by W. Z., "Kaczynski's Presidency, A Year in Charge," *Warsaw Voice,* January 3, 2007.

98. "Foreign Minister Refuses to Travel to Russia," *Warsaw Voice,* May 18, 2007.

99. "Poland Agrees to Allow Russia Veterinary Inspectors to End Standoff," *Warsaw Voice,* November 8, 2007.

100. W. Z., "Monuments of Contention," *Warsaw Voice,* May 16, 2007.

101. *Romania Libera,* February 1–10, 1990.

102. Created by artist David Cerny, the hanging Lenin statue can be viewed at the following link: http://www.myczechrepublic.com/photos/prague/hanging-lenin-statue-david-cerny.jpg.html.

103. "Constitution Watch—Poland V," *East European Constitutional Review* 7, no. 3 (Summer 1998).

104. "PiS Wants Communist Records Opened," *Warsaw Voice,* May 24, 2007.

CHAPTER 3

1. By this point in time, the Baltic states already watched the Soviet Union pressure on Finland into accepting Soviet bases on Finnish territory. Finnish authorities refused to bow to pressure and the Soviet Union invaded Finland. The Soviet-Finnish war of 1939 followed, also known as the Winter War. Short-lived and ending in a Soviet victory, this war served as an example to the Baltics of what could occur if they did not agree to Soviet demands.

2. Ministry of Foreign Affairs of Latvia, "Soviet Occupation and Annexation of Latvia 1939–1940," Briefing Paper no. 2, http://www.am.gov.lv/en/latvia/History-of-Occupation/briefing-paper2/.

3. Thomas Remeikis, "The Decision of the Lithuanian Government to Accept the Soviet Ultimatum of June 14, 1940," *Lituanus, Lithuanian Quarterly Journal of Arts and Sciences* 21, no. 4 (Winter 1975), www.lituanus.org/1975/; Kenneth Christie and Robert Cribb, *Historical Injustice and Democratic Transition in Eastern Asia and Northern Europe: Ghosts at the Table of Democracy* (New York: Routledge, 2002), 79–117; and Antanas Smetona, *Told, Told: Speeches and Presentations II, 1935–1940,* ed. Leonas Sabaliunas with Vincas Rastenis, in Lithuanian (Boston: Lithuanian Encyclopedia Press, 1974).

4. O. Freivalds et al., eds., *The Latvian Soldier During World War Two,* vol. I in Latvian (Sweden: Ziemeļblāzma, Västerås, 1970–1979), 71–72 include photocopy of the secret map.

5. Visvaldis Mangulis, *Latvia in the Wars of the 20th Century* (Princeton Junction: Cognition Books, 1983), 80–94; Alfreds Berzins, *The Unpunished Crime* (New York: Robert, Speller & Sons, 1963), 88.

6. "Baltic Residents Form Human Chain in Defiance of Soviet Rule," *Associated Press,* August 23, 1989.

7. Arias-King, "From Brezhnev Doctrine to Sinatra Doctrine."

8. Constitution of the Republic of Estonia, Preamble, in *The Rebirth of Democracy,* 119.

9. Constitution of the Republic of Lithuania, Preamble, in *The Rebirth of Democracy,* 209.

10. Lettonie—Russie, Traités et documents de base, "Summary of Supreme Council's Memorandum to USSR President Gorbachev," May 10, 1990, http://www.letton.ch/lvx_ap9.htm.

11. *The Rebirth of Democracy,* 119.

12. Ibid., 209.

13. For Estonia, Chapter II, Fundamental Rights, Liberties and Duties, Art. 32, 34, 35, 40, 45, 46, 47, 48; Chapter III, The People, Art. 56 and 60. For Latvia, Section 1, General Regulations, Article 1, Section 2, The Saeima (Parliament), Art. 6 and 8. For Lithuania, chapter 2, Art. 20, 22, 23, 25, 26, 32, 35, and 36.

14. Election results from Estonian National Electoral Committee, www.vvk.ee/engindex.html.

15. Central Election Commission, 5th, 6th, 7th, 8th, and 9th Saeima elections, http://web.cvk.lv/pub/public/28334.html.

16. Central Statistical Office, http://www3.lrs.lt/n/rinkimai/20001008/partsara.htm-13.htm.

17. Central Statistical Office, http://www3.lrs.lt/rinkimai/2004/seimas/rezultatai/rez_pgl_part_e_20.htm.

18. Karatnycky, Motyl, and Graybow, *Nations in Transit 1998,* 345 and 373.

19. *Transition Report 1998,* 164, 176, 178.

20. The Estonian Institute, "Non-Governmental Organizations in Estonia," Publications archive, 1997, www.einst.ee/factsheets/factsheets_uus_kuju/non_governmental_organisations _in_estonia.htm.

21. The Latvian Institute, "History, From the 1980s," www.li.lv/index.php?option=com _content&task=view&id=95&Itemid=173.

22. Olinka Gjigas, ed., *A Directory of Environmental Nongovernmental Organizations in Central and Eastern Europe* (Regional Environmental Center, Lithuania section, December 1997), www.rec.org/REC/Publications/NGODirIntros/index.html.

23. Karatnycky, Motyl, and Graybow, *Nations in Transit 1998,* 373.

24. Latvian Ministry of Foreign Affairs, "Number of NGOs Growing Sharply," News Archive, July 4, 2001.

25. Estonian Institute, "Non-Governmental Organizations in Estonia," Publications Archive, 1997, www.einst.ee/factsheets/factsheets_uus_kuju/non_governmental_organisations _in_estonia.htm.

26. Estonia and Lithuania are ranked "partly free" between 1990 and 1992, and "free" afterward. Latvia is ranked "partly free" between 1990 and 1993, and "free" afterward. See country reports in Karatnycky, Motyl, and Graybow, *Nations in Transit 1998;* and in *Nations in Transit 2006.*

27. "The CIS and Baltic Press on Russia/Estonia," *Ria Novosti,* February 2, 2007.

28. "Defense Minister Ivanov: WWII Victory Will Remain with Russia," *Ria Novosti,* May 4, 2005.

29. Russian Ministry of Foreign Affairs, "Comments by the Russian Foreign Ministry Information and Press Department in Connection with Remarks by Some European Politicians Regarding the 'Occupation' of the Baltic Countries by the Soviet Union and the Need for Russia to Condemn This" (Information and Press Department, unofficial translation 913: May 4, 2005).

30. Ibid.

31. "Latvia Disagrees with History as Seen by Russia's Foreign Ministry," *Ria Novosti,* May 5, 2005.

32. "Russian Servicemen in Estonia Suffered for Support of the Bronze Soldier," *Regnum News Agency,* May 30, 2006.

33. "Estonian Premier: Monument to Soldiers, Who Fought Against Nazis, Exasperates Me," *Regnum News Agency,* May 26, 2006.

34. "Estonia Moves Soviet War Monument from Center of Tallinn, Sparking Furious Russian Response," *AFP* (Tallinn: Estonia, April 27, 2007).

35. "Estonia's WWII Memorials Demolition Law Immoral—Speaker Mironov," *Ria Novosti,* November 15, 2006.

36. "Estonian Parliament Passes Law Allowing Dismantling of Soviet Monuments," *Regnum News Agency,* February 15, 2007.

37. "Estonia President Approves Soviet Memorial Demolition Law—1," *Ria Novosti,* January 11, 2007.

38. *Ria Novosti* photo gallery, May 15, 2007, http://en.rian.ru/photolents/20070502/ 64748357_5.html.

39. Quoted in Peter Finn, "Statue's Removal Sparks Violent Protests in Estonia," *Washington Post,* April 28, 2007, A12.

40. "Russian Attacks over Bronze Soldier Affect All EU, Estonia Says," *Associated France Press,* May 2, 2007; Ian Treynor, "Russia Accused of Unleashing Cyberwar to Disable Estonia,"

Guardian, May 17, 2007; Frank Gardner, "Could the UK Face 'Cyber Attack'?" *BBC World News,* July 10, 2007.

41. "1,000 People Gather on Dome Square to Express Support for Estonia," *LETA News Agency,* May 8, 2007.

42. Ministry of Foreign Affairs of Estonia, "Foreign Ministry Summons Russian Ambassador," Press Release, May 16, 2007, www.mfa.ee.

43. Latvian Ministry of Foreign Affairs, "Latvian President Unveils Freedom Monument after Renovation," News Archive, July 25, 2001.

44. "Latvian Politicians Propose Imprisonment for Those Who Deny 'Soviet Occupation,'" *Regnum News Agency,* January 14, 2007.

45. Ministry of Foreign Affairs of Lithuania, "Lithuanian and Russian Foreign Ministers Met in Sofia," Press Release, December 8, 2004.

46. "Putin Lashes Out at Latvia amid Border Dispute," *News from Russia,* May 23, 2005, http://newsfromrussia.com/cis/2005/05/23/59917.html.

47. DG External Policies Delegations Europe, "Information Note: The Border Treaty Between the Russian Federation and the Republic of Latvia," June 8, 2006, http://www.europarl.europa.eu/meetdocs/2004_2009/documents/fd/d-ru20060615_07/d-ru20060 615_07en.pdf.

48. Ministry of Foreign Affairs of the Republic of Latvia, Speech by Minister Artis Pabriks on the question of conclusion of the Latvian-Russian border agreement at the February 1 Saeima plenary session, www.mfa.gov.lv/en/news/speeches/2007/February/01-1/.

49. "Government Secures Saeima's Mandate to Sign Border Agreement with Russia," *LETA News Agency,* February 8, 2007; "President Promulgates Law Authorizing Government to Sign Border Agreement with Russia," *LETA News Agency,* February 19, 2007.

50. Ministry of Foreign Affairs of Latvia, "Latvian and Russian Prime Ministers Sign Latvia-Russia Border Agreement," Press Release, March 27, 2007.

51. Claire Bigg, "Russia/Estonia: Milestone Border Treaty Signed," *RFE/RL,* May 18, 2005.

52. "Update: Russia Pulls Out of Border Agreement with Estonia—Kremlin," *Ria Novosti,* September 1, 2005.

53. "Estonia Will Not Renounce Preamble to Bill on Ratification of Border Treaty with Russia," *Regnum News Agency,* January 9, 2007.

54. "Putin Condemns Estonia and Latvia for Violating Human Rights of Russian-Speakers," *LETA-AFP,* May 18, 2007.

55. Refugees International, "Stateless Russians in Estonia," December 20, 2004, http://www.refugeesinternational.org/content/report/detail/4831/.

56. Patrick Jackson, "Russian Roots and an Estonian Future," *BBC News,* May 10, 2007.

57. Latvian Ministry of Foreign Affairs, "Latvian President Suggests Soviet and Nazi Occupation Research Commission Be Extended Three More Years," News Archives, June 15, 2001.

58. Latvian Ministry of Foreign Affairs, "Latvia Marks 60 Years since Communist Regime Deportations," News Archive, June 14, 2001.

59. Ministry of Foreign Affairs of Estonia, "Estonia Today: August 31st 2004, the 10th Anniversary of the Withdrawal of Russian Troops from Estonia," Press and Information Department Fact Sheet, August 2004, www.vm.ee.

60. For instance, the U.S. Congress approved housing vouchers for Russian military stationed in the Baltics who wanted to relocate in Russia in 1994.

61. See also Barry James, "Yeltsin's Problem: Where to Send the Baltic Troops," *International Herald Tribune,* July 10, 1992.

62. Lithuanian Prime Minister quoted in "Polish Oil PKN Orlen's Acquisition of Mazeikiu Nafta Improved Lithuania's Energy Security—Lithuanian PM," *Interfax Central Europe,* June 1, 2006.

63. "Mazeiku Nafta Sold," *LETA,* December 14, 2006; "PKN Orlen Buys Controlling Stake in Mazeikiu Refinery," *Warsaw Voice,* December 15, 2006.

64. "Pabriks Assesses Lithuania's Threat to Block EU-Russia Cooperation Agreement as a Tactical Move," *LETA,* May 14, 2007.

65. "Estonia Against Russia-EU Talks on New Cooperation Agreement," *Ria Novosti,* May 15, 2007.

66. Kostis Geropoulos, "Druzhba: The Not-So-Friendly Russian Oil Pipeline," *New Europe Weekly,* May 18, 2007, http://www.neurope.eu/view_news.php?id=73863.

67. "Russia Won't Fix Oil Pipeline to Lithuania," *Kommersant News,* June 1, 2007.

68. "Latvian Firms Blast Russia's Ban on Canned Fish Imports," *Ria Novosti,* October 20, 2006.

69. F. Stephen Larrabee, "The Baltic States and NATO Membership," Testimony, U.S. Senate Committee on Foreign Relations (Rand Corporation: April 3, 2003), 7.

70. "Russia Turning on the Charm," *Warsaw Voice,* July 20, 1997.

71. Harri Tiido, "NATO: The Baltic Dimension," *Baltic Times,* August 30, 2001, Ministry of Foreign Affairs of Estonia, Speeches.

72. Ministry of Foreign Affairs of Estonia, "Statement by the Ministers of Foreign Affairs of Albania, Bulgaria, Croatia, Estonia, Latvia, Lithuania, Macedonia, Romania, Slovakia and Slovenia," Estonia in NATO section, Tallinn, July 2, 2001.

73. Mart Laar, "EU and NATO: Complementarity and Partnership," Ministry of Foreign Affairs of Estonia, Speeches, Estonia in NATO section, May 11, 2001.

74. "Lithuanian President Pledges Support for Ukraine's Pro-Western Aspirations," *Kyiv Post,* November 14, 2006.

75. "Lithuania to Support Georgia on Its Way to NATO," *Georgian Times,* February 2, 2007, www.geotimes.ge/index.php?m=home&newsid=3022.

76. "Regional Opinion, Between the Devil and the Deep Blue Sea," *Warsaw Voice* (compiled from Reuters reports), April 4, 1999.

77. "'New Europe' Backs EU on Iraq," *BBC News,* February 19, 2003.

78. Handy, Pourchot, and Hatch, *Learning from Successful Cooperation,* 64–65.

79. Ministry of Foreign Affairs of Lithuania, "Lithuania's Strategic Partner, Poland to Protect the Air Space of the Baltic States," Press Release, December 30, 2005.

80. Ministry of Foreign Affairs of Lithuania, "Lithuania's Foreign Policy after 2003," Address by Minister of Foreign Affairs Antanas Valionis to the Association of American Chamber of Commerce in Lithuania, Vilnius, January 23, 2003.

81. Antanas Valionis, "Foreign Policy of Lithuania in 2005: The Year of Important Decisions," Ministry of Foreign Affairs of Lithuania, December 29, 2005.

82. Ministry of Foreign Affairs of Lithuania, "EU Welcomed Lithuanian President's Contribution to Resolving the Crisis in Ukraine," Press Release, December 14, 2004.

83. Ministry of Foreign Affairs of Lithuania, "Lithuania Supported Ukraine's Aspirations and Urged Russia to Comply with Its Obligations," Press Release, December 9, 2005.

84. Ministry of Foreign Affairs of Lithuania, "Foreign Minister Antanas Valionis Visited Moscow," Press Release, January 22, 2002.

85. In 2005, a Russian plane crashed over the territory of Lithuania. While the investigation was going on regarding the cause of the crash, the sides spoke amicably and cooperatively toward the common goal of having a resolution on the matter. There were no diplomatic incidents and no "conspiracy" incriminations on either side. Ministry of Foreign Affairs of Lithuania, "Foreign Policy of Lithuania in 2005."

86. Ministry of Foreign Affairs of Estonia, "Estonia as a Nordic Country," Estonia in NATO section, December 14, 1999.

87. Valionis, "Foreign Policy of Lithuania in 2005."

88. Ministry of Foreign Affairs of Lithuania, "Lithuanian Foreign Minister Antanas Valionis Considers the Future of Lithuania Inseparable from the Future of Europe," Press Release, December 6, 2001.

89. Valionis, "Lithuania's Foreign Policy after 2003."

90. Ministry of Foreign Affairs of Lithuania, "The United Kingdom Should Substantially Revise Its Proposal on the EU Budget, December 8, 2005.

91. "Russian Ambassador Discusses Estonian-Russian Relations," *Gateway to Russia,* November 15, 2004.

92. Lithuanian Defense Minister Juozas Olekas in the opening of a NATO-Russia Council meeting, in "Lithuanian Defense Minister Called upon Russia-NATO Council to Abandon 'Cold War' Stereotypes," *Regnum News Agency,* February 28, 2007, www.regnum.ru/english/.

CHAPTER 4

1. IPAPs were launched at the 2002 NATO Prague Summit, to respond to requests from various nonmember countries for deeper cooperation with NATO. For information on IPAP, see NATO Web site, http://www.nato.int/issues/ipap/index.html.

2. Cynthia G. Brown and Farhad Karim, eds., *Playing the "Communal Card": Communal Violence and Human Rights* (New York: Human Rights Watch, 1995), 149.

3. GUAM was named after the initial letters of each cofounding country: Georgia, Ukraine, Azerbaijan, and Moldova. In 1999, Uzbekistan joined and the group was renamed GUUAM. In 2005, Uzbekistan gave up its membership and the group reverted to its initial membership and name. In 2006, members announced expansion of member relations and renamed the group GUAM Organization for Democracy and Economic Development.

4. Helen Fedor, ed., *Belarus: A Country Study* (Washington: Government Publishing Office, the Library of Congress, 1995), "Stalin and Russification" chapter, http://countrystudies.us/belarus/.

5. Ibid., "Perestroika" chapter.

6. Jean-Christophe Peuch, "Ukraine: Regional Leaders Set Up Community of Democratic Choice," *RFE/RL,* December 2, 2005.

7. Bruce Pannier, "Kazakhstan: Astana Puts New Emphasis on Military," *RFE/RL,* June 17, 2003.

8. The symbolism of the Tulip Revolution is not as clear-cut as in the case of the Orange and Rose Revolutions. If orange was Viktor Yushchenko's electoral color and roses were offered by protesters to the Georgian police forces sent to suppress the protests during the Georgian popular revolution, tulips seem to have been picked arbitrarily in Kyrgyzstan. According to eyewitness accounts, anti-Akayev demonstrators initially wore various colors to distinguish themselves in the crowds. They wore yellow ribbons; later the color red was associated with opposition groups from the southern parts of the country. Some people called it the "almond"

revolution, the color of the trees that were blooming when the unrest started. See interview with Sergei Ryspekov, "Kyrgyzstan's Motley Revolution," *Washington Profile* online, May 4, 2005, http://www.washprofile.org/en/node/3387. Other sources indicate that in early February 2005, a wave of popular enthusiasm for democratic change led opposition groups in Kyrgyzstan and Moldova to select revolutionary symbols before actual revolutions started. The tulip was chosen by Kyrgyz groups, and grapes were picked by Moldovan groups. See Fred Weir, "Kyrgyzstan: Tiptoe through Tulips? Democracy Rising in Ex-communist States," *Christian Science Monitor,* February 10, 2005.

9. *Human Rights Watch World Report 2001,* Human Rights Watch Press Backgrounder on Tajikistan (October 5, 2001), www.hrw.org.

10. Ibid.

11. "Turkmen TV Reports Niyazov's Death at 66—Russian Embassy," *Ria Novosti,* December 21, 2006; "Most Eccentric Reforms of the Late Turkmen Leader," *Ria Novosti,* December 21, 2006.

12. Taras Kuzio, "Is Ukraine Any Nearer the Truth on Gongadze's Killing?" *RFE/RL* 3, no. 8 (February 28, 2003).

13. Russia, Kazakhstan, Azerbaijan, Turkmenistan, and Iran do not agree on which waters belong to whom. Iran wants each country bordering on the sea to be legally allocated equal shares of 20 percent of the seabed. Russia, Kazakhstan, and Azerbaijan have signed an agreement that uses the principle of the median line for shared exploration. Under this principle, Iran would get only 13 percent of the seabed, which it does not accept. Turkmenistan has not ratified the Russian-Kazakh agreement either. The dispute over shared exploration slowed down the development of pipelines and intermodal technology for Caspian oil and gas during the nineties. See Christopher Pala, "Caspian Oil to Top Summit Agenda," *International Herald Tribune,* March 12, 2001.

14. Tobias Buck and Neil Buckley, "Russian Parliament Vote Backs Gazprom Export Monopoly," *Financial Times,* June 16, 2006, 8.

15. Transcript of Vladimir Putin's press conference with Russian and foreign media (February 1, 2007), President of Russia/speeches, http://www.kremlin.ru/eng/speeches/2007/02/01/1309_type82915_117609.shtml.

16. "Kocharyan: Iran-Armenia Pipeline a New Stage in Bilateral Relations," *Regnum News Agency,* March 20, 2007; "Iran–Armenia Open Gas Pipeline," *BBC World News,* March 19, 2007.

17. "Armenia Intends to Participate in Construction of Transcaspian Gas Pipeline," *Regnum News Agency,* January 9, 2007.

18. "Baku-Tbilisi-Ceyhan Pipeline Overview," BP Web site, http://www.bp.com/genericarticle.do?categoryId=9006669&contentId=7014358.

19. "AIOC: Oil Production Up, BTC Now Handling All Exports," *FSU Oil and Gas Monitor,* April 25, 2007.

20. Matthew Collin, "Azeris Stop Oil Exports to Russia," *BBC World News,* January 8, 2007.

21. "Azerbaijan Suspends Crude Supplies to Russia—Government," *Ria Novosti,* January 8, 2007.

22. "Belarus to Pay $460 mln Gas Bill to Gazprom Soon—President," *Ria Novosti,* August 2, 2007.

23. Igor Tomberg, "Who Needs the Tariff War?" *Ria Novosti,* February 8, 2007.

24. "Belarus Hits Russia with Oil Tax," *BBC World News,* January 3, 2007.

25. "Belarus Says Informed Russia of Imposing Oil Transit Duty—2," *Ria Novosti,* January 4, 2007.

26. News of the disruption in oil supplies drove the world oil prices from $55 the previous week to $57. See "Russia Oil Row Hits Europe Supply," *BBC World News,* January 8, 2007.

27. "Russia Slashes Belarus Oil Export Duty from $180.7 to $53 per mt," *Ria Novosti,* January 12, 2007.

28. "Belarus to Demand Russia Pay Rent for Land Under Gas, Oil Pipes," *Ria Novosti,* January 23, 2007.

29. "Russia-Belarus Disputes Should Not Affect Military Cooperation—Ivanov," *Ria Novosti,* January 6, 2007.

30. "Tblisi Won't Buy Russian Gas at $230—Georgian President," *Ria Novosti,* November 14, 2006.

31. "Minister Speaks of Diversified Energy Supplies," *Civil Georgia,* October 1, 2006; "Azerbaijan to Become Georgia's Main Gas Supplier from 2007—PM," *Ria Novosti,* December 20, 2006.

32. "Georgia Yields to Gas Prices of Gazprom," *Kommersant,* December 25, 2006.

33. "Gazprom Sets Price for Georgia at $235 per 1,000 cu m," *Ria Novosti,* December 20, 2006.

34. "Nogaideli: Georgia Will Receive Azerbaijani Gas at Price of $120," *Regnum News Agency,* December 29, 2006; "Saakashvili: Georgia Will Turn Down Russian Gas as soon as It Starts Receiving It from Azerbaijan," *Regnum News Agency,* December 28, 2006.

35. "Azerbaijani Natural Gas Starts Flowing into Georgia," *Ria Novosti,* January 10, 2007.

36. "Azerbaijan's Shah Deniz Field on Stream," *Oil Voice* press release, December 15, 2006, http://www.oilvoice.com/n/Azerbaijans_Shah_Deniz_Field_On_Stream/6f7f7be8.aspx; "SCP Commissioning Commences," BP press release, June 1, 2006, http://www.bp.com/genericarticle.do?categoryId=9006615&contentId=7018471.

37. "Georgia, Iran Sign Barter Agreement on Electricity Supplies," *Ria Novosti,* October 24, 2006. "Iran, Georgia Sign Electricity Deal," *Civil Georgia,* October 24, 2006.

38. "Discours Succint du Président Nursultan Nazarbayev devant le Corps Diplomatique, Accrédité au Kazakhstan, le 21 Octobre 2005 à Astana," Actualites, Bulletin Special no. 40, Ambassade du Kazakhstan en France (November 3, 2005), http://www.amb-kazakhstan.fr/news_view/103.

39. "While Russia Watches, Kazakhstan and Azerbaijan Explore New Ties," *Eurasia Net,* March 3, 2004.

40. "Kazakhstan Inks BTC Deal," *Oil Daily,* June 19, 2006, 7.

41. "While Russia Watches, Kazakhstan and Azerbaijan Explore New Ties."

42. "Central Asia: Russian, Turkmen, Kazak Leaders Agree on Caspian Pipeline," *RFE/RL,* May 12, 2007.

43. "Kazakhstan, China Consider Gas Pipeline Construction," *FSU Oil and Gas Monitor,* December 7, 2005.

44. "Kazakhstan, China Agree to Extend Oil Pipeline 'Almost' to Caspian Sea," *BBC World News,* December 25, 2006.

45. "Kazakhstan Seeks Higher Gas Transit Prices for Russia," *Ria Novosti,* November 30, 2006.

46. Nursultan Nazarbayev, "A New Kazakhstan in a New World: President Nazarbayev's Strategic Vision," excerpts from the February 28, 2007 State of the Union Address, *Kazakhstan's Echo* 36 (Embassy of Kazakhstan to the United States, March 2, 2007).

47. Andrey Kolesnikov, "Vladimir Putin Charged Ukraine," *Kommersant* (Moscow, December 9, 2005), www.kommersant.com.

48. "Comment on Naftogaz Ukrainy's Statement from 7 December 2005," *Gazprom Information Division,* December 7, 2005, http://www.gazprom.com/eng/news/2005/12/18443.shtml.

49. Maria Danilova, "No More Cheap Gas, Russia Tells Neighbors," *Associated Press,* November 28, 2005.

50. Kolesnikov, "Vladimir Putin Charged Ukraine."

51. See "Mittal Steel Company Acquires a 93% Stake in Kryvorizhstal in Ukraine," Mittal Press Release, October 24, 2005. The sale was possible after Viktor Yushchenko came to power and reversed several shady privatizations of state assets by his predecessor, Leonid Kuchma, to pro-Kremlin businessmen. Kryvorizhstal had been previously sold to Kuchma's son-in-law for $800 million, in what was largely seen as a case of high-level state corruption in the Ukrainian government. A Court reversed the sale of the steel mill, upon Yushchenko's and Prime Minister Yulia Tymoshenko's request for a reevaluation of the privatization process. As the Orange government of Yushchenko and Tymoshenko planned to dispute further shady privatizations that seemed to indicate strong connections to Moscow, the Kremlin may have become nervous about how far and how deep the process would go.

52. "Russia Approves Plan to Double Domestic Natural Gas Prices," *Reuters,* November 30, 2006.

53. "Pledging to Restore Supplies," *BBC World News,* January 3, 2005.

54. "Ukraine Looking to Feed Energy Needs by Developing Coal, Nuclear," *Ria Novosti,* March 23, 2006.

55. "Moldovan Government Approves National Energy Strategy until 2020," *Infotag,* July 26, 2007; "2007 to Become a Turning Point in Moldova's Energy System's Development," *Moldpres,* January 10, 2007.

56. "Official: Ukraine Won't Buy Russian Gas Next Year in Favor," *Associated Press,* October 9, 2006.

57. Legislation was proposed by BYuT (Yulia Tymoshenko Bloc) and Our Ukraine, who forced the issue to be put on the parliamentary agenda by blocking the podium in the Verkhovna Rada. The bill was supported by 408 out of 448 registered deputies, according to BYuT, *INFORM Newsletter* 30 (Kyiv, February 12, 2007).

58. "Ukraine Accuses Russia of Applying Political Pressure in Gas Dispute," *Associated Press,* October 11, 2007.

59. Olga Mordyushenko and Oleg Gavrish, "Gazprom Calls on Ukraine to Clear Debt," *Kommersant,* October 3, 2007.

60. "Turkmenistan Agrees Russian Gas Deal," *BBC World News,* December 18, 1999.

61. "Turkmenistan Invites U.S. Firm to Work in Energy Sector," *RFE/RL,* May 4, 2007.

62. "Petro-China Plans Massive Gas Pipeline," *Herald News,* August 24, 2007.

63. Statement by the President of Turkmenistan, His Excellency Gurbanguly Berdymukhammedov, at the 62nd Session of the UN General Assembly (New York: September 26, 2007), 8.

64. Antoine Blua, "Turkmenistan: Environmentalists Concerned about Oil, Gas Development," *RFE/RL,* September 27, 2007.

65. "Central Asia: Russian, Turkmen, Kazakh Leaders Agree on Caspian Pipeline."

66. *Komsomol'skaia Pravda,* January 22, 1992.

67. *Izvestia,* May 26, 1992, quoted in the evening edition.

68. Articles in *Nezavisimaia Gazeta,* May 5, 1994 and March 24, 1995.

69. Quoted in *Literaturnaya Gazeta,* December 11, 1996, and *Narodna Armiya,* December 11, 1996.

70. *Reuters,* March 20, 1995.

71. *Kievskie Vedomosti,* July 21, 1998.

72. Julie A. Corwin and Jan Maksymiuk, "Sparring Over Sevastopol," *RFE/RL,* February 11, 1999.

73. "Lebed Says Moscow-Kyiv Treaty Needs Changes," *RFE/RL,* February 11, 1999.

74. "Ukraine's Foreign Ministry: Russia Must Obey Court Order to Return Crimean Lighthouses," *Kyiv Post,* January 26, 2007.

75. Vladimir Putin, "Transcript of the Hot Line with President of Russia Vladimir Putin," October 25, 2006, http://www.kremlin.ru.

76. "Ukrainian Foreign Minister Is Calming Russia: Terms of Rent of Bases by Russian Black Sea Fleet Will Not Be Revised Until 2017," *Regnum News Agency,* August 27, 2007.

77. The two most widely known and quoted sources on the topic are Robert Conquest, *The Harvest of Sorrow: Soviet Collectivization and the Terror-Famine* (New York: Oxford University Press, 1986), and R. W. Davies and Stephen G. Wheatcroft, *The Years of Hunger: Soviet Agriculture, 1931–1933* (Houndmills, Basingstoke, Hampshire, and NY: Palgrave Macmillan, 2004). Conquest argues that the Holodomor was intentional Soviet policy of extermination of undesirable nationalist Ukrainians. Davies and Wheatcroft argue that the Holodomor was a by-product of Soviet inept agricultural planning, overzealousness, and poor economic management. Davies and Wheatcroft gained access to recently declassified Soviet archives to make the case that the death toll was not nearly as high as 10 million, although they recognized that a million and a half dead from famine is a tremendous figure.

78. Strobe Talbott, ed., *Khrushchev Remembers,* with an Introduction, Commentary and Notes by Edward Crankshaw (Boston: Little, Brown & Comp., 1970), 71–75.

79. Davies and Wheatcroft, *Years of Hunger,* 134.

80. Ibid., 133.

81. Ibid., 436–41.

82. Conquest, *Harvest of Sorrow,* 325–26.

83. Ibid., 322–30.

84. "Russia Bristles at Ukrainian Officials Push for Declaring Soviet-Era Famine as Genocide," *AP Moscow,* October 25, 2006.

85. Borys Tarasiuk, "Address at the General Debate of the Sixty-First Session of the General Assembly of the United Nations," 5 (September 25, 2006), http://www.un.org/webcast/ga/61/pdfs/ukraine-e.pdf.

86. "President Yushchenko Proposes Parliament Recognize 1932–1933 Holodomor as Genocide of the Ukrainian People," and "Yushchenko Suggests Parliament Pass Law Establishing Fines for Public Denial of 1932–1933 Famine," *Ukrainian News Agency,* Kyiv, November 2, 2006.

87. "Ukraine Marks 73rd Anniversary of Forced Soviet-Era Famine that Killed 10 Million," *Kyiv Post,* November 27, 2006.

88. Taras Kuzio, "Ukrainian Parliament Prepares Bill on Recognition of OUN-UPA," *Ukrainian Weekly* 70, no. 30 (July 28, 2002).

89. Jan Maksymiuk, "Poland President Expresses Regret over 1947 Akcja Wisla," *Ukrainian Weekly* 70, no. 17 (April 28, 2002).

90. "President Yushchenko Blames Communist Regime for Its Crimes Especially for Operation Wisla," *Interfax,* Ukraine, April 27, 2007; and "President Yushchenko & President

Kaczynski Honor Memory of Victims of Operation Wisla," *Ukrainian News Agency,* Kyiv, April 27, 2007.

91. "Lviv to Bury the Remains of NKVD Victims at the Lychakivsky Cemetery on 7 November," Kharkiv Human Rights Protection Group Web site, Human Rights in Ukraine, October 22, 2006, http://www.khpg.org/en/index.php?id=1161553853.

92. Tadeusz Barzdo, "Ukraine: Rapprochement with Russia," *Warsaw Voice,* March 22, 1998.

93. Gennady Chuffrin, deputy director of the Institute of World Economy and International Relations in Moscow, quoted in Fred Weir, "Color Revolutions Wane," *Christian Science Monitor,* March 7, 2006.

94. Tatiana Poloskova, deputy director of the independent Institute of Modern Diaspora, quoted in Weir, "Tiptoe through Tulips?"

95. Interview with CBS anchor Mike Wallace, Ministry of Foreign Affairs, Information and Press Department Web site, May 9, 2005.

96. Vladimir Simonov, "Russia Devises Protection Against Color Revolutions," *Ria Novosti,* December 26, 2005.

97. M.K. Bhadrakumar, "Kyrgyzstan Caught in U.S.-Russia Squeeze," *Asia Times,* November 7, 2006.

99. In 1922, the Union of Soviet Socialist Republics was agreed by three founding states, the Republic of Belarus, the Russian Federation, and Ukraine, who called themselves "the High Contracting Parties." In the Agreement on the Establishment of the Commonwealth of Independent States, the three countries retain this terminology and resolve that "the Union of Soviet Socialist Republics, as a subject of international law and a geopolitical reality, hereby terminates its existence." The same High Contracting Parties agree to establish the CIS.

98. Interview with Sergei Ryspekov, "Kyrgyzstan's Motley Revolution," *Washington Profile,* May 4, 2005.

100. Agreement on the Establishment of the Commonwealth of Independent States, protocol signed on December 8, 1991 in the city of Minsk, Belarus, http://therussiasite.org/legal/laws/CISagreement.html.

101. "Moldovan President Criticizes Single Economic Space Decision," *RFE/RL* 7, no. 180 (September 22, 2003).

102. "Experts Hears Death Bells Ringing for Russia's CIS," *Agency France Press,* April 4, 2004.

103. *Interfax,* April 9, 2005, http://www.interfax.ru/e/B/politics/28.html?id_issue =11267754.

104. "Saakashvili Comments on CIS," *Civil Georgia,* May 2, 2006, http://www.civil.ge/eng/article.php?id=12463.

105. "Georgia Still Mulling Exit from CIS—Deputy Premier," *Ria Novosti,* May 25, 2006.

106. "What the Russian Newspaper Say: CIS Unable to Carry Out Reforms," *Ria Novosti,* October 11, 2006.

107. "Mikhail Saakshvili Would Not Come to Moscow for Victory Celebrations," *Ria Novosti,* May 6, 2005.

108. "Georgia Claims that Russia Stops Supporting Abkhazia," *Regnum News Agency,* August 28, 2007.

109. Statement by H.E. Mr. Mikheil Saakashvili, President of Georgia at the 61st session of the United Nations General Assembly (New York: September 22, 2006).

110. "Russia Urges Solution to Transdnestr Conflict—Ambassador," *Ria Novosti,* March 20, 2006.

111. "Moldovan Minister Blasts Russian Ambassador over Allegations," *Ria Novosti,* March 23, 2006.

112. "Russian Aid Convoy to Transdnestr a Provocation—Ukraine," *Ria Novosti,* March 24, 2006.

113. Sarah Rainsford, "Ukraine Demands Russia's Respect," *BBC World News,* April 15, 2005.

114. Martha Brill Olcott, "The Shanghai Cooperation Organization: Changing the 'Playing Field' in Central Asia," testimony before the Helsinki Commission (Washington DC: September 26, 2006), 11.

115. Claire Bigg, "East: Making Sense of Post-Soviet Alphabet Soup," *RFE/RL,* October 10, 2007.

116. Peuch, "Ukraine: Regional Leaders Set Up Community of Democratic Choice."

117. Erika Weinthal, "Water Conflict and Cooperation in Central Asia," Occasional Paper for *UN Human Development Report 2006* (UNDP: 2006/32).

118. Pannier, "Kazakhstan: Astana Puts New Emphasis on Military."

119. "Rice to Visit Pakistan: U.S. Reaches Airbase Agreement with Kyrgyzstan," *CNN News,* October 12, 2005.

120. Charles Carlson, "Uzbekistan: Karimov Says Improved Relations with Russia Not at Expense of U.S. Ties," *RFE/RL,* September 4, 2003.

121. Venera Djumataeva, "Kyrgyzstan: Politicians Underline Pro-Russian Stances Ahead of SCO Summit," *RFE/RL,* August 10, 2007.

122. *Interfax,* July 5, 2005.

123. Bruce Pannier, "Kyrgyzstan: U.S. Defense Secretary Seeking Support for Air Base," *RFE/RL,* June 5, 2007.

124. Statement by the President of Turkmenistan at the 62nd Session of the UN General Assembly, UN Web site, 3–4.

125. European Commission External Relations, "EU-Moldova Action Plan," http://ec.europa.eu/external_relations/moldova/index_en.htm.

126. James Rodgers, "Georgia's NATO Bid Irks Russia," *BBC World News,* November 28, 2006.

127. "Georgia Allowed to Join EU Political Statements," *Ria Novosti,* June 4, 2007.

128. "EU Forges Closer Cooperation with Ukraine Over Free Trade," *Europa Newsletter* 92 (November 10, 2006).

129. "Ukrainian Defense Minister: Joining NATO, Securing Gas Supplies Are Country's Priorities," *Kyiv Post,* October 13, 2006.

130. "Ukraine Parliament Backs PM Yanukovych on NATO Reluctance," *Ria Novosti,* September 19, 2006.

131. "Ukraine's PM Says His Nation Hopes to Join WTO Next February," *Kyiv Post,* October 20, 2006.

132. "Ukrainian Parliament Suddenly Gives First Reading Approval to Seven WTO Related Bills," *BBC,* Ukraine, November 2, 2006.

133. "Yushchenko: Bad Relations with Russia Will Hurt Ukraine's Bid to Join the European Union," *Kyiv Post,* November 15, 2006.

134. Barzdo, "Ukraine: Rapprochement with Russia."

135. "Russia Blamed Over Poison Probe," *BBC,* September 11, 2007.

CHAPTER 5

1. Andrei Kortunov in "Uneasy Alliance," *PBS News Hour,* February 7, 1997.

2. Pavel Felgenhauer quoted in James Rodgers, "Georgia's NATO Bid Irks Russia," *BBC World News,* November 28, 2006.

3. Gennady Gerasimov in "Uneasy Alliance."

4. Krzysztof Pilawski, "Russia Turning on the Charm," *Warsaw Voice,* July 20, 1997.

5. "Putin Attacks West Ahead of G-8 Summit," *Associated Press,* June 4, 2007.

6. "Putin Warns of Measures Against U.S. Missile Shield in Europe," *Ria Novosti,* June 4, 2007.

7. Few official pronouncements have been made by Russian politicians regarding EU membership. One of the strongest supporters of Russia in EU was former Italian Silvio Berlusconi, who raised the issue after meeting with Vladimir Putin in Moscow in 2003. See "EU Membership Next Step for Russia after NATO," *Associated France Press,* May 28, 2002; and Jeff Israeli, "Do Not Adjust Your Seats," *Time World,* June 29, 2003, http://www.time.com/time/magazine/article/0,9171,901030707-461792,00.html.

8. A ten-year PCA came in force in 1997, establishing the formal framework for bilateral cooperation. An Energy Dialogue framework came in force in 2000, for issues related to nuclear energy, natural resources, science and research bilateral issues. Four "common spaces" were agreed in 2003: a common economic space; a space of freedom, security, and justice; a space of cooperation in the field of external security; and a space for research, education, and cultural work together. See overview and details on the European Commission's Web site, external relations, http://ec.europa.eu/external_relations/russia/intro/index.htm.

9. Prime Minister Mikhail Fradkov at a CIS meeting in Ukraine, quoted in Maria Danilova, "No More Cheap Gas, Russia Tells Neighbors," *Associated Press,* Moscow, November 28, 2005.

10. "Russian Government Raises Export Duties for Oil Shipments to Belarus," *Kyiv Post,* December 13, 2006.

11. Oleg Gavrish and Natalia Grib, "The Price of the Vote," *Kommersant,* October 20, 2007.

12. Transcript of press conference with Russian and foreign media (February 1, 2007), President of Russia/speeches, http://www.kremlin.ru/eng/speeches/2007/02/01/1309_type82915_117609.shtml.

13. "No More Free Natural Gas for Anyone—First Deputy PM Medvedev," *Ria Novosti,* January 27, 2007.

14. "Interview with Javier Solana, the European Union's High Representative for the Common Foreign and Security Policy, ahead of the Russia-EU summit in Samara," *Ria Novosti,* May 15, 2007.

15. "Wrap: Russia-EU Summit Highlights Divisions with New EU Members," *Ria Novosti,* May 18, 2007.

16. Jose Manuel Barroso, "Energizing Europe: A Real Market with Secure Supply," Opening Remarks at Press Conference on the Commission's Energy Package, Speech 07/553 (Brussels: September 19, 2007), 3.

17. Alexander Radugin, "Europe Takes Effort to Dismember Russia's Gazprom," translated by Dmitry Sudakov, *Pravda,* September 20, 2007, http://english.pravda.ru.

18. Yekaterina Kuznetsova, "Why Is Europe Powerless to Do Anything?" *Ria Novosti,* May 17, 2007.

19. Nikolai Mezhevich, Director of the Center for Transborder Studies in St. Petersburg, in an interview with Regnum news agency, "Expert: Estonia Is Winning 'International Contest' in Worsening Relations with Russia," *Regnum News Agency,* September 20, 2007.

20. "Putin Says Russia Not Dramatizing Delay in Talks on Deal with EU—1," *Ria Novosti,* May 18, 2007.

21. Speech and the following discussion at the Munich conference on security policy, President of Russia official Web portal, February 10, 2007, www.kremlin.ru/eng/text/themes/2007/02/101158_118075.shtml.

22. Vladimir Putin, "Annual Address to the Federal Assembly of the Russian Federation," April 25, 2005, President of Russia Web site, speeches, www.kremlin.ru/eng/.

23. "Putin Defends His 'Democracy,'" interview with CBS anchor Mike Wallace, May 9, 2005, www.cbsnews.com/stories/2005/05/06/60minutes/main693422_page3.shtml.

24. Ibid.

25. "Excerpts from Transcript of Meeting with Participants in the National Russian Conference of Humanities and Social Sciences Teachers," President of Russia Web site, speeches, June 21, 2007, www.kremlin.ru.

26. Interview with CBS's Mike Wallace.

27. Ibid.

28. "Arrests over Russia Writer Murder," *BBC World News,* August 28, 2007.

29. Anna Politkovskaya, "J'Accuse: Her Own Death Foretold," translated from Russian by Arch Tait, *Washington Post,* October 15, 2006, B01. This article was written two months before Politkovskaya's murder.

30. "Over 600 NGOs Closed in Russia This Year," *Kommersant,* August 20, 2007, www.kommersant.com.

31. "NGOs Face Suspension in Russia," *BBC World News,* October 18, 2006. "Russia's Re-Registration Deadline Met by 108 Foreign NGOs," *Ria Novosti,* October 19, 2006.

32. Patrick Jackson, "From Fake Rocks to Dummy NGOs," *BBC News,* Moscow, February 2, 2006.

33. Speech and the following discussion at the Munich conference.

34. Peter Baker and Peter Finn, "Bush Reaches to Putin as Relations Continue to Slide," *Washington Post,* May 31, 2007, A01.

35. Gorbachev, *Perestroika,* 192.

36. Ibid., 200.

37. Ibid., 193.

38. "Excerpts from Transcript of Meeting with Participants in the National Russian Conference of Humanities and Social Sciences Teachers."

39. Ibid.

40. The history book in question is not available at the time of this writing. It is titled *A Book for Teachers: The Modern History of Russia, 1945–2006.* The last chapter, "Sovereign Democracy," seems to embody Putin's vision for the country, as strong, proud of its heritage, no-nonsense, no apologies needed type of country. See Dmitry Babich, "On the Wrong Side of History: A New Teachers' Manual Provokes Debate," *Johnson's Russia List* 6, no. 161 (July 25, 2007); and Tony Halpin, "Textbooks Rewrite History to Fit Putin's Vision," *Times,* July 30, 2007, http://www.timesonline.co.uk/tol/news/world/europe/article2163481.ece.

41. Vladimir Putin, "Annual Address to the Federal Assembly of the Russian Federation," April 25, 2005, President of Russia Web site, speeches, www.kremlin.ru/eng/.

42. Putin-Wallace interview.

43. "President Rejects Comparisons between Economic and Soviet Unions," *RFL/RL* 7, no. 180 (September 22, 2003).

44. "Russian Senators Commemorate Hungary's 1956 Revolution," *Ria Novosti,* October 20, 2006.

45. W.Z., "Massacre Remembered," *Warsaw Voice,* September 26, 2007.

46. "Ascribing Victory to Stalin Denigrates Popular Feat," *Ria Novosti,* May 3, 2005.

47. "It's a Lie that We Fought Without Skill," *Ria Novosti,* May 3, 2005.

48. Ibid.

49. Ibid.

50. Fyodor Lukyanov in an interview with BBC, "Viewpoint: Russia's Missile Fears," *BBC World News,* June 7, 2007.

51. M.K. Bhadrakumar, "Fergana's Ghosts Haunt Central Asia," *Asia Times Online,* March 24, 2005.

52. "Igor Ivanov: Georgia, Kyrgyzstan and Ukraine Revolutions Have Nothing in Common with Democracy," *Ria Novosti,* May 4, 2005.

53. Luke Harding, "Kremlin Accuses U.S. of Deception on East European Interceptor Bases," *Guardian,* April 11, 2007.

54. "Russia Defeated Totalitarianism in Cold War—Kremlin Official," *Ria Novosti,* June 28, 2006.

55. Gennady Gerasimov in "Uneasy Alliance."

56. Putin-Wallace interview.

57. "Russia Defeated Totalitarianism in Cold War."

58. "No More Free Natural Gas for Anyone—First Deputy PM Medvedev."

Index

Abkhazia, 68–69, 106, 108, 123
Acquis communautaire, 31
Adamkus, Valdas, 59
Akayev, Askar, 5, 71
Aliyev, Heydar, 66
Aliyev, Ilham, 67, 82, 86
alternative realities, 118–36, 140–42
Andijan, 78, 113
annexation of Baltic countries. *See* Soviet
    Union
Ansip, Andrus, 50
Armenia: energy issues, 81; history, 65–66
assertive sovereignty, 1, 7, 11, 30–31, 37,
    40, 48, 54, 57–60, 62, 65, 69, 82, 86–
    87, 92, 107–10, 113–19, 139–42. *See
    also* sovereign assertiveness;
    sovereign-mindedness
August coup, 2–3, 25, 40, 71, 76
Azerbaijan: energy issues, 81–83; history,
    66–67

Balcerowitz, Lecek, 18; plan, 19
Baltic states: Baltic Way, 42–43, 51, 76;
    borders, 52–53; Council of the Baltic
    Sea States, 40; history, 41–44; security
    arrangements, 60. *See also* Bronze
    Soldier; EU; NATO

Belarus: energy issues,
    83–84; history, 67–68
Berdymukhammedov, Gurbanguly, 92, 114
Black January, 66
Black Sea Fleet, 93–96, 123
borders. *See* Baltic states
Bronze Soldier, 49–51
BTC (Baku-Tbilisi-Ceyhan pipeline), 67,
    81–82, 84–86

CDC, 110
Central Europe, 12–14
Charter 77, 13
Chechnya, 129
Chernobyl (cultural), 67
Chirac, François, 34–35, 60, 136
CIS (Commonwealth of Independent
    States), 3, 65, 68, 77, 105–7, 113;
    demise, 105–6; withdrawal from, 75,
    106
citizenship: for Russians living in Baltic
    states, 53–54, 133
civil and political rights: in Central Europe,
    15–16, 22–24. *See also* civil society
civil society: in the Baltic states, 47–48; in
    Central Europe, 22–24. *See also* civil and
    political rights; media freedom

civil war: in Tajikistan, 5, 73–74, 78; in Yugoslavia, 3, 30. *See also names of specific countries*

Clark, Wesley, 30

Cold Peace, 121

Cold War, 12, 21, 28, 32, 35, 63, 93, 119, 122, 136–37; second, 1, 10, 118, 120, 136–38; "new," 36, 39

collectivization, 76

color revolutions, 1, 64, 101, 103, 106, 122; financed by the West, 103–4, 136; Orange, 5, 27, 61, 77, 88, 89, 115; Rose, 5, 69; Tulip, 5, 71, 104. *See also names of specific countries*

Common Security and Foreign Policy, 31

communism: anticommunism, 13; collapse, 1–2, 12, 25

conspiracy theories, 118, 124, 140–42; Central Europe as a U.S. tool against Russia, 126; crime in Russia as a Western plot, 129; encirclement of Russia, 119; NGOs in Russia as Western spies, 129–30; West's double standards toward Russia, 126–27

constitutional reform: in the Baltic states, 43–45; in Belarus, 68; in Central Europe, 14–17. *See also* civil and political rights; elections

core-periphery relations, 1, 3–4, 63, 89, 122; in Central Asia, 78, 105–10; decoupling from core, 4, 55–56, 59, 64, 81

crime: in Tajikistan, 74; in Ukraine, 76, 101; in Uzbekistan, 78. *See also* Politkovskaya, Anna; Russia

Crimea, 93–96. *See also* Sevastopol

Curzon line, 35

democratization, 14–17; Central Asia, 100–104; Central Europe, early 90s, 6; Russia's role in Central Europe, 119. *See also* constitutional reform; political pluralism

deportations: of Balts, 42, 55; of Belarusians, 67; of Georgians, 68; of Jews, 42, 76; of Kazakhs, 70; of Moldovans, 72; of Tartars, 93; of

Ukrainians, 76, 93. *See also* Great Purge; Operation Visla

Druzhba pipeline, 56, 79, 83, 84, 124

Eastern Europe: after WWII, Russia's version, 132; history, 2–5

economic freedom, 21–22, 46. *See also* appendix II

economic pressure: by Russia on the Baltic states, 56–57; on Belarus, 83; on Central Asia, 79; on Georgia, 85; on Ukraine, 88–89. *See also* Russia

economic reforms: in the Baltic states, 45–46; in Central Asia, 102–3; in Central Europe, 18–22; in Georgia, 69

economy: economic crisis in Bulgaria, 20; privatization, in the Baltics, 45–46; privatization, in Central Europe, 19–20; recession, in Czech Republic, 19; recession, in Romania, 20; state-run, 15–16. *See also* economic reforms; free markets; market economy; shock therapy

education: bilingual in Baltic states, 54; programs for Russians, 53–54

elections: "double majority" system, 33–34; in Azerbaijan, 67; in Central Asia, 101; in Georgia, 69; in Kyrgyzstan, 71–72; in Tajikistan, 74; in Ukraine, 61; post-1990, 14–16, 70; Soviet Union rigging in the Baltic countries, 41; Soviet Union rigging in Central Europe, 11. *See also* appendix I

energy: Charter, 125; dependence on Russia, Armenia, 66; Belarus, 68, 83; Georgia, 69, 84; Moldova, 73, 87–88; Ukraine, 87–88; diversification, Armenia, 81; Moldova, 90; Ukraine, 90; independence from Russia, 82, 85, 86, 91; interdependence, Russia and Central Asia, 79–80, 83, 86, 91; security, for Central Asia, 79

Estonia: Internet attacks, 50–51, 124; Students Society, 47

EU: constitutional debate, 32–34; energy charter with Russia, 125; enlargement, 4, 119, 123; *euro,* 31, 46;

intergovernmental conference, 33–34;
Ioannina mechanisms, 34; Lisbon
Strategy, 31; Maastricht Treaty, 31;
membership for Baltic states, 56–57;
membership for Central Europe, 31–32;
for Georgia, 114; for Moldova, 88, 114;
for Ukraine, 116; Nice Treaty, 33;
PHARE, 31; Russia agreements, 123;
solidarity with new members, 124
Europe: old versus new, 34–35, 62

Fotyga, Anna, 37
free markets: in Central Europe, 15–20. *See
also* market economy
Freedom Monument, 51
Fulton Address, 11

gas crises: Moldova, 87; Ukraine, 77, 89,
91. *See also* economic pressure; Gazprom
Gazprom: fees, 80, 123; to Kazakhstan, 87;
to Turkmenistan, 91; monopoly, 79,
125; price increases for Armenia, 81; for
Azerbaijan, 82; for Belarus, 83; for
Georgia, 69, 84–85; for Moldova, 73,
88; for Ukraine, 88. *See also* appendix IV
Georgia: energy issues,
84–85; history, 68–69
Gerasimov, Gennady, 7, 121, 137
Germany: occupation of Baltic countries,
42; occupation of Ukraine, 76;
reunification, 3–4; Russia's version of
post-WWII, 131
Glasnost, 4, 7, 42, 66, 68, 71, 72, 76
Gorbachev, Mikhail, 2–4, 7, 36, 43, 67,
131, 136, 141
Great Famine. *See* Holodomor
Great Game, 64
Great Purge, 133
GUAM, 67, 69, 73, 77, 78, 110

Havel, Vaclav, 13, 28
history: controversy over Baltic states
annexation, 41–44, 133; controversy
over Ukraine, 77, 93–100;
Russia-Central Europe reconciliation,
134, 141–42; Russian revisionism, 131–
36; Soviet Union in WWII, 134–35. *See*

also Black Sea Fleet; Central Europe;
deportations; Eastern Europe; Holodo-
mor; monuments; Russia
Holocaust, 54, 97
Holodomor, 76, 93, 96–99
Horn, Gyula, 28

IGC (intergovernmental conference).
See EU
Iliescu, Ion, 21, 28, 34
Ilves, Hendrik Toomas, 50, 62
independence: Armenia, 65; Azerbaijan,
66; Baltic states, 40, 43; Belarus, 68;
Central Asia, 64; Crimea, 93; Estonia,
59; Georgia, 68; Kazakhstan, 70;
Kyrgyzstan, 71; Lithuania, 2; Moldova,
72; Turkmenistan, 75; Ukraine, 3, 76,
99; Uzbekistan, 77.
See also names of break away republics
Internet attacks. *See* Estonia
Ioannina mechanisms. *See* EU
IPAP (Individual Partnership Action Plan):
for Armenia, 66; for Azerbaijan, 67; for
Georgia, 69, 114; for Kazakhstan, 71;
for Moldova, 73; for Ukraine, 77
Iraq war: Baltic support, 60; Central
Europe support, 34

Jaunlatgale/Abrene district, 52. *See also*
Pytalovo district

Kaczyński, Jarosław, 33, 35–37
Kaczyński, Lech, 35, 133
Karimov, Islam, 78, 113
Kavan, Jan, 32
Kazakhstan: energy issues, 86–87; history,
70–71
Khrushchev, Nikita, 12, 67, 93
Kosovo, 3, 30, 59
Kravchuk, Leonid, 76
Kuchma, Leonid, 27, 61, 76–77, 94, 102
Kukan, Eduard, 34
Kupa, Mihaly, 19
Kwaśniewski, Aleksander, 32, 99
Kyrgyzstan: U.S. bases in, 112

Language: law in Moldova, 72;

Russification in the Baltic states, 53; in Belarus, 67; in Ukraine, 76
Latvia: Environmental Protection Club, 47
Lavrov, Sergei, 51
Lisbon Strategy. *See* EU
Lithuania Green Movement, 47
London Declaration. *See* NATO
Lukashenko, Alexander, 64, 68, 83, 84
Lukin, Vladimir, 94

Maastricht Treaty. *See* EU
market economy, 17–18
Marx, Karl, 7
Mazeikiu Nafta, 56
Meciar, Vladimir, 20
media freedom, 23–24, 47, 75–76, 101–2. *See also* appendix III
Military bases, placement of U.S., 1, 72, 78, 112, 119
missile defense shield in Central Europe, 36–37, 122, 136
Moldova: energy issues, 89–90; history, 72–73; new customs regulations on Trans-Dniester, 109
Molotov-Ribbentrop secret protocol, 41–42, 72, 131
monuments: dismantling symbols of communism, 37–38; war of, 49–51, 122. *See also* Bronze Soldier; Freedom Monument; Parnu

Nagorno-Karabakh, 65, 66
Nashi, 50
NATO: enlargement, 4, 119; enlargement to the Baltic countries, 57–59; enlargement to Central Europe, 27–31; enlargement versus expansion, 58, 120–26; first combat operation, 3, 30, 32, 59; London Declaration, 27; membership for Georgia, 114; membership for Ukraine, 115; Russia consultative arrangements, 4; Russia Council, 63, 121; *Study on Enlargement,* 28
Nice Treaty. *See* EU
Niyazov, Saparmurat, 5, 64, 75, 91, 113

Oder-Neisse line, 35

Operation Visla, 99–100
Ossetia: North, 69, 108; South, 68–69, 108, 123

Parnu, 49
perestroika, 4, 7, 42, 67, 68
PfP (Partnership for Peace), 30, 112; Armenia, 65; Azerbaijan, 67; Georgia, 69; Kazakhstan, 71; Kyrgyzstan, 72; Moldova, 73; Tajikistan, 74; Turkmenistan, 75; Ukraine, 77; Uzbekistan, 78
PHARE. *See* EU
pipelines: Atasu-Alashankou, 87; Baku-Novorossiysk, 82; CTC (Caspian Pipeline Consortium), 86; Gadzhigabul-Gazakh, 85; Iran-Armenia, 81; Yamal, 79, 83. *See also* BTC; Druzhba pipeline
Polish Claims Society, 35
political pluralism: in the Baltic states, 45; in Central Europe, 16–17; in Uzbekistan, 78
Politkovskaya, Anna, 128–29
Potsdam conference, 35, 131
Prague Spring, 13, 25
Pristina, 30, 122
Prussian Claims Society, 35–36
Putin, Vladimir, 4, 7, 51, 52, 61, 69, 77, 79, 80, 84, 88–89, 95, 103, 105, 122, 124, 126–28, 130, 132–33, 136–37
Pytalovo district, 52. *See also* Jaunlatgale/Abrene district

Rakhmonov, Emomali, 74
Red Army: occupation of Baltics, 41–42; occupation of Georgia, 68; occupation of Ukraine, 76; sacrifice, 48
referendum: to approve a renewed Soviet Union, 2, 71, 75, 93; on EU membership, Poland, 33; for independence, Azerbaijan, 66; for independence, Ukraine, 3; to reunite with Russia, Trans-Dniester, 73. *See also* independence
restitutions: material claims, for Baltic states, 49, 52; property, for Germans, 35

revolutions: in Czechoslovakia, 13, 25; in Hungary, 12, 25, 133–34. *See also* color revolutions; Prague Spring; Velvet Revolution
Rosati, Dariusz, 29
Roundtable Talks, 13
Rukhnama, 75
Russia: ban on Georgian wine, 69, 106; ban on Polish food, 37, 124, 126; blockade of cargo, Baltics, 51; civil society, 104, 129–30; crime, 128–29; crisis in banking system, 46; democracy, 126–31; EU negotiations, 124; great power status, 4, 127, 133, 138–39; media freedom, 128; military bases, 65, 69, 74, 84, 95, 107–8; NATO Council, 121, 140; neo-expansionism, 1, 108, 118, 138; new history book, 132–33; opposition to NATO enlargement, 29, 57–58; pressure on Eurasian countries, 122; on Kazakhstan, 87; on Ukraine, 90–91; relations with Baltic states, 63; reliability as energy provider, 73, 81, 87, 88; restraint from military or political interference, 4–5, 7, 16, 17, 45, 46, 65; role in the democratization of Central Europe, 132; (military) support for breakaway republics, 74, 123; withdrawal of military, 61, 73, 106. *See also* Politkovskaya, Anna; Sinatra doctrine

Saakashvili, Mikhail, 69, 84–85, 106, 108
Sachs, Jeffrey, 18
Schroeder, Gerhard, 33, 136
Screening Law, 38
secessionist movements: in Azerbaijan, 5; in Georgia, 5; in Moldova, 5; in Russia, 5. *See also names of specific countries*
secret speech, 12
Securitate, 13
Sevastopol, 93–96
Shevardnadze, Eduard, 5, 68–69, 136
shock therapy, 18, 22, 45
Sikorski, Radoslaw, 36–37
Sinatra doctrine, 7
Solidarity movement, 13, 15
sovereign assertiveness, 14; toward

Euro-Atlantic allies, 32–39, 60–63; toward Russia, 37–39, 62, 78, 83–84, 100. *See also* assertive sovereignty; Sikorski, Radoslaw; sovereign-mindedness
sovereign-mindedness, 1, 104, 107, 113; non-Kremlin mindedness, 125. *See also* assertive sovereignty; sovereign assertiveness
Soviet Union: annexation (occupation) of Baltic countries, 41–42, 48–49, 52, 54; of Ukraine, 99–100; de-Stalinization, 12; disintegration, 3, 7, 66, 100, 133; military bases in Baltic territories, 41; military intervention, 2, 12–13, 25, 40, 43, 66, 68, 70, 134; New Union Treaty (also Treaty of the Union), 2, 40, 64; occupation of Belarus, 67; purges, in Baltic countries, 42; purges, in Belarus, 68; role to end WWII, 135; withdrawal of troops, 3–4, 55–56, 69. *See also* deportations; history
Stalin, Josef, 12, 35, 76, 96–97, 133–35
Surkov, Vladislav, 137

Tajikistan: history, 73–74
Tarasiuk, Borys, 98
Tartu Peace Treaty, 52, 53
Topolánek, Mirek, 36
Trans-Dniester, 72–73, 88, 108–9
Turkmenistan: energy issues, 91–92; history, 75
Tymoshenko, Yulia, 90–91, 109

Ukraine: energy issues, 89–91; history, 75–77
Uzbekistan: history, 77–78; Manas base, 112

Velvet Revolution, 13
Vetting Law, 38
Vike-Freiberga, Vaira, 51, 52
Visegrad Group, 18–20, 26
Voronin, Vladimir, 73
Voting. *See* elections
Vyshinsky, Andrey, 17, 41

Walesa, Lech, 27

Warsaw Pact, 28; creation, 25;
    self-dissolution, 3, 25

Yalta, 11–12, 35, 41–42, 131, 135
Yanukovych, Viktor, 61, 77, 90, 102, 115,
    123

Yeltsin, Boris, 3–4, 7, 55, 57, 94, 121, 136
Yukos, 125
Yushchenko, Viktor, 27, 59, 61, 77, 90, 98;
    attempt on life, 116–17

Zhelev, Zhelyu, 28

About the Author

GEORGETA POURCHOT is Adjunct Professor of Foreign Policy and International Relations and Director of the online MA program in Political Science Northern Capital Region at Virginia Polytechnic Institute and State University. She is a fellow at the Center for Strategic and International Studies, where she directed the Euro-Atlantic Security Project. She was a founding member of the Romanian Green Party and served in the Romanian Chamber of Deputies. She is the coauthor of *Learning from Successful Cooperation in the Expanding Euro-Atlantic Region* and *Future Security Roles of NATO and the EU: Central and Eastern European Contributions.*